Recovering Historical Christology for Today's Church

Recovering Historical Christology for Today's Church

EDITED BY MARVIN JONES
Foreword by Daniel L. Akin

WIPF & STOCK · Eugene, Oregon

RECOVERING HISTORICAL CHRISTOLOGY FOR TODAY'S CHURCH

Copyright © 2019 Wipf and Stock Publishers. All rights reserved. Except for brief quotations in critical publications or reviews, no part of this book may be reproduced in any manner without prior written permission from the publisher. Write: Permissions, Wipf and Stock Publishers, 199 W. 8th Ave., Suite 3, Eugene, OR 97401.

Wipf & Stock
An Imprint of Wipf and Stock Publishers
199 W. 8th Ave., Suite 3
Eugene, OR 97401

www.wipfandstock.com

PAPERBACK ISBN: 978-1-5326-5032-1
HARDCOVER ISBN: 978-1-5326-5033-8
EBOOK ISBN: 978-1-5326-5034-5

Manufactured in the U.S.A.   MAY 30, 2019

Contents

Contributors | ix
Foreword by Daniel L. Akin | xi
Preface by Marvin Jones | xiii

Section I: Primary Christological Passages | 3

Chapter 1. The Christology of Colossians and Hebrews | 3
by Marvin Jones & Justin Langford

> This chapter reviews the basic description of Jesus Christ as God with the focus upon the meaning of the Incarnation.

Chapter 2. The Christology of Philippians and John | 25
by Marvin Jones & Justin Langford

> This chapter depicts the incarnation from the vantage point of 1) the ethical considerations of the incarnation, 2) the eternal nature of the Son as incarnate.

Section II: Historical Christological Councils | 47

Chapter 3. The deity of Christ in Christian thought before Nicæa | 49
by Michael Haykin

> This chapter reviews Christological thought from Pagans, who inadvertently, stood as witnesses to the deity of Christ. The chapter concludes with reviews of Ignatius of Antioch and the "Letter of Diognetius."

Chapter 4. The Road to Orthodoxy leads to Nicaea | 62
by Marvin Jones

> Nicea was the first ecumenical council to wrestle with the heresy of Arianism. This chapter will review the context of the challenge and examine the conclusions of the Nicene Council.

Chapter 5. The Council of Constantinople (381) | 83
by Stephen Presley

> The Council at Constantinople continued to deal with heretical issues concerning the Christology and the Trinity. This chapter will examine the historical christological issues and summarize the solution to the heresy.

Chapter 6. The Council of Ephesus | 104
by Peter Beck

> Ephesus examined the theological issues that arose from the teachings of Nestorius. This chapter will review the context and content of the Nestorian challenge and then examine its proposed solution.

Chapter 7. Christology and The Chalcedon Council | 121
by Marvin Jones and Justin Carter

> This Council of Chalcedon examined and settled the orthodox issues concerning the relationship of the two natures of Christ and the relationship between Christ and the Trinity. This chapter will review the details and the proposed solution of Chalcedon.

SECTION III: CONTEMPORARY CHRISTOLOGICAL APPLICATIONS | 141

Chapter 8. The Person and Work of Jesus | 143
by Adam Harwood

> This chapter will synthesize the conclusions of the council with the biblical evidence. It will present a unified approach to Christology that honors the conclusions of the councils along with the teachings of the Scriptures.

Chapter 9. Christological Preaching in the
    Contemporary Church | 168
    by Philip Caples

> This chapter will discuss the process of preaching (and teaching) Christology to the contemporary church. The preacher, pastor, education and youth director will be able to design sermons (and lessons) that influence discipleship based upon Christological content.

Chapter 10. Christology for the Twenty-First Century | 182
    by Marvin Jones

Addendum 1. Sermon Brief: Col. 1:15–20 | 185

Addendum 2. Propositional Outline of Col. 1:15–20 | 189

Bibliography | 191

Contributors

Dr. Peter Beck is serving in the College of Christian Studies at Charleston Southern University. He teaches in the fields of Historical and Systematic Theology, as well as philosophy and worldviews. Additionally, he served adjunctively for Boyce College (Ky.) and Southeastern Baptist Theological Seminary. Dr. Beck earned his Ph.D. (2007) and M.Div. (2003) in Historical Theology from Southern Baptist Theological Seminary in Louisville, Kentucky. Dr. Beck contributed Chapter Six, *The Council of Ephesus*.

Dr. Philip Caples is Vice President for the Integration of Faith and Learning, Dean of the School of Missions and Ministries, and Associate Professor of Preaching and Pastoral Ministry, holding the Lyndon E. Dawson Professorship in Religion at Louisiana College. He completed the Th.M. (2010) and Ph.D. (2012) at New Orleans Baptist Theological Seminary. His areas of academic interest include: preaching, pastoral ministry, hermeneutics, and biblical studies. Dr. Caples contributed Chapter Nine, *Preaching Christology in the Contemporary Church*.

Dr. Adam Harwood is Associate Professor of Theology, McFarland Chair of Theology, Director of the Baptist Center for Theology & Ministry, and editor of the *Journal for Baptist Theology & Ministry* at New Orleans Baptist Theological Seminary. He completed the M.Div. (2001) and Ph.D. (2007) at Southwestern Baptist Theological Seminary. His special areas of interest are the Doctrines of God, Sin, and Salvation. Dr. Harwood contributed Chapter Eight, *The Person and Work of Jesus: From New Testament Portraits to Theological Statements*.

Dr. Michael Haykin is Professor of Church History and Biblical Spirituality and Director of the Andrew Fuller Center for Baptist Studies at The

Contributors

Southern Baptist Theological Seminary, Louisville, Kentucky. His areas of interest are focused on Baptist History and Patristics. He earned the Master of Religion from Wycliffe College, the University of Toronto (1977), and a Th.D. (1982) in Church History from Wycliffe College and the University of Toronto. Dr. Haykin contributed Chapter Three, *The deity of Christ in Christian thought before Nicæa*

DR. MARVIN JONES serves as Assistant Professor of Theology and Church History at Louisiana College. Additionally, he served adjunctively for Liberty University and New Orleans Baptist Theological Seminary. His areas of interest include Patristics, Baptist History, Christology, Theology Proper, and Systematic Theology. He earned the Ph.D., (2014) Southwestern Baptist Theological Seminary, D.Th., (2005) University of South Africa, and the STM (2001) at Dallas Theological Seminary. Dr. Jones served as general editor of this volume and contributed Chapters One, Two, Four, and Sevento this volume.

DR. JUSTIN LANGFORD is Holder of the William Peterson Carter, Jr. Professorship in Biblical Studies and Coordinator of Faculty Development at Louisiana College. He completed the Th.M. (2009) and the Ph.D., (2012) New Orleans Baptist Theological Seminary. Chapter One, *The Christology of Colossians and Hebrews* and Chapter Two, *The Christology of Philippians and John*, were written in consultation with Dr. Justin Langford, New Testament Professor at Louisiana College.

PASTOR JUSTIN CARTER serves as Senior Pastor of First Baptist Church, Gordon, Texas. He received the Th.M. (2017) at Southwestern Baptist Theological Seminary. He is currently considering options for entering Ph.D. work in Patristics. Chapter Seven, *Christology and the Council of Chalcedon* was enhanced by the writing contribution of Pastor Justin Carter. He wrote the section *Prelude to Chalcedon* to *Leo's Tome*. This is his first publication.

DR. STEPHEN PRESLEY serves as Associate Professor of Church History and Director of the Center for Early Christian Studies at Southwestern Baptist Theological Seminary. His areas of research include early Christian Theology, Exegesis, the Church Fathers, Historical Theology, Biblical Theology, and the History of Biblical Interpretation. He earned the Th.M. (2006) from Dallas Theological Seminary, and the Ph.D. (2012) at the University of St. Andrews, Scotland. Dr. Presley contributed Chapter Five, *The Council of Constantinople*.

Foreword

CHRISTIANITY IS CHRIST. WITHOUT the Lord Jesus Christ there is no Christianity. Without his person we have no one to talk about. Without his person we have nothing to talk about. Fortunately and graciously, God has provided a true, trustworthy, and reliable revelation concerning his Son who is the Savior of the world. The source of this revelation is the Holy Scriptures. From Genesis to Revelation they tell the story of the hero of the whole Bible, the hero who is King Jesus.

For almost 2000 years the church has thought hard and reflected upon the person and work of Jesus Christ. This is what we call Christology. This reflection has rightly taken many forms. In particular the church has thought and written about Jesus from a biblical, historical and theological perspective. Each of these approaches is helpful and legitimate in their own right, and when brought together they provide for us a well-rounded and well-informed portrait of the Lord Jesus Christ. With so many false perspectives and inaccurate understandings of Jesus circulating in the twenty-first century, it is imperative and essential that we formulate a Christology that is true to Scripture and faithful to the rich history and heritage of orthodox Christianity.

Recovering Historical Christology for Today's Church endeavors to fulfill in a faithful way this holy assignment. I believe it capably accomplishes this assignment and so I am delighted to commend it to you. The book proceeds in an orderly and logical fashion from the biblical to the historical to the practical. Each of the contributors is a faithful, orthodox, evangelical who honors Scripture as the supreme authority for the Christian faith and for the task of doing theology. You can trust what you will read in this book!

The impact of Jesus Christ upon history and the modern world is still reverberating today, even if his status is lampooned and diminished by cynics and skeptics who all too often fail to take seriously the biblical record.

Foreword

However, the Christ of the Bible simply cannot be ignored or brushed aside. Perhaps no one has said it more succinctly than C.S. Lewis who writes in his classic *Mere Christianity*, "Among these Jews there suddenly turns up a man who goes about talking as if he was God. He claims to forgive sins. He says he has always existed. He says he is coming to judge the world at the end of time. Now let us get this clear. Among Pantheists, like the Indians, anyone might say that he was part of God, or one with God: there would be nothing very odd about it. But this man, since he was a Jew, could not mean that kind of God. God, in their language, meant the Being outside the world who had made it and was infinitely different from anything else. And when you have grasped that, you will see that what this man said was, quite simply, the most shocking thing that has ever been uttered by human lips."

Fully grasping who Jesus is presents a challenge. What you discover upon a careful investigating is shocking. It is also decisive. You cannot encounter the true and living Christ and remain neutral or undecided. You will be forced to respond. That is the ultimate goal and purpose of this book. Our prayer is God will do a work in your life through its chapters so that you might join John Knox in saying, "No one holds or had held the place in the heart of the world which Jesus holds. Other gods have been as devoutly worshipped; no other man has been so devotedly worshiped." I hope *Recovering Historical Christology for Today's Church* will help you better know Jesus. I hope this book will help you better love Jesus. I hope this book will help you more devoutly worship Jesus.

Daniel L. Akin
President, Southeastern Baptist Theological Seminary
Wake Forest, NC
Summer 2018

Preface

THE PASSION FOR CHRISTOLOGY captured my heart during my student days at the Criswell College. Three decades ago I enrolled in my first Church History Course with Dr. Danny Akin. His influence and passion for the subject matter was "caught" by me in those formative years. Dr. Akin introduced the role of historical theology along with the linear concept of church history. The professor's unique approach to church history compelled me to sense the struggle of earlier Christians as they were pressed by their own culture to define the person of Jesus Christ.

One semester later I enrolled in Dr. Akin's Systematic Theology Course. In this class I learned to work through the problems of contemporary theological and christological issues while remaining faithful to earlier Christian orthodox conclusions. In my very last semester, I registered for Dr. Paige Patterson's Christology class. The demand of stating and understanding Christ's dual natures, re-examining the early councils with critical thinking skills, and listening to the classroom discussions and debates while struggling to answer the many faceted questions—from classmates and professor—served to compound my desire to study Christology. Dr. Patterson introduced us to the theological complexities of *enhypostasis, homoousios, and homoiousios*. The master teacher taught his students well!

In all honesty, I probably could not have mentally grasped Dr. Patterson's Christology class without Dr. Akin's Church History and Systematic theology classes. Those three classes, at the Criswell College, had the lasting impact of allowing theology, and the subset study of Christology, come alive in ways, which thirty years later, still consumes my heart and mind.

Thirty years later, those preparatory years were used by the Lord not only in my pastorates but also in the academic ministry, teaching at the college level, and preparing future pastors. One of my frustrations is that there is not an entry-level Christology textbook that covers a broad range

Preface

of topics. I also know that the typical pastor, after graduation from college (even seminary) has typically relegated his knowledge of Christology to a backburner mindset.

My experience as a pastor and certainly as an educator motivated me to edit and contribute to an entry-level Christology textbook. The book is written with the Bachelor of Arts student in mind. It will also appeal to the pastor who wants to teach Christology in his Wednesday service and it may even help guide the church member into a deeper appreciation of his/her understanding of Jesus Christ. One caveat about this work: It is not intended to be an exhaustive study on Christology. The focus is simply to be an introduction of the topic with the desire that the contents will inform all three target audiences and hopefully compel further study from those who read it.

The book is divided into three sections. The first section, entitled *Primary Christological Passages*, reviews the four primary New Testament christological Scriptures. This section deals with with Colossians, Hebrews, Philippians, and the Gospel of John. The approach of these chapters was not to produce and in-depth exegesis of each text. There are many commentaries that function quite well for that purpose. Instead, the method was to give an introduction to the background of each book (in the broadest sense), key terms, and applications of the text as they pertain to Christology. As a result, the exegesis is limited in scope but adequate to inform the reader establishing his/her own biblical foundation for Christology study.

The second section is entitled *Historical Christological Councils*. This section begins with the Pre-Nicene Christology of the Church Fathers. This section proceeds to review the Councils of Nicaea, Constantinople, Ephesus, and Chalcedon. These four councils defined orthodox Christology not only for the early church but for contemporary Christians. Each chapter not only reviews church antiquity but contains applications for the modern church. These chapters are designed to be "stand alone" information for the student to have an academic resource on the specific council, for the pastor to have a teaching platform in his Wednesday night service, and for the church member to have an informative read on doctrinal matters.

Contemporary Christological Applications is the title of the third section. These chapters include: a correlation of the biblical data with the councils and an expositional approach so that the pastor or teacher may know how to deliver the christological text. The section and book will conclude with a summary chapter on the topic.

Preface

I want to say a personal word of appreciation to the following scholars: Dr. Philip Caples, Dr. Justin Langford, Dr. Peter Beck, Dr. Adam Harwood, Dr. Michael Haykin, Dr. Stephen Presley, and Pastor Justin Carter. These men have written significant chapters that have contributed to the contents of the book. All are personal friends, one is a former student, and one is a new acquaintance all of whom I am blessed to know. My deep love for each of you may never be known in the limited expression of words. Please realize that you have my profound respect and admiration. I count it a personal blessing that you considered this volume worthy of your time.

I would be remiss if I did not say a warm and heartfelt "thank you" to Dr. Lil Purdy of Louisiana College for her editing. Dr. Purdy has truly been God's blessing to me at Louisiana College. I also want to say "thank you" to Mrs. Haley Warren for proofreading and formatting of the manuscript. She has worked tirelessly to produce a fine product for the publication of this volume. I also want to express my gratitude to Mrs. Morgan Clark for compiling the Bibliography. A warm "thank you" to Mr. Brandon Smith as he suggested the title for the book. Without these wonderful contributors and editors this book would have never seen the publisher. Regardless of the work of these fine people I admit that any errors of the text are mine.

MARVIN JONES
Louisiana College
Pineville, LA
Summer 2018

Section I

Primary Christological Passages

1

The Christology of Colossians and Hebrews

Marvin Jones & Justin Langford

INTRODUCTION

The New Testament reveals the person and work of Jesus Christ. He is the central person that not only unifies the Old with the New Testament but also dominates the revelation of the New Testament. The person of Jesus Christ is the focal point and central theme of the Christian faith. Craig Bartholomew states, ". . . any biblical hermeneutic worth its salt must be Christocentric . . . This . . . is of great importance to biblical hermeneutics because 'prime reality' for the Christian is the God who has come to us in Jesus."[1] Without Jesus Christ there is no Christianity. Therefore a study of the person of Jesus Christ is crucial to the understanding of Christianity.

---

1. Bartholomew, *Introducing Biblical Hermeneutics*, 5–7. Bartholomew builds his hermeneutic on a Trinitarian basis. He makes the statement "It is the Trinitarian view of God that distinguishes the Christian Church from other communities," (7).

Section I—Primary Christological Passages

The study of Christ is known as Christology. Christological studies typically separate and review the person of Christ from his work.[2] While some aspects of that approach are acceptable, this work seeks to understand the person of Christ in a holistic manner. In other words, Christ performed the works of the Father because of who he is as God rather than doing his ministry as a mechanical means of accomplishment. The present study seeks 1) to honor the person of Jesus as an ontological being within the Godhead and 2) to understand that Jesus, as God, is a unified being in his person. It is heretical to suggest that Jesus Christ does not have two distinct natures. The problem for Christological studies is whether to begin with the human nature or the divine nature.

Christology has been considered from two vantage points: 1) from above and 2) from below. The first approach recognizes that Christ is God and a member of the Godhead. He is ontologically the same as the Father but distinct in his mode of existence. The Father generates the Son, whereas the Father exists ingenerate.[3] Thus, Christology from above declares the Son as God but distinct from the Father. Christology recognizes the deity of Jesus Christ.

Christology, from below, declares the incarnational aspect of the person of Jesus Christ. The starting point for this category reviews the earthly ministry of Christ as God the Son who came from above to live on earth. The incarnation means that God lived among his own people to minister to them. This paradigm takes the position that Christ as a human is the viable means to study Christology. The focal point of Christology from below is therefore the humanity of Jesus Christ. Wolfhart Pannenberg has correctly stated the hermeneutical issue of "from above" and "from below."

---

2. Even though the study and categorizations of Christ's person from his work is valid it does have innate restrictions. Richard Bauckham, *Jesus and the God of Israel*, 31 argues that the New Testament does not necessarily focus upon the being of Christ. "The whole category of divine identity and Jesus' inclusion in it has been fundamentally obscured by the alternative of 'functional' and 'ontic,' understood to mean that either Christology speaks simply of what Jesus does or else it speaks of his divine nature . . . We can see that, throughout the New Testament texts, there is a clear and deliberate use of the characteristics of the unique divine identity to include Jesus in that identity. Once we rid ourselves of the prejudice that high Christology must speak of Christ's divine nature, we can see the obvious fact that the Christology of divine identity common to the whole New Testament is the highest Christology. It identifies Jesus as intrinsic to who God is."

3. For a good discussion of this issue see, Macleod, *The Person of Christ*. Also review the classic work of Panneberg, *Jesus: God and Man*.

Rightly understood, then, the two lines of argument from above and from below are complementary. A systematic reconstruction of the history of the Christological tradition in terms of its origin, however, at least permits us to differentiate critically between the essential content of Christological dogma and secondary features of distortions. In so doing it has furthered development of an interpretation of the dogma in the light of biblical witness, as classical christology also did.[4]

The New Testament recognizes both vantage points but unites them in the mission of the Lord Jesus Christ. He was sent from the Father into the world for the redemption of humanity (Matt 4:23, Luke 19:10, John 20:21). The question that arises from the mission of the New Testament church has become the same question for the modern church: Who is Jesus Christ whom the Father sent? How is he both God and man? How does the church respond to this claim that he is unique as man and also God? Colossians and Hebrews give insight into these questions.

COLOSSIAN CHURCH AND CHRISTOLOGY

Colossians contains a highly developed Christology. The letter encourages the church to praise the Savior as Creator, Savior and Lord. Interestingly, the Colossian church was divided over the person of Jesus Christ. The church struggled with a heresy focused primarily upon some form of esoteric Judaism.[5] However, there were other heretical issues that invaded the life of the church such as a form of Gnosticism and Hellenism. These

---

4. Pannenberg, *Systematic Theology*, 289.

5. Bruce, *The Epistles*, 23 basically refers to the Colossian heresy as being a deviant form of Judaism with mixtures of Greek Hellenism with aspects of Gnosticism contributing to the confusion of the church. This train of thought led the heretical factions to view themselves as the "spiritual elite." Bruce advances the position that a sect of Judaism (acting within the church) propagated "merkabah mysticism." Bruce quotes Gersgom Scholem as he states the *merkabah* is a, "Jewish variation on one of the chief preoccupations of the second and third century Gnostics and hermetics: the ascent of the soul from the earth, through the spheres of the hostile planet-angels and ruler of the cosmos, and its return to its divine home in the fullness of God's light, a return which, to the Gnostic's mind, signified Redemption." Another alternative has been posted by Melick, *Philippians, Colossians, Philemon*, 183. He states, "Even if the incipient Gnostic elements surfaced, they were secondary. The deeper problem may have been the age-old clash of the human mind versus the Spirit or human tradition versus the revelation in Christ."

Section I—Primary Christological Passages

heresies threatened the inner life of the church as they challenged the identity of Jesus Christ.[6]

THE COLOSSIAN HERESY

The real issue for the Colossian church is the identity of Jesus Christ. The church was in grave danger of losing the biblical identity of Jesus Christ by blending him with the heretical streams of Judaism, Hellenism and Gnosticism. Basically, the church had three cultures clashing in the form of Christianity, Judaism, and Hellenism. Each culture was scuffling for its own identity.

Paul warned the church about following vain philosophy (2:8). It is highly possible that a philosophical presence that had permeated the region had now invaded the congregation. However, Colossians does not present a clear exposition of a philosophical heresy. Therefore, a concise review of the three prominent positions mentioned earlier (Judaism, Gnosticism and Hellenism) is warranted.

Judaism

Markus Barth has demonstrated that the Lycus Valley—where the Colossae was located—contained a large Jewish settlement. He states:

> One of the successors of Alexander the Great, Seleucus I gained control over the territories which before 330 had been Persian, including Asia Minor. Jewish immigration, which was minimal before this time, was encouraged by him and rewarded by the grant of citizenship in the new cities founded by him . . . Tombstones found in Hierapolis, as well as Egyptian papyri and ostraca, reveal that there were Jewish merchants, artisans, physicians, and scribes, and salaried higher and lower officials.[7]

As the Jewish population became established, there was a tendency to observe Judaism with a strict adherence to the Old Testament law. The life of Judaism would continue as it did in Palestine. However, as the gospel spread to the Jewish community and Jewish converts were assimilated into the Colossian Church, it is probable that those new Jewish Christians might

---

6. Ibid., 17.
7. Barth, *Colossians*, 14–15.

have difficulty in their Christian freedom of grace. The tendency would be to revert to the concepts of the Old Testament law without realizing the freedom of grace. The presence of Judaizers would account for the confusion of the issue. This would also explain Paul's address to the church concerning true circumcision (2:11) and his admonition against the observance of the dietary laws (2:16).

James Dunn, however, argues that the Jewish diaspora may have contributed to a variety of Jewish practices and eventual assimilation into contemporary society. He states:

> We cannot, however, assume from this that the Judaism of the Colossian synagogues was wholly uniform-any more than was the Judaism (or Judaisms) in the land of Israel, of which we have more information. Around their common features, the "sects" of Palestinian Judaism displayed a striking diversity of specific belief and halakhic practice.[8]

Dunn argues there was not a normal pattern of worship or practice among the Jewish synagogues. The absence of a normal worship pattern would lead to an integrated worship and lifestyle among the Jews of the region. Dunn goes on to say, "So with diaspora Judaism as well as with infant Christianity we should hesitate to expect that something at least of the diversity of Palestinian Judaism was reflected in the diaspora."[9]

The solution to the Jewish impact on the church does seem very plausible given the arguments of 2:8–23. This passage seems to reveal that a Jewish heresy did invade the Colossian church. If that were the case, the church would find itself working through the basic elements of law versus grace. The dynamic of law verses grace would be a significant problem for the young church as grace via Jesus Christ would be relegated to Jewish legalism. However, consideration must be given to the theory J. B. Lightfoot posed so many years ago: Gnosticism.

Early Form of Gnostic Syncretism

The idea of a pagan religion invading the Colossian church seems outlandish. However, J.B. Lightfoot proposed that the Colossian heresy was based upon Gnostic teachings. According to Lightfoot, Gnosticism "implies the

---

8. Dunn, *The Epistles*, 30.
9. Ibid.

possession of a superior wisdom, which is hidden from others. It makes a distinction between the select few who have this higher gift, and the vulgar many who are without it."[10] Apparently Gnosticism propagated a twofold spirit of superior knowledge and intellect. These teachings seemingly originated in the religious systems of the Iranian-Persian elements.[11]

Lightfoot also thinks there was a blending of Gnosticism with Judaism that produced a syncretistic heresy. The intellectual form of Gnosticism would naturally be given to some form of philosophical/theological speculation. The hidden wisdom of Gnosticism would be safe guarded among the intellectual elite. Thus, the Gnostic wisdom was adhered to by very few but was making a great impact on the intellectual and worship atmosphere of the church.[12]

As Paul writes the epistle to the Colossians, he seems to contradict the intellectual Gnostic tenet by arguing for the universal appeal of not only the gospel message but of Jesus Christ. In the epistle to the Galatians, Paul argues against a national exclusiveness, but in his letter to the Colossians he argues against an intellectual exclusiveness.[13]

It is not hard to imagine the spiritual components of this heresy. The common nature of any heresy is to appeal to a select few and then those few worship in a manner that seems spiritually superior to the rest of the congregation. Paul even addresses the Colossian practice of worshipping angels. There is no doubt that the theology of the Colossians was compromised, which affected the form and content of their worship.

Hellenism

Hellenism is the practice of local Jewish people accepting the Greek culture and lifestyle. Markus Barth, in his review of Hellenism, states that a form of Hellenistic Judaism may have been one of "total assimilation and acculturation."[14] He states:

10. Lightfoot, *St. Paul's Epistles*, 77.

11. O'Brian, *Colossians, Philemon*, xxxv.

12. This is my own conclusion. I arrived at this theory based upon the fact that Paul considered the heresy a threat so he, in turn, warned the church of the dangers of the heresy. The fact that Paul warns against "empty philosophy" and uses terminology such as "perfect knowledge" seem to counter the pseudo intellectual tenets of Gnosticism.

13. Lightfoot, 99.

14. Barth, 14.

> Unquestionably, Hellenistic Judaism is "syncretistic" when Yahweh is placed in the company of other gods, or when one of the pagan gods is identified with him. The substance and form of Jewish worship and daily conduct yielded to foreign influence just as in the time of the pre-exilic prophets. Colossae and its environment were not excluded from this process.[15]

Hellenism was not an intellectual approach to worship but rather a desire to blend in with the local communities. This would lead to many forms of Judaism being accepted yet altered for sake of appeal. This appeal would no doubt attract many worshipers who had retained some form of Judaism (with its form of legalism) while rejecting other aspects of the ceremonial and sacrificial system.[16] Paul addressed the Colossians in order to remind them of the preeminence of Jesus Christ. The person of Jesus and the gospel could not be undermined or denied by competing voices that claim the same preeminence.[17] Colossians serves as a vivid warning for those who would deny the Lordship of Jesus Christ. The epistle reviews the unique position of the Lord and the reverence he is due.

CHRIST: LORD OF THE UNIVERSE (COLOSSIANS 1)

The basic premise of Colossians is the depiction of Jesus Christ as Lord of the universe. Certain key words reveal the nature of the Lord Jesus Christ in relation to the world. Paul establishes his Christology as he elaborates on this issue with three key words: image (εἰκὼν), firstborn (πρωτότοκος), and fullness (πλήρωμα).

---

15. Ibid.

16. The interesting feature of the Colossian Church is that it parallels and, in fact, may well represent the typical modern church approach to solving doctrinal problems: they didn't address them at all. The Colossian church accepted anyone's teachings by incorporating them into the inner life of the church and thus were in severe danger of producing a syncretistic Christianity!

17. This is commonly referred to as Religious Pluralism. Carson, *The Gagging of God*, 26 refers to "radical religious pluralism." According to Carson, this position states, "that no religion can advance any legitimate claim to superiority over any other religion." This stance inevitably leads to the acceptance that all religions are of equal value but none are authoritative to represent God. Thus, any religion "competes" to be the voice of authority in a pluralistic society. This was the scenario at Colosse and is being repeated in twenty-first century America.

Section I—Primary Christological Passages

Image (εἰκὼν):

Paul uses image (εἰκὼν) in verse 15 to reference Jesus Christ as the "image of the invisible God." At first glance this word implies something that is not real—only an image of that which is real. This meaning can be read in the word if a twenty-first century definition is imported. However, the word in the ancient world had quite a different definition. The *Theological Dictionary of the New Testament* defines the term as follows:

> Christ is described as the εἰκὼν τοῦ Θροῦ τοῦ ἀοράτου. To modern logic this seems to be a contradiction, for how can there be an image of something which is invisible and without form? The peculiarity of the expression is related to that of the ancient concept, which does not limit image to a functional representation present to human senses but also thinks of it in terms of an emanation, of a revelation of the being with a substantial participation (μετοχή) in the object. Image is not to be understood as a magnitude which is alien to the reality and present only in the consciousness. It has a share in the reality. Indeed, it is the reality.[18]

The basic idea of "image" (εἰκὼν) is "likeness, manifestation and representation."[19] Kleinknecht goes on to say, "Thus image (εἰκὼν) does not imply a weakening or a feeble copy of something. It implies the illumination of its inner core and essence."[20]

The context suggests the word image (εἰκὼν) refers to a precise and absolute correspondence, i.e., the reality of the invisible God is evidenced in the visible person of Jesus Christ. The revelation of God via Jesus Christ is demonstrated by the present tense verb "is" (ἐστιν), which references the fact that Jesus Christ exists in the image of God. This concept strongly denies an origination point for the Lord's existence.

The meaning of the word "image" (εἰκὼν) is striking. God's invisibility does not merely mean that He cannot be seen but that He is epistemologically unknowable to humanity. Gordon Fee states:

> The Christological point, of course, is that Christ himself in his humanity perfectly bore that image, so that as believers now behold him as the risen One, they are themselves being "transformed" back into that image/likeness. But the emphasis in these passages

---

18. Kleinknecht, "*The Greek Use of* εἰκὼν," 2:389.
19. Ibid., 2:388.
20. Ibid., 2:389.

is not on Christ's humanity—that is assumed as inherent in the imagery itself. What we have, rather, is the true image being borne by the one *who shares the divine glory* (emphasis his), the one who, when turned to in devotion and obedience, transforms believers, by his Spirit, into the *image of God* that we had been created for in the first place.[21]

In the person of Christ the unknowable God becomes known through the person of Jesus Christ. In other words, Christ makes known the invisible, unknowable God.

Firstborn (πρωτότοκος):

The meaning of "firstborn" seems to imply position. The emphasis on the prefix "first" would naturally convey the idea of "first-in-line," which indicated position or succession. However, the word also has the meaning of "kind." The idea of "kind" not only refers to a position but to a hierarchical order. The issue of hierarchy refers to the idea of "supremacy in kind." Thus, the word "firstborn" (πρωτότοκος) describes the Lord's relationship to The Father. Danny Akin states, "The idea is not that Christ was ever somehow 'born' to God but rather that in his relationship to the Father in the Trinity he enjoys all of the rights and privileges the Father bestows upon him."[22]

The word "firstborn" (πρωτότοκος) also informs Christ's relationship to creation. The concept is that Jesus has the sovereign right to rule creation as the Creator. It is difficult to imagine that Paul would want the Colossians to embrace the idea that Jesus is the created firstborn who in turn created everything else.

"Firstborn" (πρωτότοκος) has the idea of priority in time and supremacy in rank is valid if the understanding is "firstborn in kind" (πρωτότοκος) and not "first-created" (πρωτότοκτιστος). If Paul wanted to communicate that Jesus was the "the supreme first of a created order" he would have used πρωτότοκτιστος which means "first created." The fact that the word was available and he did not use it means that the concept of "first-created" can be negated as a viable meaning. Wilhelm Michaelis confirms this interpretation:

---

21. Fee, *Pauline Christology*, 185.
22. Akin, "The Person of Christ," 407.

Section I—Primary Christological Passages

> The description of Christ as πρωτότοκος πάσης κτίσεως Colossians 1:15 obviously finds in the ὅτι clause of v. 16 its more precise and explanation: Christ is the Mediator at creation to whom all creatures without exception owe their creation . . . Hence πρωτότοκος πάσης κτίσεως does not simply denote the priority in time of the pre-existent Lord. If the expression refers to the mediation of creation through Christ, it cannot be saying as the same time that He was created as the first creature.[23]

"Firstborn" (πρωτότοκος) indicates that Jesus Christ exercises his Lordship over all creation. He is eternally pre-existent and being such he is creator of all creation. Verse 16 reveals that Christ is responsible for creation and all things (τὰ πάντα) were created in him. Therefore, Jesus is Lord over creation as he is unique and different from creation. The Colossian passage purports that Christ is the unrivaled supreme God of creation.

Fullness (πλήρωμα):

The idea of "fullness" refers to the divine attributes of being and essence residing in the person of Jesus Christ. A. T. Robertson quoting Lightfoot states, "A recognized technical term in theology, denoting the totality of the Divine powers and attributes."[24] Robertson also states, "It is an old word from *pleroo*, to fill full, used in various senses as in Mark 8:20 of the baskets, Gal. 4:10 of time, etc. The Gnostics distributed the divine powers among various aeons. Paul gathers them all up in Christ, a full and flat statement of the deity of Christ."[25]

The word "fullness" (πλήρωμα) is also used in 2:9. The context there is also a direct statement about Christ's deity. This passage supports the meaning of the "fullness of deity" of 1:19. The text reveals that Jesus is completely God. There was no work of grace on the Father's part to promote the Son to the position of deity, as he is deity by his very essence.

Jesus has the same essence and attributes that belong to the Trinity. His essence is the same as the Godhead. The Godhead is more than Jesus but no less than Jesus. Richard Melick gives insight on this issue when he states, "The fullness refers to the completeness of the divine nature, but it

---

23. Michaelis, "πρωτότοκος," 6:878. I am indebted to Dr. Ken Keathley, of Southeastern Baptist Theological Seminary, for this insight.

24. Robertson, "*Colossians*," 4:480.

25. Ibid.

does not means that Christ is all there is of God . . . Jesus is every bit God but does not mean that Christ is all there is of God."[26] The relationship between Father, Son, and Holy Spirit is that they are deity and share the same properties. Robert Letham comments on this issue, "Each person of the Trinity, when considered in himself, is absolutely, one hundred percent God, and at the same time one hundred percent of God is in each person. The whole of God is in each person, and each person is the whole God."[27]

CONCLUSION TO COLOSSIAN STUDY

Colossians presents Christ as preeminent over creation. He is creator of all things that exist and all things find their summation in him. The word "firstborn" (πρωτότοκος) reveals an epistemological difference between the creator Jesus Christ and the created world. Not only is the world created by Christ but he is ontologically different from his own creation. Thus, he is not subsumed in creation but is distinct from it. He relates to his creation as the creator but not as a part of it. This idea is demonstrated in the word "image" (εἰκών).

The idea of Christ as "image" (εἰκών) of the Father does not mean mere replica. Paul's meaning is that Jesus Christ not only created the world but brought God into the world as the invisible became visible. The revelation of Christ is that humanity can visibly see and perceive God's existence. In other words, Jesus Christ was the personal manifestation of deity.[28] The incarnation of Christ into bodily form means that Christ, as God ("fullness" i.e. πλήρωμα), has come into his own created world.

CHRIST: THE FATHER'S REVELATION (HEBREWS 1)

The book of Hebrews addresses a Jewish audience that seemed to be in danger of abandoning Christianity (and Christ) in favor of Judaism.[29] The

---

26. Melick, *Philippians, Colossians, Philemon*, 255. In his footnote, Dr. Melick explains that God exists in three different modes at the same time. Thus, all three persons are equally God. Jesus Christ is God and as such he has the same properties as the other members of the Godhead.

27. Letham, *The Holy Trinity*, 176.

28. Melick, *Philippians, Colossians, Philemon*, 215.

29. The popular opinion is that the Epistle to the Hebrews was written to a church in the province of Rome. However, Daniel Wallace thinks that the church was in the

Section I—Primary Christological Passages

response to the Jewish Christian who contemplates such a decision is the superiority of Jesus Christ. In fact, that is the theme of the book of Hebrews: Jesus is superior to anything Judaism could possibly offer. Donald Guthrie states:

> The Christian faith pronounced a complete fulfillment of all that the old order strove to do . . . The warning passages would then set out the serious consequences for any who deliberately turned their backs on this superior way. It would be tantamount of asserting the superiority of the old and identifying with those who were responsible for crucifying the Son of God.[30]

The possible Jewish defection is the basis for a renewed consideration of the deity and humanity of Jesus Christ. Chapter 1 emphasizes the deity of Christ while chapter 2 focuses upon his humanity. The result is a comprehensive depiction of the person of Jesus Christ. In order to understand the Book of Hebrews's christological presentation, the two key words and seven phrases of both chapters will be reviewed within their context.

God's Historic Communication

The word "spoke" (λαλήσας) has a significant meaning. Hebrews 1:1 reveals that God did speak to the fathers and prophets of Judaism. This clearly points out the Old Testament patriarchs and prophets as the men to whom God communicated his will for the nation and the rest of humanity. The idea is that even though the styles of communication were different they originated from the same source. Thus, the communication to the individual was divergent but not contradictory because the theme of the communication was the same.

God did not leave people to grope in the dark trying to find him as though he were silent and distant from any contact with humanity. The Lord took the initiative to communicate to Israel. Therefore, in the previous times and in different styles—God spoke!

---

infamous Lycus Valley which had a heavy Jewish population. See *Hebrews: Introduction, Argument, and Outline*. Allen, *Hebrews*, 64–71, proposes the opinion of J.V. Brown that the recipient was converted Priest living near Antioch in Syria.

30. Guthrie, "*Hebrew*," 33. Guthrie does consider the possibility that the book of Hebrews was written to a Gentile audience but this position is dismissed for lack of serious scholarly acceptance.

God's Present Communication

The aorist tense of "spoke" (ἐλάλησεν) is used in reference to God's communication by the Son. The tense reveals the contrast between the previous revelations and the latter revelation in the Son. The idea of the aorist tense can be interpreted as "consummative." The idea of the "consummative aorist"[31] is that God has spoken in the Son and will no longer speak by other means. The overused statement "once and for all" may actually apply here. The meaning seems to be that the Son is the pinnacle of God's progressive revelation.[32] The aorist—and more specifically the context of verse 2—depicts a final and full revelation from God in the Son.

The basic idea is difficult to miss: God did speak to the fathers and the prophets through various means in times past. The communication of the Lord in the Old Testament was valid and certainly valuable, but it was incomplete. The meaning of verse 1 is that communication did take place in partial forms in the past. Verse 2 reveals that the Son is the final form of God's communication. In other words, the Son completes the communication of the Godhead.

The phrase "in the Son" (ἐν υἱῷ) yields an interesting meaning. The Greek phrase is literally "in a Son." There is no exact English equivalent meaning that is capable of translating the phrase. The definite article is supplied in most English translations but it is notably absent in the Greek manuscripts. Daniel Wallace states:

> Although this should probably be translated "a Son" (there is no decent way to express this compactly in English), the force is clearly qualitative (though, of course, on the continuum it would be closer to the indefinite than the definite category). The point is that God, in his final revelation, has spoken to us in one who has the characteristics of a son. His credentials are vastly different from the credentials of the prophets (or from the angels, as the following context indicates).[33]

---

31. Wallace, *Greek Grammar*, 559 states that the consummative aorist is "often used to stress the cessation of an act or state." The idea of the context seems to argue that revelation was progressive in the Old Testament but reached its zenith and completion in the person of Jesus Christ in the New Testament. Again, the argument is more from the point of context than linguistic.

32. Erickson, ed., *Concise Dictionary of Christian Theology*.

33. Wallace, *Grammar*, 245.

Section I—Primary Christological Passages

The meaning is obvious! The nature of the Son leaves no question to the fact that he is God! Marcus Dods validates this conclusion as he goes onto state:

> The revelation now consisted not merely in what he said [προφήταις] but in what He was [υἱός]. This revelation was final because made by one who in all He is and does, reveals the Father. By uttering himself He expresses God. A Son who be characteristically designated as son, carries in Himself the Father's nature and does not need to be instructed in purposes which are also and already His own...[34]

Several ideas develop from these concepts. The revelation of the Father is now complete in the Son. The Son, therefore, reveals the Father because their nature is the same. The revelation of the Father can be epistemologically realized because the Son, who has the same nature, can naturally reveal the Father to humanity.

This means that the fathers and prophets of the past were incapable of revealing the Father unless the Father gave them the message (which he did). However, the nature of the fathers and prophets was not the same nature as the Father. Therefore, there was an epistemological issue at stake. No one could know the Father on any basis except that the Father was gracious to reveal himself in various times and by various means.

In the latter days, though, the Son can reveal the Father because his substance is the same. The attributes of the Son are the same as the Father: they are divine attributes. Thus, epistemologically, there are no barriers to communicating the Father to humanity. The stated meaning is that both Father and Son have the same essence or being in their nature. As Craig Koester states:

> This is a forceful way of describing what the listeners experienced, since they had not actually heard Jesus of Nazareth, but received the message from early Christian evangelists...If the prophets conveyed God's Word by what they said, the Son conveyed God's word by who he was and what he did.[35]

The author of Hebrews establishes the deity of Christ in the opening verses of chapter one. He leaves no doubt about the identity of the person of Jesus Christ. He is the incarnated God come to earth. He follows this concept with seven concise Old Testament affirmations of the Lord's work that

---

34. Dods, *Hebrews*, 4:249.
35. Koester, *Hebrews*, 185.

depict the Son's relationship to creation. These affirmations flow out of his person as deity.

Seven Old Testament Affirmations of Deity[36]

The seven affirmations of the Lord's deity are derived from the Old Testament. These statements are not one quote from a single Scripture. They are, in fact, a "string of seven Old Testament quotations" that the author used to "support his claim that Jesus, as Son, is superior to the angels."[37]

The Son was appointed heir of all things
(ον εθηκεν κληρονομον παντων)

Verse 2 quotes Psalm 2:8. This psalm refers to the Anointed One as the Messiah sitting on the throne ruling from a position of authority. The emphasis is upon the "heir" of the Son receiving a people to rule over. The use of Psalm 2:8 is a direct reference to Jesus Christ's Messianic office. Once again the aorist tense is used to communicate the profound concept that the appointment as heir is timeless. This speaks to the eternal nature of the Son.

The Son made the universe
(δι ου και τους αιωνας εποιησεν)

The functionality of Christ stresses the divine activity of his deity: no prophet could create the universe! The use of "whom" (διὰ) refers to the Son being the agent of creation: the Son created the ages (αἰῶνος). The word ages or universe (αἰῶνος) refers to periods of time. The Son created the various epochs that contain the successive passing of time. This verse speaks of the Son's Lordship.

---

36. Danny Akin also gives the same list with concise detail in, "The Person of Christ," 410.

37. Allen, *Hebrews*, 161.

Section I—Primary Christological Passages

The Son is the radiance of God's Glory
(ὃς ὢν ἀπαύγασμα τῆς δόξης)

The word radiance (ἀπαύγασμα) has the meaning of "radiance."[38] The early church father, Origen, stated, "the glory of this light, proceeding inseparably from (God) Himself as brightness does from light, and illuminating the whole of creation."[39] The Son can reveal the Father's glory so intimately because both share the same nature. At the incarnation, the glory of the Father was seen in the Son. The issue at stake was the fact that Jesus could reveal the Father because the glory of the Father "shined from Jesus Christ."[40]

The Son is the exact representation of the Father's being
(καὶ χαρακτὴρ τῆς ὑποστάσεως αὐτοῦ)

"Exact representation" (χαρακτήρ) from which the English "character" is derived is a hapax-legomena. BAGD gives the meaning as follows:

> Viewing Christ's exaltation and pre-existence together they sing in hymnal style of the eternal nature of the Son. The two members of the first statement (v. 3a) are in parallelism. They thus intentionally say the same thing . . . Since God's glory has impressed itself on Him as the One exalted by God, He is its reflection and image.[41]

The meaning, in this context, is that the Son is the precise expression of the divine essence of the Godhead. Dods concurs:

> In common use . . . it denoted the impress of mark made by the graving tool, especially the mark upon a coin which determined its value; hence any distinguishing mark, identifying a thing or person, *character*. 'Express image' translates it well. The mark left on wax or metal is the 'express image' of the seal of stamp. It is a reproduction of each characteristic of the original.[42]

---

38. Bauer, *A Greek-English Lexicon of the New Testament*.
39. Origen, *De Principiis*, 4:248.
40. Athanasius, *Four Discourses*, 4:394. Athanasius used the analogy of the sun and the rays: one cannot exist without the other.
41. Wilckens, "χαρακτήρ," 9:421.
42. Dods, *Hebrews*, 4:251.

The word "being" (ὑποστάσεως) has the meaning of "substantial nature, essence, actual being, reality . . . the Son of God is an exact representation of his (= God's) real being."[43] Luke Johnson gives a concise meaning as he states "what God is, the Son is: they share the same 'imprint of being.'"[44] The meaning is clear: Jesus is divine and shares the same properties of the Godhead.

The Son upholds all things by the power of his word
(φέρων τε τὰ πάντα τῷ ῥήματι τῆς δυνάμεως)

The idea of "uphold" (φέρων) is more than simply sustaining. It has the idea of moving toward the completion of a goal. Homer Kent, Jr. states:

> The durative form of the participle, as well as the meaning of the word itself as 'bring' or 'carry,' indicates that the sense involves both upholding and movement toward some goal. It is one of Christ's functions to sustain this universe in its existence and operation, and to carry it forward to reach the consummation which God has planned.[45]

Since the Son made the universe he also guides it to its intended completion. Jesus is different from creation as its originator but he also guides it as Lord of the universe.

The Son made purification for our sins
(αὐτοῦ καθαρισμὸν τῶν ἁμαρτιῶν ποιησάμενος)

The text moves from lordship of the universe to soteriology. The relationship between God and humanity is predicated upon the work of the Son. The idea of the "purification for sin" is completed. The striking feature of this statement is that the Son did what no other person or entity could do—he cleansed humanity from their sins. He reveals the Father and forgives humanity's sins thus bringing the two together in fellowship. The soteriology of the Lord's work flows out of his divine person.

---

43. Bauer, Arndt, Gingrich, and Danker, *A Greek-English Lexicon of the New Testament*, s.v. "ὑποστάσεως."
44. Johnson, *Hebrews: A Commentary*, 70.
45. Homer, *The Epistles of the Hebrews*, 37.

Section I—Primary Christological Passages

The Son sat down at the right hand of the Father
(ἐκάθισεν ἐν δεξιᾷ τῆς μεγαλωςύνης ἐν ὑψηλοῖς)

The Son's divine position is affirmed by his place at the Father's side. His work is also highlighted as the Son takes the position of accomplishment—he sits down! The aorist tense of "sit" (ἐκάθισεν) strongly implies accomplishment. There was no work left to do so the Son could ascend the throne and be seated at the right hand of the Father. The Son is now in a place of honor. His position is in stark contrast to the earthly priests who never ceased from their work. The point is well taken—Jesus Christ finished the atonement, whereas the high priest never could.

CONCLUSION TO HEBREW STUDY

The Hebrew passages present Christ as the final communication of the Father's revelation to humanity. God now speaks in a specific manner to humanity via the Son. Christ coming from the Father into the world means that the Trinitarian nature of the Godhead is now being heard through the words and actions of the Son.

Christ is presented as the fulfillment of the Old Testament. The revelation of God in the Old Testament is the self-disclosure of God to and for his people. The idea of verbal discourse seems to be the point of "God speaking to the prophets." In the coming of Christ, God now speaks to humanity as the final aspect of his revelation. Whereas, the Old Testament understood the revelation of God as progressive, the coming of Christ is to be understood as the cumulative or final expression of God's revelation.

CONTEMPORARY SIGNIFICANCE

The above study reveals the person of Jesus Christ. The question must be asked, "Why is the identity of Jesus so important?" The answer provides the demarcation line between Christianity and other religions. The biblical concept of Christology recognizes that the Son is also God who lived in bodily form on earth and is different than any alternate god. Anthony Thiselton states, "what is remarkable about Hebrews is that in comparison with other New Testament writings it has both the highest and most explicit declarations of the deity of Christ and the clearest and most deliberate expressions of the humanness of Jesus Christ."[46] Hebrews presents the God-Man, Jesus Christ, to the contemporary church so that the christological formula distinguishes God in Christ from all other alternative religious claims.

The Colossians study depicts Christ as Lord of the universe. The result is that he is Lord of all creation. The issue of Christ's lordship is directly related to the identity of his person. The study from Colossians vividly portrays Christ as having the same essence as the Father. Consider the possibilities if that were not the case: If Christ is not God then there is no basis for his Lordship. If there is no basis for his Lordship then humanity's salvation is questionable at best and doubtful at worst. If the salvation of humanity is threatened then the way to God is open for all sorts of authoritative claims to represent God. Unfortunately, this may very well be the current state of mind in modern America.

The Colossians study depicts Christ as Lord of the universe because the Son is God. The realm of his Lordship extends to every facet of creation. The idea stemming from Colossians is that no god, no cultural icon, and certainly no philosophical assertion can pose a viable challenge to the supremacy of Jesus Christ's Lordship. Again, as my dear professor used to say, "If Jesus Christ is not Lord of all then He is not Lord at all."[47]

The Hebrew study contributes to the understanding of Jesus Christ as Lord as the final act of communication from God the Father. The author of Hebrews builds upon the progressive revelation—via the Fathers communication—starting with the Old Testament. The author progresses to establish Jesus Christ as the pinnacle of God's revelation and communication. So the undeniable fact of Hebrews is the congruency of God's revelation to humanity.

When a study of the Old Testament is undertaken, the story of Jesus unfolds in small fragments. However, the New Testament introduces the God-Man to humanity in the person of Jesus Christ. The revelation of Christ in the New Testament is not fragmentary but complete in the personal introduction of the Son. Hence, the concept of Christ as the communication of the Father recognizes that the Son is also God.

Jesus Christ is capable of such a ministry because of his personage—he is God! He is the "exactness" of the Father. There is no epistemological

---

46. Thiselton, *The Hermeneutics of Doctrine*, 391.

47. This statement is also attributed to Dr. Danny Akin in Christology Class at Southeastern Baptist Theological Seminary, winter semester 1994.

Section I—Primary Christological Passages

problem between God the Father and humanity since the Son is God and thus knows the Father. The ministry of the Son is to communicate the Father to the rest of creation. Furthermore, since Christ is the pinnacle of God's revelation and since Christ reveals the Father, there is no need for more revelation! In other words, the competing voices of Mormonism, Jehovah's Witness, or any other religion that has a new revelation from God is sheer nonsense! Hebrews describes that the revelation of God in Christ is now complete.

The application is immense: God is not hidden from humanity! In the modern world so many people are confused about God's goodness and nearness. This world questions the love of God because of the assumption that God cannot be known. Hebrews informs us that God is knowable and wants to be known.

Furthermore, the same God who spoke in the past also speaks in the present. God wants his people to know him and learn more of him. Thus, it is reassuring that God is the same today as he was yesterday. He does not change the rules of the game, nor does He love with a conditional, fickle love. He loves humanity with a constant, merciful love that flows out of his person.

INTERACTIVE PERSONAL SEMINAR

Chapter Summary

In the New Testament books, Colossians and Hebrew, the person of Christ is presented through his works. Thus, a holistic approach to the study of Christology is warranted.

Key Terms

- Christology
- Ontology
- Christology from above
- Christology from below
- Lordship
- Progressive Revelation

Advanced Questions

1. What is the theological importance of the incarnation?
2. Does Colossians and Hebrews present Jesus as equal to God, as God, or both?
3. Does the New Testament present Jesus as functionally subordinate to the Father?
4. What is the significance of God's past revelation in Hebrews 1:1?
5. How is Jesus Christ the final revelation of the Father?

Theological Questions

1. Explain the meaning of the hypostatic union?
2. Explain how the hypostatic union of the Son impacts the Trinity?

Section I—Primary Christological Passages

3. During his earthly life did Jesus possess the non-moral (natural or incommunicable) attributes? Explain the answer from the position of the hypostatic union.
4. Explain how the Lord's immanence is the focal point of the incarnation.
5. Explain how the Lord is still transcendent in the incarnation.

Issues To Research

- Evaluate the incommunicable attributes of God and determine how the incarnation impacted them.
- Evaluate the meaning of "firstborn," "image," and "radiance" as they relate to Christ's divinity
- Explain the process of existing "as a slave" as that concept relates to Christ's humanity.
- Analyze the ethical meaning of Philippians 2:5–11 and how it relates to the church and individual?
- Explain the process of "progressive revelation."
- Explain why "angels" are mentioned in Hebrews 1? What is the significance of the contrast between them and Christ?

2

The Christology of Philippians and John

MARVIN JONES & JUSTIN LANGFORD

INTRODUCTION

THE APOSTLE PAUL FOUNDED the church at Philippi on his second missionary journey. In all probability, the church began during the years of AD 50–51 which would be after the infamous Jerusalem Council (Acts 15). Acts 16:12 refers to Paul's vision and hearing of the "Macedonian Call" for help. He promptly heeded this vision as God's will for him to reach the provinces of Greece.

Paul's first attempt at presenting the gospel resulted in a successful church plant. Acts also informs the reader that at least three different social strata of people comprised the church at Philippi: the working class Philippian jailer, an affluent businesswoman, and the down-and-out demon possessed girl. The Philippian jailer is well known for his conversion to Christianity. He was so distraught at the work of God in freeing the imprisoned apostle Paul that he started to kill himself over his perceived failure of letting a prisoner loose. He may be characterized as the typical blue-collar employee.

Section I—Primary Christological Passages

A second person of interest is the businesswoman, Lydia. She is described as a retailer of purple fabric. No doubt she was in the import business as her original home was in Thyatira. Lydia was quite wealthy and very prominent. She might be characterized as the mobile, up-and-coming entrepreneur.

The third person of distinction is the demon possessed slave girl. As Richard Melick states, "The Scriptures do not state that she became a convert to Christianity, there is every reason to assume that she did."[1] The slave girl was neither wealthy nor as socially prominent as Lydia. In fact, she was used by men who made profit from her demonic possession. This young woman may be characterized as living at a lower economic level. She could be deemed as one of the victims of societal oppression. Yet, these three people comprised the core of the Philippian church. Their various social and economic lifestyles reveal the gospel had crossed these restrictive boundaries. Donald Guthrie calls this phenomenon "the power of Christianity in Philippi."[2]

One would think that the various social and economic differences within the membership would mean that the church would not and could not produce sustained unity. Based upon the differing social strata, the divergent ministry focuses would be natural. However, the church not only sustained unity but was very generous in giving to Paul's ministry.[3] Their willingness to contribute financially to Paul indicates the unity within the church body.

Paul writes a letter to this generous church to thank them for the financial assistance. This letter addresses such issues of Paul's personal condition (1:12–26), news about Timothy and Epaphroditus (3:19–30), false teachers (3:1–21), an appeal to unify the membership (4:1–9) and an expression of his personal gratitude for the church's generosity (4:10–23). During the course of the letter, Paul addresses one of the greatest Christological themes in the New Testament—the humility of the Lord Jesus Christ (2:5–11). In

---

1. Melick, *Philippians, Colossians, Philemon*, 27.

2. Guthrie, *New Testament Introduction*, 541.

3. The Philippian Church is the antithesis to the modern church growth movement. The contemporary strategy often employed is to enlist a "core group" that is like minded in social and economic status so that cohesion and alleged unity is easily obtainable. The Philippian church serves as a model that unity can be achieved only through the gospel of the Lord Jesus Christ. The gospel message of salvation to all is sufficient to break down social, economic and racial barriers.

fact, this theme—Christ's humility as a servant—was the unifying factor within the church.

CHRIST: SERVANT CHRISTOLOGY

Philippians 2:5–11 communicates a Christological message that is both practical and ethical. Verse 5 informs the reader of Paul's intent: "Have this attitude in yourselves which was also in Christ Jesus" (NASB). Gerald Hawthorne comments on the use of this verse:

> Paul's motive in using it here is not the logical, but ethical. His object is not to give instruction in doctrine, but to reinforce instruction in Christian living. And he does this by appealing to the conduct of Christ . . . This is the most obvious and natural explanation for its appearance at this point in the letter, and it is quite in keeping with Paul's practice elsewhere of using the life/death of Christ as a pattern for Christians to follow.[4]

The passage depicts an ethical example for the Philippian church (and the rest of Christianity). The pattern of behavior was found in the person and work of Jesus Christ. The very nature of this passage affirms the adage that "what one believes one acts upon."

The apostle Paul appeals to Christ's thinking for the basis of the Philippians's moral and ethical behavior. Christians are exhorted to "think" as Christ "thought." In so doing, Christians would not only imitate the actions of the Lord Jesus Christ but they would adopt His mindset—a way of life!

The basic premise of Philippians is the depiction of Jesus Christ as the Servant—Lord. Certain key words reveal the nature of the Lord Jesus Christ in relationship to servanthood. Paul establishes his servant Christology as he elaborates on this issue with four key words: mind (φρονεῖτε), form (μορφῇ), grasp (ἁρπαγμὸν), and, emptied himself (ἑαυτὸν ἐκένωσεν).

Mind (φρονεῖτε)

As Paul is encouraging the Philippians to embrace unity, he declares that unity is based upon having the mind of Christ (v. 5). In his appeal to unity, he explains that unity consists of that which is in Christ and capable of being adopted by Christians. This is illustrated by the position of the word

---

4. Hawthorne, *Philippians*, 79–80.

"this" (Τοῦτο). Τοῦτο is the antecedent of "Ο" or "which" in the latter part of verse 5. Τοῦτο is also the direct object of the verb mind (φρονεῖτε). In fact the entire second part of verse 5 functions as a direct object. Paul is illustrating that the mind he wants the Philippians to have is the same mind that Christ had.

The meaning of mind (φρονεῖτε) is to "have thoughts or (an) attitude, be minded or disposed"[5] The phrase "having this attitude in you in you" (ἐν ὑμῖν) means that the Philippians could adopt the thinking of the Lord among themselves.[6] The goal of having the mind of Christ was they would be able to serve one another and avoid selfish motivation. This goal can only be realized as the church would begin looking at the selfless life of the Savior. The adoption of the Lord's lifestyle and thinking would, in turn, lead to an attitude of service in the church. The obvious question is: What was the Lord's mindset? What did he do to illustrate his attitude?

Form (μορφῇ)

In verse 6 Paul details the mode of Christ's preexistence and the accompanying thoughts about his preexistence. Jesus Christ "existed in the form of God" (ἐν μορφῇ θεοῦ). The interpretation of this verse depends upon the meaning of "form" (μορφῇ). Marvin Vincent states the meaning of the word, ". . . here means that expression of being which is identified with the essential nature and character of God, and which reveals it."[7]

Hawthorne concurs with Vincent.

> Thus, when the word is applied to God, his μορφῇ must refer to his deepest being, to what he is in himself. . .to the reality of God's being. . .To say, therefore, that Christ existed εν μορφῇ θεου is to say that outside his human nature Christ had no other manner of existing apart from existing 'in the form of God,' that is, apart from being in possession of all the characteristics and qualities belonging to God.[8]

---

5. BAGD, s.v. "φροωεῖτε."

6. I take the corporate meaning of "in you" (ἐν ὑμῖν). Gerald Hawthorne has an excellent discussion on this subject in his *Philippians*, 80–81.

7. Marvin Vincent, *Philippians and Philemon*, 57–58.

8. Hawthorne, 83–83.

Lightfoot also states the same meaning. "It remains then that μορφῇ must apply to the attributes of the Godhead.⁹ The meaning of μορφῇ expresses a "reality concept." The point is clear, Christ eternally exists in the very nature, essence, essential being of God. Μορφῇ denotes Christ as possessing the same qualities of God the Father—Jesus is God!

Johannes Behm determines that the meaning of Christ's μορφῇ θεου must be seen in contrast to his becoming μορφῇ δούλου.

> In the sequence of Phil 2:5–11 it is also the opposite of the μορφῇ θεου which he had before, and the opposite of κυριος which he will receive at His exaltation (vv. 9 ff)... Thus the phrase μορφῇ θεου, which Paul coins in obvious antithesis to μορφῇ δούλου, which can be understood only in the light of the context. The appearance assumed by the incarnate Lord, the image of humiliation and obedient submission, stands in the sharpest conceivable contrasts to his former appearance, the image of sovereign divine majesty... The specific outward sign of humanity of Jesus is the μορφῇ δούλου, and of his essential divine likeness the μορφῇ θεου... The μορφῇ θεου in which the pre-existent Christ was/is simply the divine δοξα.¹⁰

The fact that the Lord became a slave references the humanity that was added to his deity. Thus his μορφῇ θεου was present but veiled in the incarnation as he became μορφῇ δούλου.

Grasp (ἁρπαγμὸν)

The preexistence of the Son is also considered as Paul uses the word "grasp" (ἁρπαγμὸν). The word ἁρπαγμὸν is a *hapax legomena*. The meaning is difficult at best to determine. In all probability the apostle Paul borrowed the term from secular Greek. In order to determine the precise meaning of ἁρπαγμὸν, one must consider the use of the word within its own context, Philippians 2:5–11. Paul is trying to emphasize the meaning of Christ's humility or His attitude. The force of the passage is ethical so the meaning must reflect the ethical considerations of the text: *Christ did not think his equality with the Father a thing to be grasped but emptied himself*. Since the attitude of Christ is the focal point, the application that Paul demonstrates

---

9. Lightfoot, *Epistle to the Philippians*, 132.
10. Behm, "Μορφῇ,"4:750–51.

is that "grasping" or insisting on personal rights in the congregation does not lead to spiritual maturity.

The possible meaning of "robbery or things seized" can be easily dismissed. Jesus Christ did not have to seize his deity from the Father as he is co-equal, co-eternal, and co-existent with the Father. In the context, the idea that Christ was already in the form of God (without seizing any part of deity) and thought it not necessary to grasp it (again a reference to his deity) makes sense when the ethical implications of the context are considered. The point Paul is making is that Christ is the example of humility and submissiveness. He did not continue grasping or cling to his equality with the Father; likewise, Christians should not adopt an attitude of superiority but one of humility and service.

Emptied himself (ἑαυτὸν ἐκένωσεν)

This phrase has been the source of considerable theological speculation. The kenosis theory comes from the phrase "emptied himself," (ἑαυτὸν ἐκένωσεν). The kenosis theory—or kenotic Christology—according to Millard J. Erickson, takes the position that Christ gave up his divine attributes while taking on the form of humanity.[11]

In the nineteenth century, the proponents of Higher Criticism began to develop the doctrine of kenosis.[12] The end result is that Jesus Christ no longer possesses deity. Through the kenosis, or emptying, his deity was stripped from him (by his own initiative) and the end result is a perfect, obedient man. There are differing versions of this heresy. For example, many see Christ retaining his deity in the moral sense.[13] If Christ were to lay aside the divine attributes then His functioning as God would cease. For that matter, how could Christ "give-up" or "lay aside" divinity which was his very essence and existence? How could Christ still be God without the divine attributes that distinguish him as God?

---

11. Erickson, *The Word Became Flesh*, 552.

12. Ibid. Erickson does an outstanding survey of the Kenotic Theologians. See chapter 3, "The Development of Incarnational Christology: (2) After the Council of Chalcedon," for a survey on kenosis. The survey included Thomasius, "Christ's Person and Work" and Forsyth, The Person and Place of Jesus Christ. Erickson's chapter 22, "The Logic of the Incarnation (2)," reviews the theological positions and problems associated with kenosis.

13. This begs the questions though. Does the Lord's retention of moral attributes imply ontological essence? If so, then the theory of kenosis has invalidated itself.

Since the kenosis theory concludes that Christ divested Himself of all divine attributes, the proponents of the theory have de-deified the Lord. This position is based upon the concept that deity and humanity cannot exist in one person. The confusion arises over the meaning of "empty" (ἐκένωσεν). It is defined as "to make empty, render void or of no effect."[14] The Greek verb also can indicate the action of pouring out; thus, one understanding could be that Jesus did not empty himself but added to himself what he was not before the incarnation (that is, human form).

Examining the function of the participial phrases of verses 6–8 is instructive at this point. The structure of each verse is similar; each contains a primary indicative verb to which is attached one or more adverbial participles. In verse 6, the verb ἡγήσατο ("he considered") is preceded by the concessive participle ὑπάρχων ("being"). The resulting meaning then is that "even though" Christ was/existed in form as God, he did not consider this state of being as "a thing to be grasped or prized" or, in other words, something to use for one's own advantage. Submission and humility is the major point here, and verses 7–8 unpack the meaning further by demonstrating how Jesus illustrated that this was his mindset.

Philippians 2:7 contains one indicative verb (ἐκένωσεν) followed by three participial phrases that detail *how* Jesus "made himself nothing." Taking all three participles to communicate "means," the understanding is that Jesus made himself nothing "by taking (λαβών) the form of a servant," "by coming about (γενόμενος) in the likeness of men," and "by being found (εὑρεθείς) in outward appearance as a man." Jesus's submission is demonstrated in the action of the participles and as evidenced by the concession mentioned in verse six. In 2:8, Jesus's obedience is illustrated with another verb connected to a participle of means. He humbled (ἐταπείνωσεν) himself "by being (γενόμενος) obedient to death, even a cross death."

Returning to an earlier point, the addition of humanity to his ontological being means that now Jesus Christ resides in human form. F. F. Bruce comments on this issue by stating:

> By taking on the form of a servant He emptied Himself. Nothing is mentioned of any abandonment of divine attributes, the divine nature of the form of God, but only a divine paradox is stated here: He emptied Himself by taking something to Himself, namely the manner of being, the nature or form of a servant or slave.[15]

14. BAGD, 428.
15. Bruce, *The Epistle of Paul to the Philippians and Philemon*, 82.

Section I—Primary Christological Passages

The body of Jesus was the addition to the second person of the Godhead thus giving him a different mode of existence. Colin Brown states, "The word "emptied" (ἐκένωσεν) evokes the image of a vessel that retains its form after the contents have been poured out."[16]

The second question arises, "Of what did Christ empty himself?" Paul does not answer this question. He simply states that Christ emptied himself. The Lord's life as revealed in the Gospels must be considered if an adequate theological understanding is to be gained.

Throughout the gospel accounts the Lord's deity is seen via his miracles and his desire to forgive sins. These accounts reveal that the Lord still possessed his divine attributes and his divine personage. He did not completely divest himself of his divine attributes but he did lay aside his prerogative to use them. So when Jesus apparently did not know where Lazarus was laid, he was not using his divine attributes. He truly did not know the location of Lazarus's body (John 11:33).

Jesus did not surrender his divine attributes nor his divine glory. His glory was veiled during his earthly ministry even though at times He revealed it. For that matter the clear evidence of his glory was unveiled on the mountain (Matthew 17:2). For that matter, his glory will be unveiled when he returns (Revelation 1).

Since his attributes and glory were retained but veiled the addition of humanity did not subtract from his deity. Thus, Christ changed the form of his existence by taking on the form of a bondservant, or humanity, thus veiling his glory. Melick states:

> The contrasts between "'Lord'" (v. 11) and "'servant'" (v 7) and "'very nature of God'" (v. 6) and "'human likeness'" (v. 7) express the emptying. Thus the emptying is that God became human, Lord became servant, and obedience took him to death . . . Paradoxically, being "'made nothing'" means adding humanity to deity rather subtracting deity from his person.[17]

The form (μορφῇ) changed but the essence of God in Christ did not. The addition of humanity is permanent, but the emptying (ἐκένωσεν) is only temporary. The idea of "himself" (ἑαυτὸν) simply means that Christ imposed a self-limitation on his divine attributes—only God can impose a limit on himself! This limitation did not compromise or diminish his deity.

---

16. Brown, "Ernst Lohmeyer's *Kyrios Jesus*," 12.
17. Melick, 103.

CONCLUSION OF PHILIPPIAN STUDY

Philippians depicts an ethical application for the church that is rooted in the Lord's mindset. The basic context is that Christ humbled himself in order to achieve the work of redemption. The church was encouraged to adopt the mind (φρονεῖτε) or attitude of Christ in their personal relationships with one another. The fact that Paul urged the adoption of Christ's thinking implies that they were not thinking or relating to one another in the manner in which Christ lived his life. This does not mean that the church was in turmoil but it does mean that Paul instructed the adoption of the mindset in order for the relationships within the church to continue in harmony. This new attitude had ethical implications within the personal relationships of the Philippian church.

The ethical approach is demonstrated in the Lord's ability to "empty himself," (ἑαυτὸν ἐκένωσεν). This approach is self-abasement. The ability to "empty oneself" directly corresponds to the actions of the Savior. To achieve a humble state one must empty oneself of personal goals and ambitions. Thus, the idea of denouncing oneself or not "grasping" (ἁρπαγμὸν) or insisting on personal rights is the heart of self-denial. In fact, self-denial leads one to adopt a different "form" (μορφῇ) of existence, i.e. to go from ambition to self-denial.

The meaning of the new approach to living and thinking (new attitude) is actualizing the servanthood mentality for the church. The local church is to minister to the needs of people within and without the local body. The accomplishment of servanthood ministry is predicated upon a change within the individual (and the corporate body) to adopt the attitude of Christ that is the foundation of the gospel.

CHRIST: LOGOS CHRISTOLOGY

The book of John was most likely written to Gentile Churches.[18] The opening chapter strongly emphasizes the deity of Christ. In fact, John's Gospel utilizes Christology more so than any other Gospel. Erickson comments,

---

18. Wallace, *The Gospel of John: Introduction, Argument, Outline*. Wallace, gives the possibility that John wrote this epistles to the Gentile Churches of Paul's ministry. The occasion for the writing was the death of Paul. John wanted to clearly communicate the Gospel of Jesus Christ to the churches so that their hope would not die with Paul but live on in Christ.

Section I—Primary Christological Passages

"One reason for the early church's dependence on the Gospel of John is the strong Christological emphasis of the writer."[19]

The destination of John's Gospel has been traditionally thought to be Asia Minor and perhaps the church at Ephesus and the nearby churches. The apparent reason for the letter is to strengthen the church so that, in turn, the church can respond to the person of Jesus Christ. Gerald Borchert states that he believes that John's purpose is stated in John 20: 30–31, "Therefore many other signs Jesus also performed in the presence of the disciples, which are not written in this book; but these have been written so that you may believe that Jesus is the Christ, the Son of God; and that believing you may have life in His name."[20] Borchert writes:

> When this verse is set in the context of the entire Gospel, it becomes a magnificent door through which the studied reader can gain access to the motives behind the writing of this document, which Clement of Alexandria well designated as the "Spiritual Gospel."[21]

The interesting issue for the present discussion is that the purpose of John indicates that a correct theological foundation will lead to appropriate action. In other words, the church is confronted with the maxim that belief proceeds action. To use a cliché, orthodoxy leads to orthopraxy.

John is writing to the church so that their faith would be strengthened. The content of their faith is based upon their knowledge of Jesus Christ. It is hard to miss this point! Evidently John understood the need of correctly identifying Jesus Christ as the Son of God. This theme is picked up throughout the book but the opening chapter highlights the depth of John's desire for the reader to acknowledge the deity of Christ. He uses four key words to illustrate this fact. They are: beginning (ἐν ἀρχῇ), logos (λόγος), with (πρὸς), became (ἐγένετο).

Beginning (ἀρχῇ):

There is a parallel concept between Genesis 1:1 and John 1:1 as a "beginning" is referenced in both verses. However, the "beginning" that John

---

19. Erickson, 25.

20. John 20:30–31.

21. Borchert, *John 1–11*, 30. Borchert is not the only scholar who adheres to this position: see Kostenberger, *John*; Carson, *The Gospel According to John*.

refers to precedes the creation account. Genesis 1:1 refers to the beginning of creation but John 1:1 refers to an epoch before creation (commonly called "eternity past").

C.K. Barrett argues that John set the reference of his gospel in manner that depicts the activity of Jesus in its origin.[22] Barrett believes that John understood that the only theological perspective that could adequately explain Jesus and his relationship to the Father was eternity.[23] This "beginning" (ἀρχῇ) provides a cosmological background in order to interpret the person of Jesus Christ. The use of the preposition "in" (ἐν) establishes the existence of the Lord—He was not the beginning or from the beginning but existed "in" the beginning. The eternal nature of the Lord is further demonstrated by the word "was" (ἦν).

> Although the meanings of ἦν (was) and ἐγένετο (rendered "were made" in v. 3, "came" in v. 6. and "became" on v. 14) often overlap, John repeatedly uses the two verbs side by side to establish something of a contrast . . . when John uses the two verbs in the same context, ἦν (was) frequently signals existence, whereas ἐγένετο signals "coming into being" of "coming into use." In the beginning, the Word was already in existence.[24]

The word "was" (ἦν) is indicative mood, active voice, and the imperfect tense. The indicative mood demonstrates a presentation of certainty or authenticity and realness. Wallace states that "in the active voice the subject performs, produces, or experiences the action or exists in the state expressed by the verb."[25] The imperfect tense indicates on going action in the past. The word "was" (ἦν) reveals that the Lord existed in eternity past (imperfect tense).

John establishes the Lord's preexistence by making the case, rather vividly, that Jesus Christ "was existing" when the beginning actually started. Murray J. Harris comments:

> In itself ἐν ἀρχῇ ἦν ὁ λογος speaks only of the pretemporality or supratemporality of the Logos, but by the conjunction of ἐν ἀρχῇ and ἦν John implies the eternal preexistence of the Word whose true sphere was not time but eternity. Having defined the relation

---

22. Barrett, *The Gospel According to St. John*, 149.
23. Ibid.
24. Carson, *The Gospel According to John*, 114.
25. Wallace, *Greek Grammar Beyond the Basics*, 410.

of the Word to time, John then specifies his relation to the Father. There can be little doubt that τὸν θεόν designates the Father.[26]

Logos (λόγος):

This word has been the subject of much discussion. For this discussion, Kittel's *Theological Dictionary of the New Testament* will be depended upon. Klenknecht gives the meaning of the word from a Greek philosophical reference. He states:

> λόγος achieved a comprehensive and varied significance with the process of rationalization which characterized the Greek spirit. Indeed, in its manifold historical application one might almost call is symbolic of the Greek understanding of the world and existence.[27]

Klenknecht states that the basic root meaning of λόγος is "counting, reckoning, and explaining."[28] However, as Klenknecht pointed out this word began to symbolize the Greek spirit of philosophical thought. From a speculative standpoint, λόγος may well have gained its meaning from the Greek attempt to give a rational explanation for the universe.

The basic idea is that the λόγος embodied a basic philosophical life principle that attempted to explain the reason or rational for the universe's existence. Again, Klenknecht states:

> It is presupposed as self-evident by the Greek that there is in things, in the world and its course, a primary λόγος, an intelligible and recognizable law, which then makes possible knowledge and understanding in the human λόγος. But this λόγος is not taken to be something which is merely grasped theoretically. It claims a man. It determines his true life and conduct.[29]

Apparently the rational power of the λόγος was the rational component that existed in humanity. According to Heraclitus, the possibility of rational understanding was the λόγος which bridged the cosmos with humanity.[30]

---

26. Harris, *Prepositions and Theology in the Greek New Testament*, 190.
27. Kleinknecht, TDNT, "The Logos in the Greek and Hellenistic World," 4:76.
28. Ibid., 78.
29. Ibid., 81.
30. The source of this paraphrase is from Kleinkencht's article in *TDNT*, "The Logos in the Greek and Hellenistic World."

Klenknecht also stresses that the λόγος further developed in meaning through Stoic philosophy. He states:

> In Stoicism λόγος is a term for the ordered and teleologically orientated nature of the world. It is thus equated with the concept of God. As such it can no longer be rendered actively as concrete speech which is uttered on a meaningful basis, as in Socratic-Platonic philosophy. It can be identified only passively with the (cosmic) law of reason. God is ὁ πάντων τῶν ὄντων λόγος, and the basis of the unity of this world.[31]

John may have been utilizing a well-known Greek philosophical concept to express the nature of the Jesus Christ. The meaning is striking. He identifies the λόγος as the eternal God that gives life and meaning to life (this meaning is also delineated in v. 4). The λόγος is the absolute communication of God that gives meaning to all things that exist.

There is a strong possibility that John also used λόγος with the Hebrew background of "wisdom." Carson explains:

> The Wisdom of God is highly personified in some passages (especially Pr 8:22ff.) becoming the agent of creation and a wonderful gift. This personification is again extended in later Jewish writings (e.g. Wisdom 7:22–8:1; Ecclus. 24). Many scholars, finding frequent parallels to John in Wisdom literature, hold that the Evangelists assigns to λόγος some of the attributes of Wisdom.[32]

There is a link (either direct or indirect) to the Old Testament concept of "wisdom." The emphasis of the wisdom motif may well have been John's desire to demonstrate that the λόγος is the long-awaited Messiah. The meaning then is that wisdom is the Messiah who is introduced as the λόγος. This approach would speak to a Jewish audience. However, there is one other possibility concerning the meaning and usage of the word λόγος.

It could be that John is trying to communicate a distinct Christian concept to his contemporary audience. In other words, he was contextualizing the Christian message.[33] If the recipients of John's Gospel were in Asia Minor—or for that matter—outside Palestine, then it would prove

---

31. ibid., 84.

32. Carson, 115.

33. Cairns, Dictionary of Theological Terms, s.v. "Contextualization." The "contextualization" refers to "A method of literary criticism that seeks to distinguish the meaning of the text of a Scripture from the culture and historical context in which it was given. The latter is regarded as the temporary garb in which God's revelation appeared in a

Section I—Primary Christological Passages

necessary to demonstrate that Christianity is the answer to the Gentile's contemporary philosophical questions. John is building a foundation for evangelism (which is his stated purpose in John 20:30–31). Carson confirms this approach. He states:

> . . . when Christians looked around for suitable categories to express what they had come to know of Jesus Christ, many that applied to him necessarily enjoyed a plethora of antecedent associations. The terms had to be semantically related to what the Christians wanted to say, or they could not have communicated with their own age.[34]

With (πρὸς):

This preposition has significant meaning in verse 1. A. T. Robertson states that the meaning of "with" (πρὸς) is that the λόγος was literally "face to face with God."[35] The preposition yields the meaning of a distinction of persons within the Godhead. The intimacy of the λόγος with Father is a theme throughout the Gospel (3:2; 8:29, 38; 16:32). Verse 1 specifically states that the intimacy between the Father and Son was before creation. Harris comments, "When πρὸς is used of a relationship between persons, it must imply personal intercourse rather than simply denoting spatial juxtaposition or personal accompaniment."[36]

The question becomes, how does the Son relate to the Father within the distinction of the Godhead? "Face to face" indicates equality of persons, which includes not only a spatial concept but the realm of communication between the God and the Logos as being equal within their relationship. This is evidenced by that fact that "with" (πρὸς) is a transitive preposition with a stative verb ("was"; ἦν). According to Wallace, "when a stative verb is used with a transitive preposition, the preposition's natural force is neutralized; all that remains is a stative idea."[37] The stative idea is that the λόγος did not come into the presence of God as a subordinate but was constantly in intimate fellowship with God as an equal.

---

particular place at a particular time. The theory is that we may change the garb to suit another culture in which we are called to preach the gospel.

34. Carson, 116.
35. Robertson, *A Grammar of the Greek New Testament*, 623.
36. Harris, 192.
37. Wallace, 359.

The meaning of the two phrases ("In the beginning was the Word, and the Word was with God," ἐν ἀρχῇ ἦν ὁ λογος και ο λόγος ἦν πρὸς τὸν θεόν) depicts the ontological nature of the λόγος. The Logos has the same nature as the Father and as such there is no inferiority within the nature of the Son. The last phrase ("and the Word was God," καί θεὸς ἦν ὁ λόγος) states the obvious: not only was the λόγος in the presence of God (intimate fellowship), but the λόγος is God. There was never a time when the λόγος was not fully God. Andreas J. Kostenberger states:

> It is one thing for the Word to be with God (so were Isaiah's personified Word and Wisdom); it is quite another for the Word to be God. Having distinguished the Word—Jesus, not mentioned by name until 1:17—from God, John now shows what they have in common: they are God.[38]

The fellowship of the Son and Father are based upon the common nature—their deity! The basic concept is that Jesus shared in the ontological nature of the Father even though there was a distinction in the personage.

Excursus

One excursus warrants mention. The phrase "In the beginning was the Word, and the Word was with God and the Word was God" (ἐν ἀρχῇ ἦν ὁ λογος και ο λόγος ἦν πρὸς τὸν θεόν καί θεὸς ἦν ὁ λόγος) has generated much discussion among evangelicals and has given rise to cultic distortion.

The phrase is a predicate nominative. That simply means that two nouns are linked together by an equative verb. In the Greek language the terminology is more involved. A predicate nominative (a noun) can be anarthrous—without a definite article. Basically, in John 1:1 there are two definite nouns linked by an equative verb. An English example would be: "The boy is human." In this example there are two nouns linked by a stative, equative verb.

This English grammatical construction determines that the boy is a subset of humanity. The boy in question is not the sum total of humanity (girls are human too—I know I shattered the perception of every twelve-year-old boy and I do apologize for this dose of shocking reality), but he is human nonetheless.

---

38. Kostenberger, *John*, 28.

Section I—Primary Christological Passages

The same concept is true of verse one. The Son is not the totality of the Godhead, but he is God nonetheless! Wallace concludes that the predicate nominative, θεὸς (God), functions qualitatively. In other words, θεὸς (God) qualifies the primary categories, which means the subcategory of the λόγος is God. Wallace states:

> The most likely candidate for θεὸς is qualitative . . . Such an option does not impugn the deity of Christ. Rather, it stresses that, although the person of Christ is not the person of the Father, their *essence* (emphasis his) is identical . . . The idea of a qualitative θεὸς here is that the Word had all the attributes and qualities that "the God" (1:1b) had. In other words, he shared the *essence* (emphasis his) of the Father, though they differed in person. *The construction the evangelist chose to express this idea was the most concise way he could have stated that the Word was God and yet was distinct from the Father.*[39]

END OF EXCURSUS

Became (ἐγένετο):

The prologue begins with the pre-existence of the Logos established as God. John makes the point that the Logos is God but distinct from the Father and yet the Logos has the exact same nature as the Father. He is coexistent, coequal, and coeternal with the Father. The prologue also introduces the Baptist and his witness to the Logos's as the Light of the World. Nothing more is mentioned specifically about the Logos's essence or eternal nature.

However, in verse 14 ("And the Word became flesh," και ο λόγος σαρξ ἐγένετο) the passage takes an abrupt turn. The Logos is re-introduced in the prologue but with a significant difference: the Logos "became" (ἐγένετο) flesh! The Logos is now something he was not before—human.

The meaning of "became" (ἐγένετο) was discussed briefly. The term now warrants a deeper investigation. The word "became" (ἐγένετο) is an aorist tense which has the meaning of completed action. The word is defined as meaning "to become, of persons and things which change their

---

39. Wallace, 269. Wallace comments on the fact that many theologians use Colwell's rule to state that θεος is a definite noun. It is compelling to do so but if the θεος (God) is definite then the ο λογος (the Word) must also be definite. Again, Wallace states, "The problem of this argument is that the θεος in 1:1b is the Father. Thus to say that the θεος in 1:1c is the person is to say that "the Word was the *Father*." (268).

nature, to indicate their entering a new condition: become something."[40] The context yields the meaning in graphic terms: the Lord took on or added flesh to His nature and that is a permanent condition! Leon Morris writes:

> *Became* is in the aorist tense, and indicates action at a point of time. *Flesh* is a strong, almost crude way of referring to human nature. John does not say, "the Word became man," nor "the Word took a body." He chooses that form of expression which puts what he wants to say most bluntly . . . He is clear on the deity of the Word. But he is just as clear on the genuineness of His humanity.[41]

The contrast between the eternal nature and the incarnation of the Logos is apparent. The Logos existed eternally as God and in the presence of the Father. Verse 1 refers to the timelessness of the Logos's eternal nature, whereas, verse 14 speaks to a definite time centered event. The eternal Logos took on a time-bound nature and lived among humanity.

When the Logos became flesh he did not cease to be God nor was his deity ever diminished. Ben Witherington's insight is valuable. He states:

> Here one finds "*ho logos sarx egneto*." This means "the Word became flesh." It certainly does not mean that the Word turned into flesh with no remainder, because he remains the Word who is beheld by the community at the end of the hymn. Thus it might be better to say that what is mean is either the Word took on flesh, or the Word came on the human scene. The Word became more than he was before, not less. To his divine nature he added a human one.[42]

Again, the contrast cannot be dismissed between verse 1 and verse 14. The Logos existed as God with God in fellowship with God. However, in verse 14 the Logos became flesh. The rationale is that in the person of Jesus Christ, the Logos added human nature to his deity. The functional purpose is so that Jesus Christ, as God, existed as a human with humans and in fellowship with humanity.

---

40. Vine, 196.

41. Morris, *The Gospel According to John*, 102.

42. Witherington III, *John's Wisdom*, 55. Verse 14 does not support some mythical interpretations that God changed into man. Bloesch, *Jesus Christ: Savior & Lord* states it well: "The flesh was not 'changed into the nature of God nor was the ineffable nature of the Word of God transformed into the nature of flesh.' Orthodox Christianity holds neither to an appearance of God in a man nor a metamorphosis of God into man." The two natures did not co-mingle-they remained intact so that the property of each nature was undiminished in the incarnation.

Section I—Primary Christological Passages

CONCLUSION OF THE JOHANNINE STUDY

John depicts Logos Christology from an eternal perspective, i.e. "Christology from above."[43] However, John reveals that the Logos came to earth and lived among humans as a human. The Incarnation is the focal point of John's Christology. Jesus Christ is the divinely appointed mediator to creation while also expressing the Father to creation. The fellowship of humanity with God is possible only in Jesus Christ.

The possibility of humanity's relating to God (θεὸς) is realized in the person of the Logos (λόγος) as he became (ἐγένετο) fleshly. The incarnation of the Logos (λόγος) by no means implies that his activities as God ceased. Morris states "When the Word became flesh His cosmic activities did not remain in abeyance until the time of the earthly life was ended . . . we must surely hold that the incarnation meant the adding of something to what the Word was doing, rather than the cessation of most of His activities."[44] The point of the incarnation is that Jesus Christ is God.

CONTEMPORARY SIGNIFICANCE

The servanthood Christology of Philippians reveals that Christ came from above to serve below on earth. The act of service requires a humble attitude characterized in Scripture as the mind (φρονεῖτε) of Christ. The humility of Christ was demonstrated in the taking on the form (μορφῇ) of a servant. However, the action of self-denial is rooted in the thinking or attitude of Christ. The Philippian passage strongly implies that the action had its foundation in the attitude.

The ethical application for the church at Philippi is to realize Jesus Christ did not grasp or hold onto equality with the Father as though he were jealous of losing a position. Paul's focus was to transform interpersonal relationships so that the church would be transformed by adopting the same attitude Christ adopted as he incarnated into a different form (μορφῇ). The same goal and same approach is possible for the contemporary church. The action of servanthood ministry can only be accomplished by means of thinking differently than expected. The new attitude is to mimic the Savior who expressed self-denial without embracing feelings of inferiority. In

---

43. See chapter two in this volume for the definition of "Christology from above."
44. Morris, 114.

other words, humble servanthood ministries must be accompanied by a strong self-identity in Christ.

In the Johannine passage, the eternal Logos comes into the world in order to fellowship with humanity. The fellowship is based upon the revelation of the Son concerning the Father. C.F.D. Moule states, "If Jesus did not 'belong' to humankind, men and women would not find new life in him."[45] Again, the concept of "Christology from above" is evident but coupled with the fact that the Son was sent below to redeem humanity. The lasting result of God sending the Son is that eternal fellowship is possible with God.

The revelation of the Son's dual natures is hard to miss. The incarnation united both human and divine natures into the person of Jesus Christ. A full-orbed Christology is demonstrated in that the Logos was with God (ο λόγος ἦν πρὸς τὸν θεόν) but now, in the flesh, he entered the world to live with humanity. The impact for the contemporary church is to regain the theological understanding that nothing less than God is worshipped on Sunday morning. On the other hand, the contemporary church must also realize that the Savior has the ability to identify with the joys, tragedies, triumphs, sufferings, emotions, and limitations of humans. The dual natures of humanity and deity simply mean that the Son identifies with humanness and at the same time demonstrates the richness of heaven from his divine nature.

---

45. Moule, "*The Manhood of Jesus in the New Testament*," 53.

Section I—Primary Christological Passages

INTERACTIVE PERSONAL SEMINAR

Chapter Summary

In the New Testament books, Philippians and John, the person of Christ is presented throughout the works. Thus, a holistic approach to the study of Christology is warranted.

Key Terms

- Servant Christology
- Logos Christology
- The mind of Christ
- Logos
- Lordship
- Special Revelation

Advanced Questions

1. What is the theological importance of the incarnation?
2. Does Philippians and John present Jesus as equal to God, as God, or both?
3. Does the New Testament present Jesus as superior to the Father?
4. What is the significance of the Word being with the Father in John 1:1?
5. What is the significance of the two natures being incarnated?

Theological Questions

1. Explain the meaning of the hypostatic union.
2. Explain how the hypostatic union of the Son impacts the Trinity.

3. During his earthly life did Jesus possess the non-moral (natural or incommunicable) attributes? Explain the answer from the position of the hypostatic union.
4. Explain how the Lord's immanence is the focal point of the incarnation.
5. Explain how the Lord is still transcendent in the incarnation.

Issues To Research

- Evaluate the incommunicable attributes of God and determine how the incarnation impacted them.
- Evaluate the meaning of "firstborn," "image," and "radiance" as they relate to Christ's divinity.
- Explain the process of existing "as a slave" as that concept relates to Christ's humanity.
- Analyze the ethical meaning of Philippians 2:5–11 and how it relates to the church and individual.
- Explain the process of "progressive revelation."
- Explain why "angels" are mentioned in Hebrews 1. What is the significance of the contrast between them and Christ?

Section II

Historical Christological Councils

3

The Deity of Christ in Christian Thought before Nicea

Michael Haykin

A HIGH-SPEED MURDER MYSTERY, Dan Brown's monumental best-seller *The Da Vinci Code* was also a perfect example of postmodern historical revisionism in which an art historian, hero Robert Langdon, discovers that contemporary expressions of Christianity, especially that of the Roman Catholic Church, have no sound historical basis.[1] According to Brown's novel, it was not until the reign of the early fourth-century Roman emperor Constantine (r.306–337 AD) that the Bible—in particular the New Testament—was collated. In fact, it was Constantine who had the New Testament as we know it drawn up in order to suppress alternative perspectives on Jesus.[2] It was also not until the early fourth century Council of Nicæa (325 AD) that Jesus Christ was regarded as anything other than a human prophet. It was at this

---

1. Veith, "The *Da Vinci* phenomenon," 20–21.
2. Brown, *The Da Vinci Code*, 231–32.

Section II—Historical Christological Councils

council, which was astutely manipulated by the power-hungry Constantine for his own ends, that Jesus was "turned... into a deity" and became for the first time an object of worship.[3] Third, both of these events took place in order to conceal the fact that Jesus was actually married to Mary Magdalene,[4] had a child by her,[5] and that he intended that Mary be the founder of the church.[6] Key Christian teachings are thus the result of a power move by Constantine and other males in order to squash women. As Brown has one of his characters say, "It was all about power."[7]

Brown clearly intended these claims to be more than key aspects of the conspiratorial ambience of his novel. As Greg Clarke, Director of the Centre for Apologetic Scholarship and Education at New College, University of New South Wales, has rightly noted, Dan Brown's book had "evangelistic intentions" and was "meant to change our lives."[8] In the words of R. Albert Mohler, President of the Southern Baptist Theological Seminary, the book was thus a not-so-subtle denial of the central truths of biblical Christianity.[9]

Now, a goodly number of book-length responses were made to these claims.[10] What this article seeks to do is to respond to one of Brown's assertions, namely that of the person and deity of Christ, and in doing so elucidate a central motif of early Christian theology, specifically that Christ is indeed God and worthy of worship. In the words of Sir Leigh Teabing, a key figure in the novel, Christ is a "historical figure of staggering influence, perhaps the most enigmatic and inspirational leader the world has ever seen," but simply "a great and powerful man."[11] It was only at the Council

---

3. Ibid., 233–35.
4. Ibid., 244–47.
5. Ibid., 255–56.
6. Ibid., 248–49, 254.
7. *Da Vinci Code*, 233.

8. *Is it worth believing? The spiritual challenge of The Da Vinci Code* (Kingsford, New South Wales: Matthias Media, 2005), 25.

9. "Historical Propaganda", *Tabletalk*, 30, no.5 (May 2006), 12. This issue of *Tabletalk* is subtitled "The Da Vinci Hoax" and contains five articles devoted to examining Brown's book.

10. Here are some of the best, in terms of their critique of *The Da Vinci Code*: Bock, *Breaking the Da Vinci Code*; Clark, *The Da Vinci Code on Trial*; Ehrman, *Truth And Fiction in The Da Vinci Code.*; Lutzer, *The Da Vinci Deception*; Williams, *The Da Vinci Code: from Dan Brown's fiction to Mary Magdalene's faith*.

11. *Da Vinci Code*, 231, 233. See also *Da Vinci Code*, 234.

of Nicæa that Jesus's divine status was ratified by a "relatively close vote." Behind this vote was the scheming hand of Constantine and thus in a real sense Constantine "shaped the face of Christianity as we know it today."[12]

If this claim is true, it would eviscerate the heart of Christianity. Without the pre-existent deity of Christ, as American scholar Douglas McCready has shown, "every distinctive Christian belief would have to be discarded" and the Christian faith itself would become at best trivial and at worst utterly irrelevant.[13] Presbyterian theologian Benjamin B. Warfield was right to maintain, though, that the warp and woof New Testament is "saturated" with the presupposition of the deity of Christ.[14] And McCready's recent study *He Came Down From Heaven: The Preexistence of Christ and the Christian Faith* amply corroborates Warfield's claim.

SOME NEW TESTAMENT EVIDENCE

Apart from James's letter, the earliest New Testament documents are the letters of the Apostle Paul. McCready shows that a number of these letters plainly speak of Christ's divine pre-existence.[15] For instance, there is Colossians 1:15–16, which maintains that Christ is "the image of the invisible God."[16] In other words, Christ perfectly represents God. This text goes on to say that Christ created the entire universe: "by him all things were created, in heaven and on earth, visible and invisible," they were "created through him and for him." Being thus the creator of all things, Christ cannot be included in the created order.[17] Following these claims, there is also the assertion in Colossians 1:19 that in Christ dwelt "all the fullness of God," an assertion that is repeated in Colossians 2:9.[18] As McCready notes of these two latter verses, they declare "about as clearly as can be said that Jesus is God without confusing God the Father and the Son."[19]

---

12. Brown, *Da Vinci Code*, 233–34.
13. McCready, *He Came Down From Heaven*, 317.
14. "The Deity of Christ," 23–26, *passim*.
15. McCready, *He Came Down From Heaven*, 70–104.
16. Text from the Scriptures is taken from the ESV.
17. McCready, *He Came Down From Heaven*, 81–82.
18. "In him the whole fullness of deity dwells bodily."
19. McCready, *He Came Down From Heaven*, 82.

Section II—Historical Christological Councils

Paul also affirms Christ's creatorship in 1 Corinthians 8:5-6—"there is . . . one Lord, Jesus Christ, through whom are all things"[20]—and his deity in Romans 9:5 where Christ is described as "God over all, blessed forever."[21] With regard to this second Pauline text, McCready cites a comment on it by the third-century Christian exegete Origen (c.185–254): "It is clear from this passage that Christ is the God who is over all."[22]

There is also the much-discussed hymn to Christ in Philippians 2:5-11, which clearly presupposes Christ's pre-existence.[23] While the hymn is focused on the example of Christ's humility and self-sacrifice, it does make two significant ontological statements about the Lord Jesus. First, he "was in the form of God" (2:6). While there are sharp disagreements among New Testament scholars about the exact meaning of this phrase, the most consistent interpretation of this statement in the context of the hymn is that it is a declaration of Christ's enjoyment of the status or nature of God himself.[24] Then, the hymn goes on to assert that prior to his descent to the earth during the incarnation, Christ possessed "equality with God" (2:6). It was naturally his, and he willingly gave it up when he took on human existence.

McCready notes other New Testament texts that strongly assert the divinity of Christ, like Matthew 11:27[25] and Hebrews 1:1-8.[26] Understandably though, he devotes a significant amount of text to discussing the Johannine witness.[27] At the very opening of the Gospel of John, John 1:1 and 1:14 speak unequivocally of Christ as a divine being: as the Word he "was with God" and "was God (*theos*)" but he "became flesh and dwelt" in this world. In verse 1 it needs to be noted that the term for God, *theos*, does not have the definite article. As McCready points out, this syntactical construction serves to make the point that while the Word is equal with God—what God the Father is in terms of divine attributes, the Word also is—he is not identical with God. John thus emphasizes Jesus's deity without

---

20. Ibid., 86–87.
21. Ibid., 91–92.
22. McCready, *He Came Down From Heaven*, 92. See also Ehrman, *Truth And Fiction in The Da Vinci Code*, 16.
23. For extensive discussion, see McCready, *He Came Down From Heaven*, 73–80.
24. Ibid., 76–78.
25. Ibid., 108–112.
26. Ibid., 123–30.
27. Ibid., 135–62. See also Ehrman, *Truth And Fiction in The Da Vinci Code*, 16–17.

committing the error of what would later be called modalism, which removes the distinctions between the persons of the Godhead.[28]

In light of these statements about Christ's deity in the opening chapter of John's Gospel, the statement by Jesus in John 10:30 that he and "the Father are one" is probably to be read as being more than simply an assertion of his union with the Father in thought and intent. In light of the gospel context, it seems to affirm a union of being between the Father and the Son.[29] Some of Jesus's hearers who radically disagreed with him certainly understood it this way, for we are told in John 10:31–33 that they accused him of the blasphemy of making himself God.

Yet another Johannine text that is affirmative of the deity of Christ is 1 John 5:20, where Jesus is described as "the true God and eternal life." To be sure, there are difficulties with the grammatical construction of the sentence in relation to what precedes it. And while the import of the text is soteriological in intent—we can know God, "him who is true," because of the revelatory work of his Son, who "has given us understanding" of God—yet, as McCready quotes I. Howard Marshall, "it is precisely because Jesus is the true God that the person who is in him is also in the Father."[30]

McCready's examination of the New Testament witness about the person of Christ is an exhaustive one. At the end of it, he states that the evidence of the New Testament points in only one direction: it "consistently presents Jesus Christ as preexistent deity every time the subject arises."[31] Of course, by arguing that Constantine commissioned a Bible "that embellished those gospels that made Him [i.e. Christ] godlike,"[32] Dan Brown hoped to undercut any such argument from the New Testament for the deity of Christ. Therefore, the testimony of post-apostolic Christianity in the second and third centuries also needs to be considered in a response to Brown's claim that prior to the Council of Nicæa Christ was regarded only as a human being. In what follows, due to space, our focus is limited to various second and third-century witnesses to the deity of Christ, both pagan and Christian. The two Christian testimonies, it should be noted, cover a couple of genres: the epistolary writings of Ignatius of Antioch, similar in form to those of Paul; and a work of apologetics, the *Letter to Diognetus*.

28. McCready, *He Came Down From Heaven*, 141–42.
29. Ibid., 150–51.
30. Ibid., 158–59.
31. Ibid., 310.
32. Brown, *The Da Vinci Code*, 234.

Section II—Historical Christological Councils

Three pagan witnesses

Around the year 110 AD, a new governor was appointed for the Roman provinces of Pontus and Bithynia in what is now northern Turkey. His name was Caius Plinius Caecilius Secundus, better known to history as Pliny the Younger (61/62–c.113 AD). Prior to this appointment, he was in charge of the public works for the city of Rome and performed so admirably that the emperor, Trajan (r.98–117 AD), appointed him to clean up an economic mess in the province of Pontus and Bithynia. Like any good leader, Pliny sought first to find out what was happening at ground level before instituting significant changes in the infrastructure of the province. In the course of his tour of the cities and towns of the province, certain Christians were brought to him in one of the towns.[33] From the point of view of the Roman *imperium*, these men and women were members of an illegal religion, part of what Pliny called "a degenerate sort of cult carried to extravagant lengths."[34] Their crime was their steadfast refusal (*contumacia*) to heed the urging of an official of the Roman state, Pliny, to worship the Roman gods and do reverence to a statue of the emperor.

To find out more about the doings of these Christians, Pliny tortured two women whom he terms *ministrae*, that is "deaconesses."[35] In the process of his torturing these women, he learned a number of things about early Christian worship, including the fact, as he later wrote to Trajan, that these Christians would sing "an antiphonal hymn to Christ as to a god."[36] Pliny the pagan might have viewed this worship as "degenerate," but there is no gainsaying the fact that the Roman governor understood Christians to be people who offered adoration to Christ as a divine being.

Another pagan author in the second century who had a similar impression is the satirist Lucian of Samosata (c.125–c.180 AD). In his book *The Passing of Peregrinus*, which satirizes the career of the Cynic philosopher Peregrinus and was written after Pergrinus's self-immolation at the Olympic Games in 165 AD, Lucian noted that at one point Peregrinus joined the Christians. Rising rapidly in their ranks, Peregrinus was soon

---

33. For our knowledge of these events, see Pliny, *Letters*, 10.96–97. For a translation of these texts, see Henry Bettenson in his selected and ed., *Documents of the Christian Church*, 3–4.

34. *Letter*, 10.96.8.

35. Ibid., 10.96.8.

36. *Letter*, 10.96.8. See also the remarks of Clark, *Da Vinci Code on Trial*, 64–65; Gumbel, *The Da Vinci Code: A Response*,, 17.

incarcerated for his faith. Lucian poked fun at the way fellow Christians treated Peregrinus while he was in prison and noted that

> the efficiency the Christians show whenever something of community interest like this happens is unbelievable; they literally spare nothing. And so, because Peregrinus was in jail, money poured in from them; he picked up a very nice income this way. The poor wretches have convinced themselves, first and foremost, that they're all going to be immortal and live forever, which makes them take death lightly and willingly give themselves up to it. Furthermore, their first lawgiver [i.e. Christ] persuaded them that they are all brothers of one another when they deny the Greek gods (thereby breaking our law) and begin to worship him, the crucified sophist himself, and to live their lives according to his rules. They scorn all possessions without distinction and treat them as common property; doctrines like this they accept strictly on faith. Consequently, if a charlatan and trickster who knows how to capitalize on a situation comes among them, he quickly becomes exceedingly rich while laughing at the simpletons.[37]

This is a fascinating text in many ways as it touches on a number of aspects of early Christianity. What is important for the subject at hand is that Lucian, who has nothing but scorn for Christians, knew that they refused to participate in the worship of the Graeco-Roman pantheon of gods. Instead, he said they offered "worship" to a "crucified sophist," by which he obviously means Christ. It seems clear that Lucian viewed the worship of Christ as the Christian alternative to the worship of the gods of his pagan world. As such Lucian is another pagan witness to the fact that the second-century Church worshipped Christ.

A final pagan witness from the third century is an item of graffiti.[38] In the quarters of the imperial page boys on the Palatine Hill in Rome, there has been found the drawing of a figure of a man on a cross with the head of a donkey. Beneath it is another figure, the figure of a boy with his arm upraised, a typical gesture of worship found in early Christian art. Underneath these crude drawings are words in Latin, which when translated state: "Alexamenos worships his god." There is little doubt that this is an attack on one of the page boys, Alexamenos, who was a Christian. And it is clear that the one who made this attack understood Alexamenos's religious beliefs to involve worship of the one who was crucified, namely Jesus Christ. It is

37. Lucian, *The Passing of Peregrinus* 13.
38. For this piece of graffiti, see Green, *Evangelism in the Early Church*, 174–75.

interesting that another hand—possibly that of Alexamenos himself or one of his fellow page boys who was impressed with Alexamenos's witness—has scrawled below the above-mentioned statement, "Alexamenos is faithful."

Ignatius of Antioch

Apart from the Apostle Paul no other figure from the first two centuries of Christianity lays bare his soul as much as Ignatius of Antioch (died c.107–110 AD). In the words of biblical scholar Bruce Metzger, Ignatius's letters, though somewhat staccato in style and punctuated with rhetorical embellishments, manifest "such strong faith and overwhelming love of Christ as to make them one of the finest literary expressions of Christianity during the second century."[39] Moreover, although we possess only seven authentic letters of Ignatius, they provide one of our richest resources for the understanding of Christianity in the era immediately following that of the Apostles.[40]

Ignatius, the bishop of the church in Antioch, had been arrested in this city somewhere between 107 and 110 and sent to Rome for trial.[41] There are no details of the persecution in which he was arrested, though Ignatius does mention others who were probably arrested during the same persecution and who had preceded him to Rome.[42] Thus, he was brought across the great roads of southern Asia Minor in the custody of ten Roman soldiers, whom he likens to "savage leopards."[43] He expects the end of the journey in Rome to have to one certain outcome: death.

Among the concerns that were uppermost in Ignatius's mind as he wrote these letters was the heresy of Gnosticism, which was troubling a number of the churches to which he was writing and which maintained that the incarnation of Christ, and consequently his death and resurrection, did not really take place.[44] The divine status of Christ was not in debate, but

---

39. Lawyer, "Eucharist and Martyrdom," 281.

40. Williams, *Christian Spirituality*, 14. On the transmission of the text of these letters, see the brief summary by Maxwell Staniforth in his trans., *Early Christian Writings: The Apostolic Fathers*, 55–56.

41. For the date, see Trevett, *A Study of Ignatius of Antioch*, 3–9.

42. *Romans* 10.

43. *Romans* 5.

44. Lawyer, "Eucharist and Martyrdom," 281.

on a number of occasions the letters show marked evidence of a very high Christology.[45]

In his letter to the Ephesian church, for example, Ignatius describes Christ as "God incarnate" and later in the letter reminds his readers that in Christ "God was revealing himself as a man."[46] Or writing to the believers in Smyrna, Ignatius says that Christ is none other than "God the Word, the only-begotten Son."[47] And at the very outset of his letter to the church at Rome, in which Ignatius sought to convince the church there not to attempt to free him from the Roman authorities but to allow him to fulfill his calling to be a martyr, he says of Jesus Christ that he is "our God."[48] Later in this letter, he says, "leave me to imitate the Passion of my God."[49] The one who died on the cross is none other than God. In referring to Christ as "God," Ignatius evidently expected the Christians to whom he was writing to be both familiar with such a view of Christ and comfortable with it.[50]

Reinforcing all of these texts is the statement in Ignatius's letter to the church at Magnesia-on-the-Meander that "Jesus Christ . . . was with the Father (*para patri*) from all eternity."[51] This clause is parallel to the Johannine affirmation in John 1:1 that "the Word was with God (*pros ton theon*)." In *koinē* Greek at this time, the use of *para* with the dative to express the idea of "with someone" was receiving competition from *pros* with the accusative. In other words, Ignatius's statement that Jesus was "with the Father" and John's declaration that the Word "was with God" are making the same point: Jesus Christ/the Word has enjoyed an intimate, personal communion with the Father that is eternal in nature. But such a statement is ludicrous unless one believes in the deity of Christ.

---

45. For a very brief overview of Ignatius's view of Christ as preexistent deity, see McCready, *He Came Down From Heaven*, 210. For a detailed study of Ignatius's Christology, see Story, "The Christology of Ignatius of Antioch," 173–82; Brown, *The Gospel and Ignatius of Antioch*.

46. *Ephesians* 7 and 19. See also *Ephesians* 1, where Ignatius refers to the "blood of God." Williams (*Da Vinci Code*, 23) cites the first of these texts as proof of post-apostolic Christian literature speaking of "Jesus plainly as God."

47. *Smyrnaeans* 1.

48. *Romans*, Salutation.

49. *Romans* 6.

50. Brown, *Gospel and Ignatius of Antioch*, 134.

51. *Magnesians*, 6.

Section II—Historical Christological Councils

The Letter to Diognetus

The Letter to Diognetus, which is easily overlooked among second-century Christian writings, has been well described by American author Avery Dulles as "the pearl of early Christian apologetics."[52] *In nuce*, this anonymous work is the joyous expression in Pauline terms of a man who stands utterly amazed at the gracious revelation of God's love in the death of his Son for sinners and who is seeking to persuade a Graeco-Roman pagan by the name of Diognetus to make a similar commitment to the Christian faith. From the elegant Greek of the treatise it is probably correct to observe that the author had had a classical education and "possessed considerable literary skill and style."[53] Though the historical and geographical context of the work and audience is not known, it should probably be dated in the latter half of the second century.[54]

Markus Bockmuehl has rightly noted that the theological centre of the *Letter to Diognetus* is found in chapters 7–9,[55] where, among other things, an answer is given to a question asked of the author by Diognetus, "Who is the God Christians believe in and worship?" The author formulates his answer to the question in terms of a high Christology. He begins by indicating that the Christian concept of God is not the product of human thought or philosophy.[56]

> [I]t is not an earthly discovery that has been passed on to them [i.e. Christians]. That which they think it worthwhile to guard so carefully is not a result of mortal thinking, nor is what has been entrusted to them a stewardship of merely human mysteries. On

---

52. *A History of Apologetics*, 28.

53. Barnard, "The Enigma of the Epistle to Diognetus", 172. "[G]ood Hellenistic [Greek] with a marked approach to classical standards in vocabulary and diction" is the way H.G. Meecham describes the language of the letter ["The Theology of the Epistle to Diognetus", *The Expository Times*, 97]. For a list of possible authors, see Barnard, "Epistle to Diognetus", 171–72.

54. For this dating, see Grant, *Greek Apologists*, 178–179; Theofried Baumeister, "Zur Datierung der Schrift an Diognet", *Vigiliae Christianae*, 42 (1988), 105–111. Walford, *Epistle to Diognetus*, 7–9 and Barnard, "Epistle to Diognetus", 172–73 would date it no later than 140.

55. *Revelation and Mystery*, 219. Reference to the *Letter to Diognetus* is according to chapter and verse. I am following the chapter and verse divisions of Meecham, *The Epistle to Diognetus* and Thierry, *The Epistle to Diognetus*.

56. For an earlier allusion in the letter to this fact, see *Diognetus* 5.3. The same point will be made yet a third time in *Diognetu,s* 8.1–5.

> the contrary, the Almighty himself, the Creator of the universe and the invisible God, has from heaven planted the Truth, even the holy and incomprehensible Word, among men and fixed it firmly in their hearts.[57]

Here the author unequivocally affirms that Christian truth is ultimately not a matter of human reason or religious speculation. Rather, it is rooted in God's revelation of himself. Before he revealed himself to the world of paganism, God was unknown.

This revelation, the author of this treatise now maintains, was made through the incarnation of his Son. God has not, he writes,

> sent to humanity some servant, angel or ruler . . . Rather, [he has sent] the very Designer and Maker of the universe, by whom he made the heavens and confined the seas within their bounds; . . . from whom the sun is assigned the limits of its daily course and whom the moon obeys when he bids her to shine by night, and whom the stars obey as they follow the course of the moon. He is the One by whom all things have been set in order, determined, and placed in subjection—both the heavens and things in the heavens, the earth and things on the earth, the sea and the things in the sea, fire, air, abyss, the things in the heights and those in the depths and the realm between. Such was the One God sent to them. . . . In gentleness and meekness he sent him, as a King sending his son who is a king. He sent him as God, he sent him as [man] to men, he sent him as Savior.[58]

Christianity, then, is ultimately not a human attempt to find God by philosophical speculation or religious ritual. Rather, it is founded on God's revelation of himself, and that in a person, his Son. Although the personal name of the incarnate Son, Jesus, is not mentioned in this passage or even in the treatise as a whole,[59] there is no doubt that this is the person of whom the author here writes so eloquently.

Now, when many of the pagans in the Graeco-Roman world stood outside of their homes on a cloudless night and looked up to the heavens, they believed that the stars they could see were none other than divine beings. The long description of the Son's sovereignty over the entirety of creation clearly indicates that Christian theism does not believe in such

---

57. *Diognetus*, 7.1–2.
58. *Diognetus*, 7.2, 4.
59. On this fact, see Marrou, *A Diognète*, 185–87.

a multiplicity of divine beings. Yet, it does believe in the deity of the Son. For the Son is depicted in terms that one can only regard as fully divine. He clearly does not belong to the order of creation. Who then is this One whom God has sent to reveal himself? Well, he is "a son." He is sent by God "as God." As L.B. Radford has commented: "He is God so truly that His coming can be described as the coming of God."[60]

A Concluding Word

More textual evidence from the second and the third centuries than what is adduced here could have been cited.[61] It would uniformly bear out what the texts we have looked at consistently assert: Jesus Christ was viewed as a divine being in both the New Testament era as well as in the two centuries that followed. As Bart Ehrman, himself no friend to orthodox Christianity, states: "Scholars who study the history of Christianity will find it bizarre, at best, to hear [Brown] claim that Christians before the Council of Nicea did not consider Jesus to be divine."[62] What the creedal statement issued at this council declared, namely that Jesus is "true God of true God" and of "one being with the Father," had been the central conviction of the Church in the years since the Apostolic era. And this was the conviction of the Church for it ultimately derived from the Church's foundational text, the New Testament itself.

---

60. *The Epistle to Diognetus*, 39.
61. For other second-century authors, see McCready, *He Came Down From Heaven*, 211–18.
62. Ehrman, *Truth And Fiction in The Da Vinci Code*, 15.

INTERACTIVE PERSONAL SEMINAR

Chapter Summary

Pre-Nicene Theology addressed philosophical challenges to Christology. The local heresies were the harbinger of more advanced theology heresies that would plague the church internally. Yet, these external challenges proved beneficial in that the church had a strong foundation to build the case for orthodoxy.

Key Terms

- *Letter to Diognetus*
- *The Passing of Peregrinus*

Key People

- Ignatius
- Pliny the Younger
- Diognetus

Advanced Questions

1. The actions of Pliny the Younger depict the actions of imperial Rome toward the Christians. Why were the Christians so hated by governmental Rome?
2. The apologetics contained in the *Letter to Diognetus* reveals the early Christians capability of defending the faith. Why was it necessary to proclaim a defense of the faith? Is that same need still existence in the contemporary world?

4

The Road to Orthodoxy Leads to Nicaea

Marvin Jones

POLITICS AND RELIGION

The political scene at the beginning of the fourth century drastically altered the status of Christianity. Constantine has the dubious honor of being known as the first Christian Emperor.[1] He was of royal linage as his father, "Constantius Chlorus, reigned over Gaul, Spain, and Britain till his death in 306."[2] Constantius ruled during the Diocletian persecution and "refused to inflict death on anyone for his religion, maintaining that the 'the temple of God,' the human body, may not be so maltreated."[3] It may be that Constantine's mother greatly influenced Constantius as the Christian church considered her a pious woman and later a saint of the Catholic Church.[4]

---

1. Brown, *Heresies*, 108.
2. Schaff, *History of the Christian Church*, 18.
3. Renwick, *Story of the Church*, 50.
4. Schaff, *History of the Christian Church*, 19.

Constantine

Constantine proved himself a capable leader in the military, and he was proclaimed Emperor upon his father's death. Constantine stated:

> My father revered the Christian God and uniformly prospered, while the emperors who worshipped the heathen gods, died a miserable death; therefore, that I may enjoy a happy life and reign, I will imitate the example of my father and join myself to the cause of Christians, who are growing daily, while the heathen are diminishing.[5]

The battle that recognized and solidified the emperorship of Constantine was the infamous battle of the Milvian Bridge. Bruce Shelly states:

> Upon the death of Galerius, a struggle for imperial power broke loose. In the Spring of 312, Constantine, the son of Constantius Chlorus, advanced across the Alps to dislodge his rival Maxentius from Italy and to capture Rome. It was a daring gamble; and when he came upon his militarily superior enemy at the Milvian Bridge, just outside of Rome, he turned for help to the God of the Christians. In a dream he saw a cross in the sky and the words, 'In this sign conquer.' This convinced him to advance. When on 28 October 312 he achieved his brilliant victory over the troops of Maxentius, Constantine looked upon his success as proof of the power of Christ and the superiority of the Christian religion.[6]

The result of this battle was the famous "Edict of Milan." This edict gave religious toleration, even freedom, to all religions of the day. The Roman Empire now had only two rulers: (1) Constantine (who favored the Christians while tolerating the pagans) ruled in the West, (2) Licinius (who favored the pagans and tolerated the Christian Churches) ruled in the East.

Under the leadership of Constantine, the Christian Church enjoyed more freedom than at any point in its history. Constantine exempted the clergy from military duty, abolished laws that were offensive in nature to

---

5. Ibid., 19–20.

6. Shelly, *Church History in Plain Language*, 108. Galerius was a contemporary of Constantine's father, Constantius Chlorus. At the death Galerius, civil war broke out over control for the Roman Empire. This specific battle, in the life of Constantine, had full ramifications for the Council of Nicaea. If Constantine would have lost this battle, it is safe to assume that the Nicaean council would have never convened. Galerius, unlike Constantius Chlorus, continued the Diocletian persecution and passed the legacy to Maxentius. I do not wish to demean the story into a "good verses evil" epic; nonetheless, the providence of God can be clearly evidenced as witnessed by the events and outcome of this battle.

Section II—Historical Christological Councils

Christians, emancipated Christian slaves and enjoined Sunday as a day of worship. Licinius, on the other hand, not only ridiculed the Christians but also banished them from public office. These events led to open confrontation between the East and West.[7]

The inevitable clash of the two leaders of the Roman Empire took place in a series of battles. The battle of Adrianople in July 323 and the battle of Chalcedon in September gave the decisive victory to Constantine and eventually assured Christianity's acceptance into the general populace.

The Roman Empire was now politically secure in the hands of Constantine. Both the East and the West enjoyed the tranquility of a peaceful life since Constantine was now ready to rule a unified Roman Empire. The unity of the Empire was predicated on two fronts: (1) Political and military solidarity had been achieved—there was no inward nor outward threat to the Empire, (2) Christianity was now openly acceptable and Christians lived without the fear of governmental or private persecution. Thus, the religion of the people could maintain the moral climate of good citizenship. Peace and prosperity seemed to be in place for Constantine, the Roman Empire, and the Christian Church.

THEOLOGICAL CONFLICT IN THE CHRISTIAN CHURCH

The theological problems of the church surfaced very soon after the ascension of Constantine to the throne. The new Emperor had an ecclesiological issue that could prove to be divisive within the empire. Schaff comments on the problem, "No sooner had Constantine, the first Christian Emperor, gained complete control of the empire than he found the church—which he had hoped would help him reunite his vast domain—riven by bitter conflict."[8]

The major theological issue focused on the preaching of Arius as he pastored in Alexandria Egypt. He depicted Jesus Christ as lacking in the co-eternal nature of the Father. In a letter to Bishop Alexander of Alexandria, Arius states:

> God being the cause of all is without beginning, most alone; but the Son, begotten by the Father created and founded before the ages, was not before He was begotten . . . For He is not everlasting or co-everlasting or unbegotten with the Father. Nor does he

---

7. Schaff, *History of the Christian Church*, 31.
8. Brown, *Heresies*, 107–08.

have being with the Father . . . and bring into the discussion two unbegotten causes.[9]

The result of the letter was a debate that only served to frustrate the situation. Alexander went public with a ban on Arius and his teachings. This ban started the path to Nicaea where Arius, Alexander, Athanasius, and the subject of Christology became an ecumenical issue throughout the Constantinian Empire.

Arius

The central person in the theological issue was Arius. "The outset of the controversy, probably in about the year 319, was caused by Arius's preaching."[10] Arius was the presbyter of the Baucalis Church in Alexandria. The content of Arius's message is known as the Arian controversy. Basically, Arius adhered to a deviant position concerning the nature of Jesus Christ. "His dominant idea was the monotheistic principle of the Monarchians, that there is only one unbegotten God, one unoriginated Being, without any beginning existence."[11] The interesting issue about Arius is the fact that the views he exposed were not of his own origination. The theological concept that became known as Arianism had been a teaching of the famous Alexandrian School. Arius had two teachers: Paul of Samosata and Lucian.

Paul of Samosata propagated the teachings of Monarchianism. "Paul differed from the previous Monarchians in that he held that Christ, commencing as a man, was raised by progressive development to the dignity of the Son of God due to his excellent rank."[12] The fact that there are no surviving documents from Paul of Samosata reveals that any statements attributed to him are suspect for accuracy. Regardless, history has documented his teachings as the source that informed Arius's preaching content. Khaled Anatolios, referencing Saballius and Paul of Samosata, states, "their impact was such that it became *de rigueur* for the articulation of a

---

9. Arius, "Arius Letter to Alexandria," 31–32.

10. Rusch, *The Trinitarian Controversy*, 17.

11. Berkhof, *The History of Christian Doctrines*, 84.

12. Bingham, *Class Notes from History of Christian Doctrine*. "The term Monarchianism has specific reference to the sole Government or rule of God as distinct from polytheism. The term denotes, in general, the tendency that emphasizes the unity of God and rejects a plurality of disjoined persons."

Section II—Historical Christological Councils

Christian doctrine of God to reject a 'Sabellian' or 'Samosatene' interpretation of divine unity."[13]

Paul of Samosata's position is an adoptionistic view[14] of the person of Christ (he did view Jesus as God but only through a moral unity or moral perfection). His teachings were condemned at the Synod of Antioch in 269 AD. Older historical scholarship attributed Paul's teaching as foundational to Arius's theological tenets. However, recent scholarship has downplayed the influence of Paul of Samosata upon Arius. R. P. C. Hanson states "if we construct the teaching of Paul at all, his doctrine is more likely to have been the inspiration of Eustathius and Marcellus than of Arius."[15] Further studies are required to ascertain the influence of Paul of Samosata upon Arius.

Lucian, a student of Paul of Samosata, practiced his belief on interpreting the Bible literally.[16] Paul of Samosata and Lucian were of the School of Antioch. This hermeneutical school was in direct opposition of the School of Alexandria. "Lucian followed in the tradition of Paul of Samosata, emphasizing the humanity and the human will of Jesus."[17]

Lucian expounded his view that the Logos was a divine power created by God the Father. He argued that the Logos was then incarnated in the person of Jesus Christ, meaning that only the Father is full deity. He understood the Logos as a "kind of intermediate, created spiritual being between God and man."[18] Lucian emphasized the humanity of Jesus Christ rather than his deity. This emphasis led to an attempted explanation of the Logos's incarnation, without simply allowing the Logos to retain deity.

Lucian also tried to avoid the adoptionist heresy of his predecessor.[19] Paul of Samosata influenced Lucian who likewise taught his theological concepts to Arius. Lewis Ayres notes, "The ancient sources seem to identify

---

13. Anatolios, *Retrieving Nicaea*, 16.

14. Matt Slick, "Adoptionism." Adoptionists taught that Jesus was tested by God; and after passing this test and upon his baptism, he was granted supernatural powers by God and adopted as the Son. As a reward for his great accomplishments and perfect character, Jesus was raised from the dead and adopted into the Godhead.

15. Hanson, *The Search for the Christian Doctrine of God*, 71.

16. By using the word "literal" it may imply a Grammatical Historical Hermeneutic. That is not the case. Lucian imposed a narrow interpretation on the text that did not allow for symbolism or grammatical meanings. For example, he would read the word *begotten* and erroneous conclude that the Son was a creature that was made. This form of hermeneutic was taught to his student, Arius.

17. Brown, *Heresies*, 107.

18. Ibid.

19. Olsen, *The Story of Christian Theology*, 140–42.

a particular group of Euseban theologians as 'Lucianists.' Arius himself writes to Eusebius of Nicomedia using the epithet 'co-Lucianist.' . . . Philostorgius, writing in the early fifth century, presents Lucian as one of the key sources for the non-Nicene tradition."[20] Lucian's student Arius would gain notoriety that neither Paul of Samosata nor Lucian achieved: Arius's sermon content expounded the heresy outside of Antioch and directly led to the Council of Nicaea.

There is little doubt that Lucian influenced Arius. Yet it is also likely that Arius's teaching was derived from Origen. Schaff states:

> The eternal generation of the Son from the will of the Father was, with Origen, the communication of a divine but secondary substance, and this idea, in the hands of the less devout and more profound Arius, who with his more rigid logic could admit no intermediate being between God and the creature, deteriorated to the notion of the primal creature.[21]

Donald McKim also agrees with Schaff. In his book, *Theological Turning Points*, McKim states:

> The tensions in Origen's doctrine of God became more clearly focused in the teachings of Arius, a presbyter of Alexandria. Arius forced the church to define its understanding of the divine nature of the Son and to say how the Son and Father are related. For Arius the basic principle is that God must be understood absolutely as uncreated, unbegotten, and unoriginated. There is only one God, who cannot share or communicate divine being or substance with any other being or person. To do so would imply that God is divisible and subject to change.[22]

Arius, in his rigid and narrow interpretation, embraced the teaching of subordinationism of Origen. He followed the teachings of Paul of Samosata and Lucian, which in turn created an explosive controversy in Alexandria. There is no doubt that Arius tried to protect the Monarchy of the Father. However, in his zeal, he denied the deity of the Son by relegating the Son to a creature.

Arius was sincere in his task to preserve the monotheism of God the Father while trying to examine the relationship of the Logos-Christ to the Father. The only conclusion was to stress the difference of the Father and

---

20. Ayres, *Nicaea and its Legacy*, 57.
21. Schaff, *Nicene and Post-Nicean Christianity*, 620.
22. McKim, *Theological Turning Points*, 14.

Son. In doing so, the monad of the Father was protected. However, Arius forced this difference to its most logical conclusion: the Son was a created being.

The Arian doctrine can be summarized in four points. First, the Son is a creature. Second, the Son had a beginning. Third, the Son does not have direct knowledge of God the Father. Fourth, the Son is liable to son. Arius succeeded in preserving the monotheism of God the Father. However, he forfeited the deity of the second person of the Trinity, Jesus Christ. In fact, Arius introduced a half-god, half-man which means that Arius had the Christian faith worshipping a demigod!

Alexander of Alexandria

Alexander was the Bishop of Alexandria. The beginning of the controversy was the public worship service where Alexander "theologized about the Holy Trinity" in the presence of all his presbyters and clergy.[23] Contradicting the Trinitarian message of Alexander, Arius uttered the previously noted phrase. He even created jingles using the content of his theology so that the common person could sing while he worked. These jingles were recorded by Arius in a work he entitled, "The Thalia."[24] The actions of Arius infuriated Alexander.

Alexander was a brilliant orator and thus tried in vain to use the tactic of debate to persuade or at least expose Arius as a heretic. The common ground for both men at the debates focused on their belief that the Logos existed prior to the incarnation. The real issue of the controversy was the relationship between the Father and the Son. Unfortunately, Arius viewed Jesus as a man who would come to possess the Logos, as the Logos existed prior to the life of Jesus. However, in his theological system, the Logos was created and not co-eternal with the Father.

The debate centered upon the nature of God. Alexander accused Arius of worshipping something other than God. The logic of Alexander appeals to tradition and scripture in that since the inception of Christianity, Jesus had been worshipped as God. Alexander keenly understood the heresy as it relates to the heart of Christianity: if Jesus were less than God, Christians would be guilty of worshipping a created being.

23. Behr, *The Nicene Faith*, 62–63.
24. Athanasius references "*The Thalia*" in his writings. See, "Athanasius's Orations Against the Arians, Book 1," in *The Trinitarian Controversy*, 64.

The result of the debates proved futile. As Bishop of Alexandria, Alexander had the responsibility of protecting the people of his parish and—for the sake of truth—he tried to protect other parishes as well. Therefore, Alexander went public with a ban of Arius and his teachings. Anatolios states:

> It is clear that for Alexander the issue is not merely ecclesiastical politics but a crucial cornerstone of Christian faith. He summoned a council of Alexandrian clergy that presented Arius with a confession of the faith they deemed as orthodox. Upon rejecting this confession, Arius and his supporters were excommunicated by Alexander and began their campaign of soliciting support from bishops outside Egypt.[25]

The basic problem with Alexander's approach was that he underestimated the influence of Arius, who had ecclesiastical and political friends throughout the Roman Empire! Arius drew support from Eusebius, Bishop of Nicomedia. Eusebius wrote a letter supporting Arius:

> We have never heard that there are two unbegotten beings, nor that one has been divided into two, nor have we learned or believed that it has ever undergone any change of a corporeal nature; but we affirm that the unbegotten is one, and one also that which exists in truth by Him, yet was not made out of His substance, and does not at all participate in the nature or substance of the unbegotten, entirely distinct in nature and in power, and made after perfect likeness both of character and power to the maker.[26]

The result was that both Eusebius and Alexander sent letters to all the bishops of the eastern portion of Constantine's empire. The Arian conflict was now in public view. To secure a victory, Alexander excommunicated Arius at the synod of 321. It was a brief and shallow victory for Bishop Alexander as Eusebius did muster support for Arius. It would take the Council of Nicaea to resolve the problem.

Athanasius

Athanasius was born around 295 in Egypt. He was raised in the Christian faith by Alexander of Alexandria. His career was guided by the Bishop. He "served six years as a reader; by the outbreak of the Arian controversy he was already a deacon, and in close relations with the aged bishop Alexander,

---

25. Anatolios, *Retrieving Nicaea*, 79.
26. Eusebius of Nicomedia, "Letter to Arius," 42.

Section II—Historical Christological Councils

perhaps as his amanuensis."[27] Between approximately 326 and 328, Athanasius followed Alexander as Bishop "embarking on a forty-six year reign over the Church of Egypt, punctuated by sixteen years of exile."[28]

Athanasius had a reputation that preceded him before the Arian controversy. In fact, Justo Gonzalez states:

> His strong suit was in his close ties to the people among whom he lived, and in living out his faith without the subtleties of the Arians of the pomp of so many bishops of other important sees. His monastic discipline, his roots among the people, his fiery spirit, and his profound and unshakable conviction made him invincible ... The presence of God amid humankind, made human: that is the heart of Christianity as Athanasius understands it.[29]

Athanasius lived out his Christian convictions among the people of Alexandria in such a way that his lifestyle compelled the love and respect of his fellow congregants.

Prior to the Arian controversy, Athanasius was theologically working through the meaning of the incarnation and redemption. The result is one of the most celebrated works in historical theology, *On the Incarnation of the Word*.[30] This work "represents in fact the first elaborate statement made by the young bishop, after about five or six years in office, a statement by which he traces the ideological orientation of the kind of catechesis which he wanted to promote in his church in Alexandria under his ruling."[31]

The methodology Athanasius utilized to write *On the Incarnation of the Word* proved useful for the Arian controversy. Athanasius utilized the concept of Scripture and Tradition. The Canon was recognized but not yet formalized by the greater Christian church. Therefore, the early church fathers had to make an appeal to the traditions that were handed down to them and to the scriptures as they possessed them. Athanasius accepts this hermeneutical tradition as valid and often utilizes its method.

This work laid the foundation for Athanasius's soteriological evaluation of the Arian heresy. Athanasius states, "The Word of God takes to himself a body like others, and from things of the earth that is, by the works His body, so that they who would not know Him from his providence and

27. Loofs, "Athanasius."
28. Anatolios, *Retrieving Nicaea*, 20.
29. Gonzalez, *The Story of Christianity*, 174.
30. Athanasius, "*On The Incarnation of The Word.*"
31. Kannengiesser, "St Athanasius of Alexandria Rediscovered," 72.

rule over all things . . . know the Word of God which was in the body, and through him the Father."[32] The Incarnation of Christ in the flesh was to make known the Father to lost humanity. This work established the foundation by which Athanasius would confront the Arian heresy.

THE PROBLEM OF HERMENEUTICS

On the eve of the Nicaean Council the problem of interpretation took full center stage in the polemics, the proclamations, and the writings of both Arius and Athanasius. Charles Kannengiesser states, "The Crisis is essentially one of hermeneutics."[33]

The hermeneutical problem led to a deviant doctrinal position concerning the nature of the Godhead. The focus of the doctrinal issue centers upon the relationship of Jesus Christ to the Father. The basic question that arises from Arius is the nature of Jesus Christ. Basically, the question is simple: Does Jesus possess the full divinity of the Father? In other words, Is Jesus "God" in the same way as the Father? Does Jesus have the same essence as the Father? These questions reveal the heart of the Christological issue. However, the doctrine goes beyond Christology. The problem, though not addressed, is a Trinitarian issue. This is evident from the use of the Arian phrase: *There was a time when he was not.*[34]

The Arian Hermeneutic

The Arian doctrine had direct implications for the meaning of the Trinity. Arius would admit to a Trinity. However, the trinity for Arius was not one essence and three persons but three different essences. In other words, the three distinct beings in the Godhead did not share the same essence. His claim was that each person was of a different essence or substance (*heteroousios*). Thus, the Trinity was proclaimed in Tri-theistic terms! Although Arius wanted to protect the Monad of God, he inadvertently proclaimed tritheism or even polytheism in the theology of Christianity.

Preserving the Fatherhood of God in such a way meant the Arians had to explain the relationship between Father and Son. The Son was created to be adopted into the Godhead. Thus, the Son was elevated to the status

---

32. Athanasius, *On the Incarnation of the Word*, 14.8
33. Kannengiesser, *Holy Scripture and Hellenistic Hermeneutics*, 1.
34. Kelly, *Early Christian Doctrine*, 228.

of the Godhead but does not share the same essence as the Father. R.P.C. Hanson confirms the Arian position when he states:

> There is no common nature shared by Father, Son, and, Spirit, no divine 'substance' which they all possess. The Son is not ingenerate nor eternal nor invisible nor immortal as the Father is. He does not possess one by participation . . . In the end there is only one God who is good, wise, etc. We cannot number the Three, because the Father is incomparable. The three are not equal, their difference of nature entails a difference of degree.[35]

The logic of the Arians pushes the Scriptural revelation too far in its meaning. Per Arius, if the Trinity means that all have the same essence, then there are two or more ungenerated beings within the Trinity. This concept allows Arius to reject traditional Christology. He never considered the Son as eternally generated by the Father. Instead of accepting a trinitarian formula of God, Arius forced a tri-theistic Godhead upon Christianity.

Arius's position also forced a division of the Godhead into ontological subordination. The meaning of the godhead, per the Arian position, is that God is graded in his relationships within tri-theism. Robert Gregg and Dennis Groh write:

> According to the traditional view of Arius and his partisans as cosmologists preoccupied with a particular idea of God, the logical sequence of the statement is as follows: the singularity and uniqueness of God as first principle requires that he alone be counted as without beginning and eternal, so that all things, even the Son, are preceded by him. Thus, a doctrine of God is understood to control description of the Son as posterior, secondary to God, and having a beginning (ἀρχή); God's transcendence dictates the Son's subordinate status.[36]

The result of the Arian position is that the Church was worshipping a creature instead of a creator.

The Arian position is revealed in the *Thalia*.[37] Rowan Williams lists the contents of the *Thalia* from the works of Athanasius. Williams, summarizing Athanasius, states that Arius wrote, "For him it is impossible to search out the mysteries of the Father who exists in himself; for the Son

---

35. Hanson, *The Search for the Christian Doctrine of God*, 104.
36. Gregg and Groh, *Early Arianism*, 82.
37. See footnote 22 above.

does not [even] know his own substance he came into actual subsistence by a father's will."[38]

The hermeneutics of Arius not only led to a christological, trinitarian problem for the early church but ushered with it an epistemological problem of communication between Father, Son, and creature. If the Son cannot know the Father, how can the Son reveal the Father to the Father's own creation? The epistemological problem means that Soteriology was at stake.

The Athanasian Hermeneutic

The nexus between Christology and trinitarian theology is crucial for Athanasius. Following Alexander, he knows that the issue of Christ's divinity has implications for trinitarian thought. The ontological inferior Arian Christ will not advance incarnational or trinitarian theology. The incarnation of Christ means that God came to humanity. If Christ is anything but God in his ontological nature, then God could not come via incarnation to redeem humans. Thus, for Athanasius, the line of theological demarcation with the Arians goes from Christology (including incarnation), to Trinity, and then to Soteriology.

The basic Athanasian tenet is that Christ is eternal in his person and position as Son. He demonstrates the eternal nature of the Son in his work *Contra Arianos*.[39] The eternal nature of the Son establishes the coherent nature of the Trinity. The Son, as second person of the Trinity, shares in the same essence of the Father. To underscore this thought, Athanasius uses the word "proper" to describe the nature of the Son to the Father in their divine being.

In CA 1:16 Athanasius uses the words "proper Sonship" in relationship to the Father. Athanasius writes:

> We are driven to say that what is from the essence of the Father, and proper to Him, is entirely the Son; for it is all one to say that God is wholly participated, and that He begets; and what does begetting signify but a Son? And thus of the Son Himself, all things partake according to the grace of the Spirit coming from Him . . . And beholding the Son, we see the Father; for the thought and comprehension of the Son, is knowledge concerning the Father, because He is His proper offspring from His essence. And since to be partaken no one of us would ever call affection or division of God's

---

38. Williams, *Arius: Heresy and Tradition*, 103.
39. For this work the abbreviation of *CA* will be used.

> essence (for it has been shown and acknowledged that God is participated, and to be participated is the same thing as to beget); therefore that which is begotten is neither affection nor division of that blessed essence.[40]

Athanasius understands that participation of the Son in the Father is generation. The theological issue discussed is the eternal generation of the Son. This allows the Father to be Father, eternally generating the Son who has the position and role of Son.

The believer's participation in the Son is by means of grace. The believer is adopted into Sonship by means of faith in Christ. Thus, humanity is not the same ontologically as the Son or Father.

The Son knows the Father, as he is the same essence—or *ousia*—of the Father. Epistemologically, the Son can reveal the Father as both share in the same *ousia*. The shared essence is the foundation of the Trinity. The theological concept is that all persons of the Trinity have the same essence as one another.

That poses the question: How are Father and Son different in their essence or are they different? In CA 2:47 Athanasius appeals to John 1:1, 14; Galatians 3:13, and II Corinthians 5:21 as scriptural evidence that the Son does not change ontologically. The Son is not transformed by his incarnation ontologically, but he puts on a created body (allusions to Proverbs 8:22) for the sake of humanity's salvation. Athanasius writes:

> For the Lord, knowing His own Essence to be the Only-begotten Wisdom and Offspring of the Father, and other than things originate and natural creatures, says in love to man, 'The Lord created me a beginning of His ways,' as if to say, 'My Father has prepared for Me a body, and has created Me for men in behalf of their salvation.'[41]

Athanasius understands Christ comes into the world via incarnation so that humanity could know God's will for salvation. The meaning of humanity's salvation is that redeemed humans participate in the Son's divine nature, which participates in the Father's nature. Thus, the Father is always Father and the Son is always and eternally the Son.

Soteriology was the primary focus of Athanasius. The essence of God is that which was incarnated via the Son for the purpose of redemption. The incarnation did not diminish the Son's essence but added the human nature to his eternal nature via the hypostatic union.

---

40. Athanasius, "*Contra Arianos*," 1:16.
41. Ibid., 2:47.

CONSTANTINE INTERVENES

The news of the theological controversy reached Emperor Constantine and the threat of a religiously separated Empire disturbed him. From the Emperor's point of view, he had just secured the political condition of the Empire, which had been in chaos for quite some time. Now the threat that the religious fabric of the Empire would be so divisive that Constantine assumed it could have the same effect as a political upheaval. The Emperor tried to repair the rift before it had time to become irreparable. "His opening move was to send his advisor, Hosius of Cordova, to Alexandria with a letter that called for reconciliation and suggested that the issue being debated was 'unprofitable'—a minor disagreement over a point of view."[42]

Hosius's attempt at reconciliation only served to further inflame the situation. Constantine's fear was becoming a reality as the Empire began to explode over a theological issue. The controversy was so public that Constantine had no choice but to take further action.

> One bishop describes Constantinople as seething with discussion: 'If in the city you asked anyone for change he'll discuss with you whether God the Son is begotten or unbegotten. If you ask about the quality of bread, you will receive the answer that 'God is the Father is greater, God the Son is less.' If you suggest that a bath is desirable, you will be told that 'there was nothing before the Son was created.'[43]

Constantine's solution was to call the first ecumenical council.

THE COUNCIL IS CONVENED

Constantine determined that unity was essential. This fact prompted him to convene the first ecumenical council. As a result of the events in the East, Emperor Constantine decided to call a universal council of the church to settle the dispute. Lewis Ayers states, "The procedures of a council modelled on methods of Roman governance would have been familiar to Constantine, and we can assume that he saw it as the natural means to achieve consensus within the church."[44]

The synodal letter from Antioch mentions that the synod was to be held in Ancyra. But the site was transferred to Nicaea before the beginning

---

42. Walker, *A History of the Christian Church*, 133.
43. Shelly, *Church History*, 113.
44. Ayres, *Nicaea and its Legacy*, 87.

Section II—Historical Christological Councils

of the council."[45] The Emperor was so enamored with unity among the bishops that he pledged his word that the bishops and their attendants would be provided with transportation at public expense.

Three hundred and eighteen bishops and presbyters attended the council, most of whom well remembered the persecution of former days. The following is a description of some of the bishops and presbyters:

> Paul, bishop of Neo-Caesarea, a fortress situated on the banks of the Euphrates, had suffered from the frantic rage of Licinius. He had been deprived of the use of both hands by the application of a red-hot iron, by which the nerves which give motion to the muscles had been contracted and rendered dead. Some had the right eye dug out, others had lost the right arm. Among these was Paphnutius of Egypt. In short, the council looked like an assembled army of martyrs.[46]

The attendees represented three different groups. However, two primary factions dominated the discussion.

The Arians were present and represented by Arius. The Alexandrians were present and represented by Athanasius. The third group was represented by Eusebius of Caesarea and Eusebius of Nicomedia. This group formed the majority of the council. Lewis Ayres has used the term "Eusebian to designate any who would have found common ground with either of Arius's most prominent supporters, Eusebius of Nicomedia or Eusebius of Caesarea."[47]

The basic difference between the three groups was demonstrated by their adherence to differing theological persuasions. The Arians arrived at the council convinced of victory in their position that the Son was a creation of the Father. The Alexandrians, however, were just as convinced that their position was correct – the Son was equal to the Father. The third group, "had Arian leanings and was opposed to the doctrine that the Son is of the same substance with the Father (*homoiousios*) to the Father."[48]

The stage was now set to investigate the theological implications of the Arian controversy. Kelly makes this statement:

> The theological issue at stake was, or seemed to be, a much narrower one, vis. the status of the Word in His relation to the

---

45. Rusch, *The Trinitarian Controversy*, 19.
46. Theodoret, *The Ecclesiastical History of Theodoret*, 43.
47. Ayres, *Nicaea and its Legacy*, 52
48. Berkhof, *Christian Doctrines*, 86.

Godhead. Was He fully divine, in the precise sense of the term, and therefore akin to the Father? Or was He after all a creature, superior no doubt to the rest of creation, even by courtesy designated divine, but all things separated by an unbridgeable chasm from the Godhead?"[49]

The Council of Nicaea was to determine the nature of God. This may sound out of place in the modern world, but in the fourth century world, Christianity had embraced Jesus as God, and yet there was confusion as to his relationship to the Father. This council would lay the foundation, regardless of its findings, for the future of Christianity.

THE INVESTIGATION BEGINS

Constantine opened the council with an exhortation for unity among the bishops and presbyters and a hope for an easy resolution. Per Constantine's request, the Council was of divine appointment, which created the harsh position that anyone who disagreed with its final conclusions would be banished for being guilty of working against the emperor and the church. At the council, Constantine declared he would assist in the process but Hosius of Cordova would moderate the proceedings.

The Arians stated their position concerning their position of Jesus's nature to the Father in the most radical terms. "The Arians, confident that victory would be theirs, made the great mistake of beginning the council by presenting their own statement of faith, a straight forward document drawn up by Eusebius of Nicomedia. This document emphatically denied the deity of Jesus Christ.

The majority did not really understand the issues at stake, but they did recognize the Arian position was in grave error. The Arian Creed was overwhelmingly voted down and torn to pieces. The council took a unique turn of events as Eusebius of Caesarea presented a more moderate and acceptable creed.[50]

> Then the church historian Eusebius, in the name of the middle party, proposed an ancient Palestinian Confession, which was similar to the Nicene, and acknowledged the divine nature of Christ in general biblical terms, but avoided the term in question,

---

49. Kelly, *Early Christian Doctrine*, 223.
50. Ayres, *Nicaea and its Legacy*, 89.

homoousios. The emperor had already seen and approved this confession, and even the Arian minority were ready to accept it.[51]

This creed identified Christ as the Logos as God. Their hopes were that the creed would solve the problem without really addressing the nature of the problem. The plan worked as the council was ready to adopt this confession as normative for the Christian doctrine of God. The rationale for the Arians acceptance of the Eusebian Creed is that it is "extremely cautious and offers very little description of, or terminology for, the Son's generation other than to say that the Son was 'begotten from the Father before all ages.'"[52] However, Alexander and Athanasius were opposed to ratifying the document.

Constantine, whose only concern seemed to be peace among the council members, realized that any chance of unity was now remote. The Council rejected the Eusebian Creed as it had overtones of Arian theology. Instead the council wrote its own creed which, according to John Behr, greatly annoyed Eusebius. In order to ratify the council's creed the compilers added the word homoousia. Essentially this word effected the Creed significantly.[53]

The meaning of homoousia was vague and thus defining the word was problematic. Lampe's, *A Patristic Greek Lexicon,* defines *homoousios* as "expressive of the belief that what the Father is, that also the Son is."[54] The council adopted the word to mean "same essence" which thwarted any position that the Christ-Logos was a created being in any fashion. The Arian party did not agree. They refused to adopt what has become known as The Nicene Creed as it confesses the Son is the same essence as the Father. The Creed reads as follows:

> We believe in one God, the Father Almighty, Maker of all things visible and invisible: – and in one Lord Jesus Christ, the Son of God, the only-begotten of the Father, that is the substance [*homoousios*] of the Father, that is of the light, true God of true God: begotten not made, consubstantial with the Father; by whom all things were made both which are in Heaven and on Earth; who for the sake of us men, and on account of our salvation, descended, became incarnate, was made man, suffered and rose again on the

---

51. Schaff, *History of the Christian Church,* 628.
52. Ayres, *Nicaea and its Legacy,* 89.
53. Behr, *The Nicene Faith,* 155.
54. Lampe, "homoousios," 959.

> third day; he ascended into the heavens, and will come to judge the living and the dead.

And [we believe] in the Holy Spirit.

> But those who say 'there was a time when He was not,' or 'He was made of nothing,' or assert that 'He is of other substance or essence of the Father,' or that 'the Son of God is created, or mutable, or susceptible of change,' the Catholic and apostolic Church of God anathematizes.[55]

Arius's refusal to sign the Nicene Creed resulted in the Emperor sending him into exile. Even though the Council of Nicaea approved the Creed, the issue was not settled.

THE AFTERMATH OF NICAEA

The debate between the Arian and Athanasian parties continued for quite some time. In fact, it continued for the next fifty years culminating in the Council of Constantinople in 381. "The decision of the Council did not terminate the controversy but was rather only the beginning of it."[56] Part of the reason for this predicament was that the Emperor's actions forced a solution to the controversy. The consequence is that no one who signed the Nicene Creed felt ownership. For that matter, the impact of the Emperor on the Council has ramifications to this day in that the Church and State emerged into an ecclesiastical-political power.

> The Church's new relation to the State, which mean that the success or failure of a doctrine might hinge upon the favor of the reigning emperor, tended to sharpen these divisions. In fact, the dispersal of the Council marked the commencement of a protracted period of controversy lasting at least until Constantius' death in 361.[57]

The theological implications of the Council left much to be desired. Even though Arius was exiled, his teachings began to gain momentum.

The vast majority of attendees comprised the third party of the meeting. Again, they were confused by the terminology and did not understand the issues. Many of the Arian supporters joined this third party, which had

---

55. "The Nicene Creed," 11.
56. Berkhof, *Christian Doctrines*, 87.
57. Kelly, *Early Christian Doctrines*, 237.

the immediate effect of growing into a larger party. This new enlarged third party was soon to be deemed the semi-Arians whose theological content spread throughout the empire.

The fate of Arius and Athanasius, in view of the Council's decision to adopt the Nicene Creed, remains a fascinating study in contrast. After lengthy discussion and consideration, Constantine recalled Arius from exile. Athanasius, on the other hand, was banished and recalled five times throughout his life.

CONCLUSION OF NICAEA

The consequences of Nicaea cannot be overestimated or understated. For one, the doctrine of the church was not settled by clergy only but also by political magistrates who directed the process of the council. Ecclesiastical dogma was established by approval of political powers often within the church and state. This uneasy alliance often resulted in tension and even strained relations with one another.

The second issue is that the relationship between church and state was simply an after thought and not the stated purpose of the Council. The fact that an emperor intervened in ecclesiastical matters set a precedent for European relationships between church and state that—in some places—continues to this very day. This action resulted in the autonomy of the church being nationalized via the Emperor. When Europe entered the Medieval Ages after the break-up of the Roman Empire, the church was united to local governmental authorities that took national churches to new relationship levels.

Theologically, the precedent for a unified doctrinal structure was established by Nicaea. The Creed became the standard by which orthodoxy was established throughout Christianity. The precedent was so strong for ancient Christianity that the three following councils adhered to the Nicene Creed. For contemporary Christians, both Protestants and Catholics, the Nicene Creed sets the standard that a demi-god is not worshiped. The implication is that the test of orthodoxy for the modern Christian is to still adhere to the Nicene Creed, which established the boundaries of Trinitarianism.

INTERACTIVE PERSONAL SEMINAR

Chapter Summary

Nicaea addressed the problem of the Christ relationship to the Father. In essence, this council helped clarify the deity of Christ and has become known as a Trinitarian issue. Nicaea also set the standard for future ecumenical councils in that 1) the Nicene Creed was continually upheld as the standard for orthodoxy for the Trinity, 2) the council set the precedent for church/state relations for the next thousand years.

Key Terms

- Nicene Creed
- *Ousia*
- *Homoousia*
- Monarchians
- Sabellianism

Key People

- Constantine
- Arius
- Alexander of Alexandria
- Athanasius

Advanced Questions

1. What was Arius trying to protect in stating that Jesus was better than all creation but not equal to God?
2. In what way did Nicaea deny Arius position?
3. The Council of Nicaea provided the famous Nicene Creed. Why was this necessary?

Section II—Historical Christological Councils

4. Did politics have too much influence in the theology of the church?
5. Did Nicaea intentionally try to set the standard for Christianity or was it a by – product of the Council? Depending on your answer, is the Nicene Creed still valid for contemporary Christianity?

Theological Questions

1. Explain the theological difference between Arius's view of Christ as a creation (creature) and Athanasius's (via Nicaea) that Christ is the same substance as the Father?
2. If the Lord could attend the council in person do you think he would condemn the relationship between the Church and State? Do you think he would uphold the Nicene Creed and approve the process of Church and State working together? Or perhaps, do you think he would condemn the process but like the results of the Nicene Creed?
3. In what way[s] does one's theological presuppositions drive his/her hermeneutical method?

Issues to Research

- Consider the role of political allegiances in the life of the church during the early days of Christendom.
- Would Arius be considered heretical in the contemporary expressions of Christianity?
- Are there similarities between Arianism and Jehovah's Witnesses?
- Should contemporary Christians refer to the Nicene Creed to settle modern Trinitarian issues?

5

The Council of Constantinople (381)

Stephen Presley

INTRODUCTION

In the years following the Council of Nicaea (325 AD), the church continued to struggle with the Arian cause. While the Nicene Creed handed the church a unified statement of faith that had Constantine's imperial approval, those who opposed the creed continued to resist the statement as a standard for orthodoxy. As the fourth century wore on, each new emperor, either in the East or the West, varied in their sympathies to the competing factions of the church. Bishops and other ecclesiastical leaders faced persecution for their views and many were exiled (many more than once) as power shifted hands back and forth. Those who supported the Nicene faith were now realizing that the wording of the creed alone was not sufficient enough to deal with some of the new challenges; another ecumenical council was needed. Therefore, in 381 the Emperor Theodosius called the Council of Constantinople—commonly known as the Second Ecumenical Council—as a way to bring unity to the theologically fractured church. After meeting for three months, the council produced a creed known as the Nicene-Constantinopolitan Creed and from the fourth century through to the present day, this creed has been a touchstone for the orthodox Christian view of the doctrine of God.[1]

There is, however, a rather complex relationship between the Nicene Creed and the creed articulated at Constantinople, both in terms of history and theology. This chapter will discuss the issues surrounding the Council of Constantinople, including the historical background of the council, the proceedings—at least what we can reconstruct from extant sources—, and finally the theological contents of the creed. This council, especially the theological discussions implied in the language of the creed and the reaffirmation of Nicene faith, are paramount for understanding the nature of God in the early church. The theological framework of this creed sets a paradigm for trinitarian discussions that developed throughout the rest of the history of Christianity. The main theological issues discussed at the council include the deity of the Holy Spirit against the Macedonians (Pneumatomachians) and the christological errors of Apollinarianism. There were other practical matters discussed that intended to help promote the creed by stabilizing some institutional structures and practices in the church. In the end, any recounting of the history of the doctrine of God must consider the decisive events of the Council of Constantinople and the creed it affirmed.

HISTORICAL BACKGROUND OF THE COUNCIL OF CONSTANTINOPLE

There is no doubt that the Nicene Creed brought a degree of unity to the Christian church and helped articulate an orthodox understanding of God. The emperor and all the bishops present at the council approved a confession that they believed would guide the faith of the church in the Constantinian era. Yet underneath this statement of theological unity, conflicts precipitated throughout the empire. Those who were sympathetic to the Arian cause still found the language of *homoousios* suspicious. Things become volatile after the death of Constantine in 337. The faith of the church oscillated between the Nicene confession and the Arian response depending upon the emperor in power and the theological commitments of the any given bishop. At various times it seemed as if the Arian party would

---

1. Studer, *Trinity and the Incarnation*, 159.

ultimately triumph in the fourth century, and the whole church would officially deny the unity of the Father and the Son.[2]

The situation changed when Theodosius assumed power over the Eastern Empire on January 19, 379. After his coronation, he published several edits aimed at establishing the Nicene faith. The first was *Cunctos populos* published on February 27, 380 that made the Nicene faith the official faith of the empire and his subjects were required to confess Nicene theology.[3] By November of that same year, Theodosius moved to Constantinople to begin shoring up the Eastern part of the empire. The city of Constantinople had been the primary center of religious and political power in the East ever since Constantine moved the capitol there in the fourth century.[4] But when Theodosius arrived, he found that Demophilus, the current bishop of Constantinople, was an avowed Arian so he offered him the opportunity to confess the Nicene faith or face exile. Demophilus chose the latter, so he ordered him to leave the city.[5] In his place he appointed the well-known theologian Gregory of Nazianzus as Bishop of Constantinople. A rival Bishop, Maximus the Cynic, was also chosen by the Arian community, though he was rejected later at the council the following year.

By end of 380 the thought of an ecumenical council was well under way. Meletius, the bishop of Antioch—a position that was highly contested at the time—made his way to Constantinople in January 381, apparently to meet with Theodosius and conceive of a new council to settle the theological and ecclesiastical disputes that pervaded the East. Meletius had already convened a council in 379 in Antioch (after returning from his third exile by various Arian authorities), which served as something of a "dress rehearsal" for the ecumenical council in Constantinople.[6] On January 10, 381, Theodosius continued pressing the imperial adgeda toward adherence to the Nicene Creed and issued another edit called *Nullis haereticis*, which

---

2. Hanson, *The Search for the Christian Doctrine of God*, 791. Hanson's work traces the narrative of the Arian crisis of the fourth century and provides extensive historical and theological analysis of this period. See also: Ritter, *Das Konzil von Konstantinopel und sein Symbol.*

3. Hanson, *The Search*, 804. See also Sozomen, *Ecclesiastical History*, 7.4.

4. Constantinople would become the site of several ecumenical councils including: the Second (Constantinople I, 381 AD), the Fifth (Constantinople II, 553 AD), and the Sixth (Constantinople III, 680–81 AD). For background on the city see Valeva and Vionis, "The Balkan Peninsula," 366–67.

5. Socrates, *EH*, 7.5.

6. Hanson, *The Search*, 806.

Section II—Historical Christological Councils

restricted any anti-Nicene groups from gathering for worship in churches or in towns.[7] The document specifically calls out Arians, Eunomians, and the Photinians, though there was no mention of the Macedonians (Pneumatomachians) at this point. Theodosius was likely hoping to win over some from the latter groups and bring them back into communion with the pro-Nicene party.

At some point around the end of 380 or beginning of 381, Theodosius summoned a synod at Constantinople and the council convened in May 381.[8] There were 150 bishops present, all from the East.[9] Meletius of Antioch was the presiding officer and other notable participants included Gregory of Nazianzus, Gregory of Nyssa, Peter of Sebaste, Cyril of Jerusalem, and Diodore of Tarsus. In his summary of the conciliar events, the ancient Christian historian Socrates writes,

> The emperor making no delay summoned a Synod of the prelates of his own faith, in order that he might establish the Nicene Creed, and appoint a bishop of Constantinople: and inasmuch as he was not without hope that me might win the Macedonians over to his own views, he invited those who presided over that sect to be present also. There met therefore, on this occasion of the Homoousian party, Timothy from Alexandria, Cyril from Jerusalem, who at the time recognized the doctrine of homoousion, having retracted his former opinion; Melitius from Antioch, he having arrived there previously to assist at the installation of Gregory; Ascholius also from Thessalonica and many others, amounting in all to one hundred and fifty.[10]

From Socrates's account we can presume that the motivation of the council was to establish the theological unity and appoint a pro-Nicene bishop at Constantinople who would ensure allegiance to that faith. At the same time, the council also intended to consider some heterodox perspectives that were opposed to the wording of the creed, particularly of the statements on Christ and the Spirit.

---

7. Ibid., 805.

8. Three ancient historians, Socrates, Sozomen, and Theodoret, all record an account of the events of the council and together give a general outline of the proceedings. See Sozomen, *EH* 7.6–11; Socrates, *EH* 5.6–10; Theodoret, *EH*, 5.6–9.

9. Sozomen, *EH* 7.6; Socrates, *EH* 5.8; Theodoret *EH* 5.7.

10. Socrates, *EH* 5.8.

THE COUNCIL OF CONSTANTINOPLE

There is little that survives from the actions of the council outside the brief accounts in the ancient historians, such as Socrates mentioned above, and scattered allusions to the council amid the writings of the church fathers. In fact, explicit discussions of the Creed of Constantinople remain obscure until Aetius, the archdeacon of Constantinople, read the proceedings of the Council of Constantinople at the opening of the Council of Chalcedon in 451. From these extant accounts, it seems that the main issues discussed at the council include the Meletian schism of Antioch (that saw the bishopric of Antioch split into four rival factions in the early part of 360), the deity of the Holy Spirit (especially in connection with the Macedonians), and a discussion of the christological errors of Apollinarianism. There were other ecclesiastical matters discussed in the canons that addressed some administrative issues in the church.

Early in the proceedings there were serious discussions with about thirty Macedonian bishops, led by Eleusius of Cyzicus and Marcion of Lampsacus.[11] These Macedonians, also known as the Pneumatomachians or "Spirit-fighters," repelled any notion that the Spirit might be *homoousios* with the Son and the Father. Most were willing to concede the consubstantiality of the Son and the Father against the Arians, but affirming the deity of the Spirit was just going too far. It appears these initial discussions did not go as the Macedonians were hoping so they left the council early, which may have motivated the remaining bishops to clarify the brief statement on the Holy Spirit in the Nicene Creed.[12] As we will see, the final Chalcedonian Creed produced from the council did not mention the Spirit as consubstantial with the Father and Son, which may have been some kind of concession for the Macedonians, but it did confess that the Spirit was worthy of the same worship and glory due to the Father and the Son.

In the beginning Meletius presided over the council, but at some point, he died suddenly and Gregory Nazianzus was appointed president. His tenure did not last long either, and his frustration with the council began with resolution of the Melitian schism. Gregory debated the schism with a delegation of Egyptian bishops who arrived late to the council. Sources do not explain why this contingent from Egypt, led by Timothy of Alexandria the newly appointed bishop of Alexandria, arrived late, but

---

11. Hanson, *The Search*, 807; Sozomen, *EH* 7.7.
12. Socrates, *EH* 5.8; Sozomen, *EH* 7.7.

Section II—Historical Christological Councils

there is some indication that Theodosius encouraged their attendance in order to secure a pro-Nicene outcome.[13] This contingent was also the only loose connection to the West represented at the council, given the close association between the bishop of Alexandria and the bishop of Rome.[14] Ancient sources discuss an agreement between Paulinus and Meletius (both vying for the position of bishop in Antioch in 379) to end the schism in Antioch.[15] The terms of their agreement were that each recognized the other as bishop so that whomever died first, the other would succeed him. Since Meletius died, Paulinus was the apparent heir to the positon in Antioch, and Gregory Nazianzus supported him. However, most of the bishops, especially the Syrian bishops, rejected this agreement and decided, against Gregory's recommendation, to appoint Flavian.[16] To make matters worse, the Egyptian Bishops also raised questions about the succession of the bishop of Constantinople and the legitimacy of Gregory's position. These bishops wanted to prohibit the movement, or translation, of a bishop from one ministry center to another. As the discussions turned to the creed, Gregory was not satisfied with the council's statement of the Holy Spirit either. He believed it did not go far enough in affirming the Spirit's deity and declared it a "half-way" doctrine.[17]

Together, these decisions left Gregory frustrated with the entire conciliar process and not wishing to cause any further divisions, he submitted his resignation to the council.[18] Before he did so, however, he delivered one of his most famous orations, *Oration 42*, before the council. The moving oration left the bishops with a series of final thoughts and farewells, including one closing image where he implores them to walk the narrow path of orthodoxy and not succumb to the heresies that lay on either side, saying:

> Let us then bid farewell to all contentious shiftings and balancings of the truth on either side, neither, like the Sabellians, assailing the Trinity in the interest of the Unity, and so destroying the distinction by a wicked confusion; nor, like the Arians, assailing the Unity in the interest of the Trinity, and by an impious distinction overthrowing the Oneness. For our object is not to exchange

---

13. Hanson, *The Search*, 807.
14. Ibid., 807.
15. Socrates, *EH* 5.5; Sozomen, *EH* 7.3.
16. Hanson, *The Search*, 810.
17. Ibid., 819.
18. Socrates, *EH* 5.8; Sozomen, *EH* 7.7; *Thodoret*, EH 5.7.

one evil for another, but to ensure our attainment of that which is good. These are the playthings of the Wicked One, who is ever swaying our fortunes towards the evil. But we, walking along the royal road which lies between the two extremes, which is the seat of the virtues, as the authorities say, believe in the Father, the Son and the Holy Ghost, of one Substance and glory.[19]

After Gregory resigned, Nectarius, an unbaptized civil servant and catechumen in Constantinople, was appointed bishop of Constantinople and presided over the remainder of the council.[20] While it might seem odd to appoint a figure of low ecclesiastical standing, Nectarius was by no means an unknown figure; he was the *praetor urbanus* in Constantinople, which is sort of like choosing the city mayor as bishop.[21] In reality, after the discussions of the translation of bishops, there was no one present at the council who could be appointed to the position.

Following the conciliar deliberations, the council issued 4 canons.[22] The first canon reaffirmed Nicaea and anathematized the Arian, Semi-Arian, or other heretical groups including: the Eunomians, Arians, Eudoxians, Macedonians, Sabellians, Marcellians, Photinians, and Apollinarians.[23] Many of these views, to one degree or another, are rejected with the various statements of the creed. The second canon limited the boundaries of episcopal activity and the translations between one ministry center and another so that each bishop was restricted from ministering outside the region where they were appointed. The third canon asserted that the bishop of Constantinople had the prerogatives of honor after the bishop of Rome. This was a point of particular interest to Theodosius, who was ruling the East from Constantinople and elevated that city over Alexandria and Antioch. The fourth canon ruled that Maximus the Cynic, who was appointed as a rival bishop to Gregory in Constantinople, was never properly ordained as bishop and that any ordination performed by him was invalid. With all these canons, the council was able to bring a greater sense of clarity to the Nicene faith and the theological unity to the churches of the East. These canons also arranged some of the practical matters of the church to ensure that the creed was promoted in preaching, catechism, and baptism.

19. Gregory of Nazianzus, *Oration* 42.
20. Sozomen, *EH* 7.8.
21. Hanson, *The Search*, 811.
22. Ibid., 807. See also Need, *Truly Divine and Truly Human*, 77.
23. Hanson, *The Search*, 807.

The council concluded on July 30, 381 and Theodosius issued an edict that served as the imperial confirmation of the creed as the official theological position of the empire.[24] The edict stated that all churches and ecclesiastical positions should be handed over to those who confess the faith of the creed. It also named those who were the examples of orthodoxy including: Nectarius of Constantinople, Timothy of Alexandria, Diodore of Tarsus, and Gregory of Nyssa.[25] The writings and teaching of these bishops and theologians would serve as the exemplars of Nicene orthodoxy reaffirmed at the Council of Constantinople and ensure the defense of the faith.

CREED OF THE COUNCIL OF CONSTANTINOPLE

Along with the conciliar discussions listed above, the council also drafted the Creed of Constantinople. Later Christian tradition will recognize a close association between this one and the Nicene Creed, which is why it is often called the Nicene-Constantinopolitan Creed or even simply "the Creed of Nicaea."[26] The universality of this creed is unparalleled, as J.N.D Kelly writes, "[o]f all existing creeds it [the Creed of Constantinople] is the only one for which ecumenicity, or universal acceptance, can be plausibly claimed . . . It is thus one of the few threads by which the tattered fragments of the divided robe of Christendom are held together."[27] In other words, this creed was, and continues to be, a highly significant unifying statement on the doctrine of God that is affirmed by every major Christian tradition and denomination throughout the history of the church. It is one of the few creeds often recited in worship settings and consistently appears as a statement for orthodoxy in later creeds and confessions.

The traditional view of the Creed of Constantinople held that it was an expansion of Nicaea, especially in terms of the statement on the Holy Spirit.[28] There is, however, a good bit of mystery surrounding this creed and several scholars have brought forward serious questions about its provenance; some going so far as to doubt that the council even produced a creed. The view that the Creed of Constantinople was a myth was posited by Hort and Harnack, who argued this assertion primarily on three grounds:

24. Ibid., 820.
25. Ibid., 821.
26. Behr, *The Nicene Faith*, 74.
27. Kelly, *Early Christian Creeds*, 296.
28. Ibid., 300–01.

1) the differences or notable omissions in key terms or phrases, especially the phrase "*ousia* of the father", 2) the significant differences in word order and structure, and 3) statistical comparisons between the wording of the creed.[29] These points led them—and a good many others—to conclude that Constantinople is not a modified version of Nicaea but in fact two radically different creeds. As mentioned above, the history of the creed also becomes more complex when we realize that the first clear identification of a Creed of Constantinople is when Aetius reads it aloud in the opening proceedings of the Council of Chalcedon in 451. There is no explicit mention of the creed during the seventy years in between 381 and 451. There are even other councils, such as the Council of Ephesus in 431, Council of Constantinople in 448, and "Robbers Synod" in 449, which all mention the Nicene Creed, but not the Creed of Constantinople. For these reasons, Hort and Harnack argued that the fathers of Chalcedon were mistaken in assuming there was a creed composed at Constantinople and, as a result, they also misled the rest of the Christian tradition.

The work of J.N.D Kelly remains the best analysis of the creed and its history, and he brings serious charges against the Hort-Harnack thesis. Kelly's response recognizes that their criticisms are far from convincing and his rebuttal has shifted the scholarly tide back in the direction of the traditional view. The simple fact is that the bishops who gathered at Constantinople in 381 never imagined they were composing a new creed; they were clarifying the faith articulated and received in the Nicene Creed. Kelly reminds us of the need to distinguish between the faithfulness to the wording in the creed and faithfulness to the "faith" of the creed or the distinction between the "Nicene teaching" and the "literal wording" of the creed.[30] The council never imaged that they would produce a new creed but that their particular formulation of the creed was a reaffirmation of the Nicene faith with a few additions clarifying the wording of the creed. In reality the phrase the "faith of Nicaea" could apply to any number of variations of the creed composed at Nicaea so long as the variations adhered to the faith confessed in words of the Nicene Creed.

We can note that both ancient historians Socrates and Sozomen state that the Council of Constantinople confirmed the Creed of Nicaea, which probably means that their affirmation took the form of the Creed

---

29. Ibid., 302.
30. Ibid., 325.

Section II—Historical Christological Councils

of Constantinople.[31] As Behr observes, "Not even the bishops who has met at Constantinople, some would argue, considered that they had produced a creed."[32] Instead, the Council of Constantinople "did not consider itself to have introduced a new creed but merely to have reaffirmed 'the faith of the three hundred and eighteen fathers gathered at Nicaea.'"[33] Ayres also makes a similar point saying that the reason there is the "lack of reference to this creed until the council of Chalcedon in 451 is the lack of intention of its framers that Constantinople creed serve as a precise marker of orthodoxy."[34] That is to say, the orthodox faith was set forth at Nicaea and this council only envisioned that they were reaffirming and clarifying the faith articulated there, which explains the relative silence of the creed in the years before Chalcedon.[35] At the same time, there is not as much historical silence as some have been led to believe, in the years before and after Constantinople, there are discussions about the clarification of the Nicene Creed and even some subtle references to the work of the council that indicates they were refining or discussing the content of the Nicene Creed.[36]

It is clear, then, that by the time of the Council of Chalcedon, the fathers of the church were now recognizing the Creed of Constantinople as an authoritative standard for orthodoxy and a statement in complete accord with the Nicene Creed. Aetius described this continuity when he introduces the creed saying:

> We decree that the exposition of the right and blameless faith of the three hundred and eighteen holy and blessed fathers assembled in Nicaea, in the time of Emperor Constantine of orthodox memory be pre-eminent, and, moreover, that the definitions made by the one hundred and fifty holy fathers in Constantinople, for the removal of the heresies then rife, and for the confirmation of the same catholic and apostolic faith, remain valid.[37]

---

31. Socrates, *EH* 5.8 and Sozomen, *EH* 7.9.
32. Behr, *The Nicene Faith*, 372.
33. Ibid., 376.
34. Ayres, *Nicaea and its Legacy*, 256.
35. Studer, *Trinity and the Incarnation*, 159.
36. Kelly, *Early Christian Creeds*, 226. Hanson goes on to show that there is some evidence that the creed was known before 451. For example there are references to additions to the Nicene Creed in the Second Macedonian Dialogue and Gregory of Nazianzus complains about the council adding to the creed. Hanson, *The search*, 813.
37. Behr, *The Nicene Faith*, 377.

For those gathered at Chalcedon, there is a recognizable orthodox trajectory moving from Nicaea in 325 to Constantinople in 381 to Chalcedon in 451. From this introduction, there is little doubt that the bishops present at the Council of Chalcedon believed that the Council of Constantinople had produced a creed that clarified the faith expressed at Nicaea.

One can only assume that when Aetius, the archdeacon of Constantinople, recited the creed, he was reading from copies of the proceedings of the Council of Constantinople that were held in his ecclesiastical archives.[38] The following is the authorized version of the creed he read at the Council of Chalcedon in 451:

> We believe in one God, the Father Almighty maker of heaven and earth and of all things visible and invisible;
>
> And in one Lord Jesus Christ, the Son of God, the Only Begotten, begotten by his Father before all ages, Light from light, true God from true God, begotten not made, consubstantial with the Father, through whom all things came into existence, who for us men and for our salvation came down from the heavens and became incarnate by the Holy Spirit and the Virgin Mary and became man, and was crucified for us under Pontius Pilate and suffered and was buried and rose again on the third day in accordance with the Scriptures and ascended into the heavens and is seated at the right hand of the Father and will come again with glory to judge the living and the dead, and there will be no end to his kingdom;
>
> And in the Holy Spirit, the Lord and Life-giver, who proceeds from the Father, who is worshipped and glorified together with the Father and the Son, who spoke by the prophets;
>
> And in one holy Catholic and apostolic Church;
>
> We confess one baptism for the forgiveness of sins;
>
> We wait for the resurrection of the dead and the life of the coming age. Amen.[39]

Even a cursory comparison of this creed with the Nicene Creed reveals many minor differences between them. This does not imply that we are dealing with two radically different creeds, but a clarification of the Nicene Creed, especially in the case of the person and work of Christ and the deity

---

38. Hanson, *The Search*, 813.
39. Ibid., 816.

of the Spirit. Hanson provides a helpful list of twelve specific ways that they differ in any substantive way:[40]

1. Maker of heaven and earth is added in Constantinople
2. "only-begotten" is added after "Son of God" in Constantinople instead of after 'from the Father" as in Nicaea
3. "that is, from the substance of the Father" of Nicaea is omitted in Constantinople
4. "the things in heaven and the things on earth" after "through whom all things are made" which stands in Nicaea is omitted in Constantinople
5. "by the Holy Spirit and the Virgin Mary" is added in Constantinople after "became incarnate"
6. "was crucified for us under Pontius Pilate" is added in Constantinople
7. "and was buried" is added in Constantinople
8. "according to the Scriptures" and "is seated at the right hand of the Father" is added in Constantinople
9. "in glory" is added in Constantinople to "will come again"
10. "and there will be no end to his kingdom" is added in Constantinople
11. Everything in Constantinople after "and in the Holy Spirit" is added
12. Constantinople omits the anathemas of Nicaea

Most of these differences are entirely inconsequential and can be attributed to the natural shaping of the creedal language through its use within the liturgical (especially baptismal) setting during the years between 325 and 381. One can easily imagine how some of these minor qualifications might develop as bishops taught, explained, and passed down the creed within their churches. So, for example, clarifying statements that Father is the "Maker of heaven and earth" or that Christ "was crucified under Pontius Pilate" and "was buried" are not controversial among either those affirming the Nicene faith or other heretical groups.

There are, however, five differences that have some potential significance: 1) the omission of Nicaea's anathemas, 2) the reference to the Son's kingdom which will have no end, 3) the omission of 'from the *ousia* of the Father", 4) the addition of the phrase "from the Holy Spirit and the Virgin

---

40. Ibid., 816. This list is adapted from Hanson's list of the differences between the creeds.

Mary," and 5) the addition of the extended statement about the Spirit.[41] The first difference is not too difficult to reconcile. There is no need to reaffirm Nicaea's anathemas because they served their purpose and there was no one at the Council of Constantinople to exclude or anathematize with those statements.[42] At the same time, the final lines of the creed (which are another addition) are indicative of the purpose of the creed as a confession to be used in liturgical contexts. They point to the unity of the church under this confession of "one holy catholic [or universal] and apostolic Church," "one baptism for the forgiveness of sins," and the hope of "the resurrection of the dead and the life of the coming age." These lines must be a standard way to conclude a creed and a way to reaffirm the unity of the faith expressed in the statement. For Kelly, "The creed was, above all, a formula for liturgical purposes, and while it was desirable to bring it into line with Nicene orthodoxy, it was unnecessary to incorporate all the Nicene phrases."[43]

The second difference, the reference that "there will be no end to his [Christ's] kingdom," is certainly a rejection of the teaching of Marcellus of Ancyra. Marcellus had been known to teach—though he later rejected this view—that the Son would be absorbed back into the divine Monad in the eschatological state.[44] He assumed that Sonship was limited to the economic relationship during the incarnation. After the Son completed his earthly ministry, the Word of God would return to be imminent with the Father. Marcellus died a few years before Constantinople, but it seems that by the time of the council this anti-Marcellus saying, which is probably derived from Luke 1:33, had become a traditional part of the creed.

The third significant difference is the omission of 'from the *ousia* of the Father," which has caused a good bit of discussion among scholars. It seems possible, as Hanson argues, that this phrase was just overlooked, and given that the creed affirms that the Son is *homoousios* with the Father, it is not altogether necessary.[45] Furthermore, this council was more attentive to the defending of the humanity of Christ and the deity of the Holy Spirit rather than narrowly focused on the deity of the Son. Ayres also suggests

---

41. Ibid., 817.
42. Ayres, *Nicaea and its Legacy*, 256.
43. Kelly, *Early Christian Creeds*, 333.
44. Hanson, *The Search*, 817. Kelly, *Early Christian Creeds*, 338.
45. Ayres, *Nicaea and its Legacy*, 257; Hanson, *The Search*, 817.

Section II—Historical Christological Councils

that the language of *ousia* in this case was probably more important in Athanasian circles that it was in those of Basil and Meletius.[46]

We should also note that in the years between Nicaea and Constantinople, there was a good bit of discussion about the terms *ousia* and *hypostasis*. The Cappadocian Fathers in particular helped clarify the distinction between the terms. For example, Basil writes:

> The distinction between *ousia* and *hypostasis* is the same as between the general and the particular; as, for instance, between the animal and the particular man. Wherefore, in the case of the Godhead, we confess one essence or substance so as not to give a variant definition of existence, but we confess a particular *hypostasis*, in order that our conception of Father, Son, and Holy Spirit may be without confusion and clear. If we have no distinct perception of the separate characteristics, namely, fatherhood, sonship, and sanctification, but form our conception of God from the general idea of existence, we cannot possibly give a sound account of our faith. We must, therefore, confess the faith by adding the particular to the common. The Godhead is common; the fatherhood is particular. We must therefore combine the two and say, 'I believe in God the Father.' The like course must be pursued in the confession of the Son; we must combine the particular with the common and say 'I believe in God the Son,' so in the case of the Holy Ghost we must make our utterance conform to the appellation and say 'in God the Holy Ghost.'[47]

This key distinction would be vital for the council as evidenced in the final synodal letter composed after the creed. In that document, the council summarizes their work and remarks that this statement was not intended to be a replacement for the Nicene Creed, but merely a restatement of the faith confessed at Nicaea with the clarification of the distinction between the one *ousia* and the three *hypostases*. A key portion of the letter reads:

> This is the faith which ought to be sufficient for you, for us, for all who wrest not the word of the true faith; for it is the ancient faith; it is the faith of our baptism; it is the faith that teaches us to believe in the name of the Father, of the Son, and of the Holy Ghost. According to this faith there is one Godhead, Power and Substance of the Father and of the Son and of the Holy Ghost; the dignity being equal, and the majesty being equal in three perfect essences

---

46. Ibid., 257.
47. Basil, *Letter 236*, 6. See also Kelly, *Early Christian Doctrines*, 263–69.

and three perfect persons. Thus there is neither room for the heresy of Sabellius by the confusion of the essences or destruction of the individualities; thus the blasphemy of the Eunomians, of the Arians, and of the Pneumatomachi is nullified, which divides the substance, the nature and the godhead and superinduces on the uncreated consubstantial and co-eternal trinity a nature posterior, created and of a different substance.[48]

The letter expresses in no uncertain terms that God exists as one "Power and Substance" and "three perfect essences and three perfect persons," which finalizes the distinction for which the Cappadocian's had been laboring. So while the removal of the phrase "from the ousia of the Father" is curious, it does not detract from the Christology of the creed.

The fourth difference is the clarification of the incarnation with the line that he "became incarnate by the Holy Spirit and the virgin Mary," which seems to be based upon Luke 1:27 and 35 and appears as a response to Apollinarianism. On one hand, Apollinaris, the bishop of Laodicea, affirmed the Nicene Creed and rejected Arianism, but on the other hand his view of the humanity of Christ was problematic. He believed that Christ did not have two natures, but one; and he argued that "the Logos took the place of the human soul," thereby becoming the animating principle in the person of Jesus.[49] In other words, "the Word was the sole life of the God-man, infusing vital energy and movement into Him even at the purely physical and biological levels."[50] Apollinaris rejected any discussion of the "two natures" of Christ, which is implied in the statement that Christ was born of the Spirit and Mary. Kelly, though, is not entirely convinced that this statement is directed against Apollinarianism and without more explanation of the deliberations during the council it is hard to know for certain, but clearly the later tradition took this phrase in the creed as a reference to a two-natures Christology.[51] At the same time, the synodical letter the bishops composed after the council has a strong condemnation of Apollinarianism saying, "We moreover preserve unperverted the doctrine of the incarnation of the Lord, holding the tradition that the dispensation of the flesh is neither soulless nor mindless nor imperfect; and knowing full well that God's Word was perfect before the ages, and became perfect man in the

---

48. Theodoret, *EH*, 5.9.
49. Drobner, *The Fathers of the Church*, 293.
50. Kelly, *Early Christian Doctrines*, 292.
51. Kelly, *Early Christian Creeds*, 335–36.

last days for our salvation."[52] The first canon of the council also condemned Apollinarianism, so the council was obviously concerned with the rejecting this christological error. Thus the statement "Christ born of the Spirit and Mary" was a preliminary step that anticipates the discussions of the two natures Christology at the Council of Chalcedon in 451.

The final major difference, and probably the most important qualification of the creed, is the extended statement on the Spirit. This language about the Holy Spirit is a summary of the contribution of the Cappadocian Fathers during the years between the councils of Nicaea and Constantinople, including Basil of Caesarea, Gregory of Nazianzus, and Gregory of Nyssa. With the additional statements on the Spirit, the consubstantiality of the Spirit and the Son was affirmed—even if it does not use this language. During the Arian controversy in the early years of the fourth century, the deity of the Spirit took a backseat to the deity of the Son, though figures such as Athanasius defended the deity of the Spirit.[53] By 381 the issue had come to the forefront through the teaching of the Macedonians who were particularly unreceptive to the idea of the procession of the Spirit from the Father.[54] The Macedonians, also known as the Pneumatomachians, received their name from Macedonius the *homoiousian* bishop of Constantinople from 342–360, though there is actually little that connects him directly to this group.[55] Socrates reports that their most prominent leader was Eustathius of Sebaste, saying, "But when the Macedonians began to deny the Divinity of the Holy Spirit in the Trinity, Eustathius said: 'I can neither admit that the Holy Spirit is God, nor can I dare affirm him to be a creature.' For this reason those who hold the *homoousion* of the Son call these heretics 'Pneumatomachi.'"[56] Eustathius and the Macedonians believed the Spirit must occupy some intermediate position less than God but more than a mere creature. They often cited Scripture passages they believed taught the inferiority of the Spirit and suggested that in order to be divine the Spirit must be some sort of "coordinate unoriginate principle with the Father or else the brother of the Son," neither of which was an option, so the Spirit must be like other spirits and in no way God.[57]

52. Theodoret, *EH*, 5.9.
53. Kelly, *Early Christian Creeds*, 339.
54. Ibid., 344.
55. Kelly, *Early Christian Doctrines*, 259.
56. Socrates, *EH*, 2.45.
57. Kelly, *Early Christian Doctrines*, 260.

Basil of Caesarea and the other Cappadocian Fathers responded forcefully to this view and argued that the Spirit should be glorified together with the Father and the Son. They grounded their arguments in Scripture's testimony to the divinity and dignity of the Spirit, as well as the descriptions of the economic and personal relationship between the Father, Son, and Spirit.[58] Gregory of Nazianzus captures this thought in one of his famous theological orations saying, "What then? Is the Spirit God? Most certainly. Well then, is He Consubstantial? Yes, if He is God."[59] In a similar way, Basil writes that to deny the deity of the Spirit is to reject the Son and the Father as well saying:

> I testify to every man who is confessing Christ and denying God, that Christ will profit him nothing; to every man that calls upon God but rejects the Son, that his faith is vain; to every man that sets aside the Spirit, that his faith in the Father and the Son will be useless, for he cannot even hold it without the presence of the Spirit. For he who does not believe the Spirit does not believe in the Son, and he who has not believed in the Son does not believe in the Father.[60]

These affirmations of the Spirit and the detailed analysis of Scripture that supported these views, eventually influenced the composition of the Creed at Constantinople.

In the words of the creed, the initial reference to the Spirit as "the Lord" indicates that "the Spirit is no serving but a ruling spirit, thus belonging to the divine sphere."[61] The language, which is certainly dependent on 2 Cor 3:17, "Now the Lord is the Spirit; and where the Spirit of the Lord is, there is liberty," already indicates that the Spirit bears the same title and is likewise consubstantial with the Father and Son. This is supported with the reference to the Spirit as the "Life-giver" (see 2 Cor 3:6) that points to the Spirit's creative activities within the divine economy.[62] Similarly, the language that the Spirit "proceeds from the Father" comes from the words of

---

58. Ibid., 261.
59. Gregory of Nazianzus, *Oration* 31, 10.
60. Basil, *On the Holy Spirit*, 11.
61. Studer, *Trinity and Incarnation*, 157.
62. See also John 6:63.

Christ in John 15:26 and argues that the Spirit is not a creature, but comes from the Father's hypostasis.[63]

Perhaps the most important phrase is the statement that the Spirit "is worshipped and glorified together with the Father and the Son." This is implied in Lord's command in Matt 28:19 where the disciples are called to baptize in the name of the Father, Son, and Spirit.[64] Unlike the decision of the Son at Nicaea, the council avoided applying the language *homoousios* to the Spirit. Though the council probably believed this, the fact that they avoided it seems to indicate that they were compromising for the sake of the Macedonians who left earlier in the council. As mentioned above, Gregory certainly felt that the creed did not go far enough, but Ayres recently argued that when it comes to this statement in the creed a "desire to accommodate need not also mean a willingness to compromise."[65] In the process of composing the statement on the Spirit, Basil, and the other Cappadocians, were trying to work with the *homoiousians* to bring unity and clarity to the role of the Spirit. Even though they did not use the word *homoousios*, they did argue that the Spirit is also "worshipped and glorified together with the Father and the Son." For these fathers, the common worship of the Spirit with the Father and the Son necessitates "equal ontological status."[66] Finally, the closing line of the Spirit's work upholds that the prophets spoke by means of the Spirit. The language comes from 1 Pet 1:21 and insists that the Scriptures—both Old and New Testaments—are inspired by the same Spirit."[67] Together, all this language of the Spirit provided a way to affirm that the Spirit was *homoousios* with the Father and the Son without using the precise language and clearly demonstrating that the Spirit is of equal adoration and reverence.

Immediately following the council in July 381, Theodosius issued the edict *Episcopis tradi* that officially ordered all churches to be turned over to those who profess the faith of the church articulated at the council.[68] At this point, the Nicene faith became the official religion of the Roman

---

63. Studer, *Trinity and Incarnation*, 157. See 1 Cor 2:12. There is no mention here of the *filioque* clause "and the Son," which will be an issue in later versions of the creed.

64. See 2 Cor 13:14.

65. Ayres, *Nicaea and its Legacy*, 258. See also Studer, *Trinity and the Incarnation*, 157.

66. Ayres, *Nicaea and its Legacy*, 258.

67. See Acts 28:25.

68. Hanson, *The Search*, 820.

Empire and the Nicene-Constantinopolitan Creed the official statement of orthodoxy. As mentioned above, one year later the bishops at Constantinople also produced a letter to share their conclusions with the bishops in the West.[69] The contents of the letters reflects the faith of the church described by the council and hopes that the church will continue to reject the errors of Sabellius, Arius, and the Macedonians (Pneumatomachians). At the same time, this council, with its conclusions about the Son and the Spirit, sets the stage for subsequent conciliar discussions about the nature of God and Christ. Eventually the bishops in the West affirmed the conclusions of the council and from at least the fifth century onwards this gathering is retrospectively called the Second Ecumenical Council.[70]

CONCLUSION

The Creed of Constantinople remains one of the most important statements of faith in the early church and a definitive statement of orthodox Trinitarianism. As we have seen, there is certainly a complex historical relationship between the Councils of Nicaea and Constantinople, but these issues should not cloud the important theological continuity that exists between them and the way they continue to guide the church's reflection on her doctrine of God. Though we do not possess all the proceedings from the council, there is enough to piece together the events with relative confidence and to recognize the important theological contributions of the council. These include the affirmation of the deity of the Holy Spirit against the Macedonians and the initial discussions of the humanity of Christ against Apollinarianism. This creed, like the others before and after it, is part of the grand theological conversation that began in the earliest days of the church. As Hanson remarks, these creeds are "accurate sign-posts rather than to exhaustive charts;" they point the church in the right direction to guide her faith as she marches on to face new challenges.[71]

---

69. Theodoret, *EH*, 5.9.
70. Hanson, *The Search*, 821.
71. Ibid., 820.

Section II—Historical Christological Councils

INTERACTIVE PERSONAL SEMINAR

Chapter Summary

In 381 AD a group of 150 bishops gathered in Constantinople for what is now known as the Second Ecumenical Council. The council produced a creed that reaffirmed the creed of Nicaea and also clarified that creed on several points, especially the deity of the Holy Spirit and the humanity of Christ.

Key Terms

- Deity of the Holy Spirit
- Faith of Nicaea
- Melitian Schism
- Apollinarianism
- Macedonians or Pneumatomachians ("Spirit Fighters")

Key People

- Gregory of Nazianzus
- Theodosius
- Basil of Caesarea
- Nectarius of Constantinople
- Marcellus of Ancyra

Advanced Questions

1. Describe the historical context of the creed and the role of the emperor Theodosius.
2. Describe the various groups and figures present at the council and the ways they reacted to the deliberations.

3. What were the major decisions of the council and what steps did they take to ensure that the Nicene faith was affirmed?
4. What were the key terms and phrases added to the Nicene Creed at the council of Constantinople?

Theological Questions

1. Explain how the creed of Constantinople portrays the relationship between the Spirit and the Father and the Son?
2. Does the creed use the language *homoousios* to describe the relationship between the Spirit and the Father and Son? If not, is the language of the creed sufficient?
3. In what ways does the Creed of Constantinople address Apollinarianism and does the discussion of the Christ's two natures need even more clarification?
4. Explain the difference between the "wording" of the creed of Nicaea and the "faith" or "teaching" of the creed.

Issues To Research

1. Evaluate all the specific differences between the Creed of Nicaea and Constantinople and explain why the latter council made their decisions
2. Explain the important theological contributions of the Cappadocian Fathers (Basil of Caesarea, Gregory of Nazianzus, and Gregory of Nyssa) and how they influenced the wording of the creed.
3. Explain the key Biblical terms and phrases in the creed and the way they use them to defend the deity of the Spirit?

6

The Council of Ephesus

Peter Beck

IMAGINE YOU'RE DRIVING DOWN a long, lonely stretch of highway at night. No one to talk to. Nothing to look at. The constant, rhythmic flashing of the reflectors in the pavement hypnotically lull you into a mental haze. You grow more and more tired. Slowly you drift off to sleep. Just as slowly you begin to drift off to the right, your tires dropping off the pavement.

BOOM! You awake with a start and immediately recognize the peril of your situation. You do the only logical thing. You pull the steering wheel to the left to get yourself back onto the road, back to safety. The problem gets worse, however, if you overreact. You yank to the left too hard. You overcorrect. Now you're out of the right ditch and heading to the left. Things have gone from bad to worse. The results may be catastrophic.

Theologians drive this same stretch of highway all the time. Periodically new ideas arise. They challenge the status quo. They wake the church from its theological slumber. The theologians interact with these new ideas. They react to the situation at hand with intellectual aplomb. They solve the problem. They answer the questions. They embrace the good while rejecting the bad. Sometimes. Sometimes they overreact. Sometimes they accidentally create new problems while attempting to solve the old.

Such is the tale of the christological controversies of the fourth and fifth centuries. Once the canon of Scripture was finally closed and the church was firmly and safely entrenched in the life of the Roman Empire, theologians embraced the opportunity to test the deeper theological waters of the Bible. The first order of business, as it should have been, was questions about the person and work of Christ.

Each successive council closed the books on the theological debate of its age. In doing so, however, they left some questions unresolved and begged yet others. Nicaea answered Arius's challenge. They resolved the question of Christ's deity but failed to address his humanity with any certainty. The Council of Constantinople (381) dealt with that, rightly arguing against Apollinarianism that Jesus was fully human, possessing all the attributes native to humanity. That generation failed however, to explain the relationship between Christ's deity and his humanity. Exactly how is Jesus both fully God and fully man, the creator and the created, at the same time? How do these two natures exist simultaneously in one person? Yet again, the church reacted to a problem but only partially, responding to the crisis at hand while failing to see around the next theological bend. The coming generation would have to correct its course without overcorrecting. Thus, the road to Ephesus was paved with good intentions and unforeseen dangers.

FROM CONSTANTINOPLE TO EPHESUS

The journey from Constantinople to Ephesus spans a greater distance than the 341 miles between the two ancient cities. It is a theological odyssey that spanned more than fifty years between the two councils and crossed two diverse theological traditions. In the West, basking in the glow of Athanasius's victory at Nicaea, Alexandrian theology set off on an eventual and accidental collision course with that of the Antiochenes in the East. Along the way to defining her orthodoxy, the church struggled to avoid the ditch of Apollinarianism on one side and that of Nestorianism on the other. In the end, the Council of Ephesus (431) provided another much needed theological course correction.

Following Athanasius's triumph in Nicaea the church began to weigh the implications of those decisions. Confident of the full divinity of Christ, the church necessarily grappled with the next logical question: In what ways was Jesus human? Those in Athanasius's tradition, the Alexandrians, followed in his stead and, even as they pondered this question, carefully sought to do so by preserving the supremacy of his deity. Occasionally their Word-Flesh Christology emphasized his deity at the expense of his humanity. Within that broader tradition, Apollinarius pushed the bounds of orthodoxy as he pondered this relationship.

Apollinarius (310–390) served as the bishop of Laodicea. He defended the fullness of Christ's deity in keeping with the findings of Nicaea. In doing so, he sought to explain the humanity of Jesus in a way that would not undermine those conclusions. In the process he undermined the fullness of that humanity instead. Convinced that the human nature was necessarily inferior to the divine, just as the creature is inferior to his creator, Apollinarius wished to avoid the mistake of diminishing the latter by glorifying the former. "Just as we attribute glory to the body by reason of the divine conjunction and its unity with God," he wrote, "so we ought not to deny the inglorious attributes that stem from the body."[1]

Because of the imperfections of the flesh, Apollinarius contended, Christ's divine nature subsumed rather than assumed the flesh. That is, the *logos*, the Word, the divine spirit of Jesus, "contributes a special energy to the whole together with the divine perfection" by overwhelming the human side of the equation, replacing the human spirit with the divine. As a result, the human became less than fully human.[2] Or, as Apollinarius argued elsewhere, "[Jesus] is not a human being but is *like* a human being" (emphasis mine).[3] Christ, Apollinarius held, emptied himself in the incarnation not by becoming human but by "being clothed" in the human.[4] Thus, the divinity of Christ as the second person of the Godhead remained unchanged while the humanity of the man named Jesus changed to suit its divine occupant. The Council of Constantinople condemned Apollinarius's view in 381 while strongly affirming the full humanity of Christ without satisfactorily answering the question of relationship.

At the same time, another theological tradition provided influence in the East. Rather than the Word-Flesh Christology of Alexandria that arguably gave birth to the likes of Apollinarius and his emphasis on the divinity of Christ over that of his humanity, the Antiochenes's Word-Man Christology sought to highlight the humanity of Jesus without denigrating his deity.

---

1. Apollinarius of Laodicea, "On the Union in Christ of the Body with the Godhead," 103.
2. Ibid., 104.
3. Ibid., 109.
4. Ibid., 111.

This emphasis on the humanity, taken too far, eventually led to the rise of new Christological problems.

According to Cyril of Alexandria, Diodore (d. 390)—the bishop of Tarsus and a participant at the Council of Constantinople—stood at the trailhead of these new problems. Diodore held to both the full deity and the full humanity of Christ but did so by maintaining a strong distinction between Jesus as the Son of God and Jesus as the Son of David. The former, he believed, pointed to Jesus's eternality while the latter his humanity. Thus, there were two sons of God, one in nature (the divine) and one by grace (the human). The two should not be theologically or ontologically confused, Diodore reasoned. The Word, he argued, should never be thought of as Mary's son. She was not the *theotokos*, the God-bearer. In the incarnation both retained the fullness of their individual natures. The Son of God was fully God. The Son of David was fully human. Both natures resided in the one individual, Jesus, working together to fulfill the will of God for the Messiah.

Also an Antiochene, Theodore of Mopsuestia (~350–428) made much of Jesus's humanity as well. A staunch defender of orthodoxy, he wrote frequently on the decretals of both Nicaea and Constantinople. Yet Theodore's Christology was confusing at best and problematic at worst. Like Diodore before him, he rejected the idea that Mary was the *theotokos*. She was, according to Theodore's estimation, *anthropotokos*, the man-bearer and the mother of the human Jesus. Also echoing Diodore, he argued that the *logos*, the divine, lived within the human.[5] He wrote of this union between Christ's deity and humanity as the "Word and assumed man," one being with two different individual natures, the human at the disposal of the divine.[6] Theodore contended the two natures shared a unity of will derived from the divine spirit functioning together in a union of these two natures. However, in order to preserve the freedom of the human nature's will, something he considered essential to human nature, Theodore spoke of the two natures cooperating "at will." That is, the two natures could have chosen to operate together or at odds as they saw fit. Thus, in his effort to hold to the full deity and full humanity of Christ, both with their incumbent and diverse natures, Theodore may have undermined the very Christological unity that he sought to protect. His precise legacy confounded contemporary theologians of his day and still confounds scholars today.

5. Ferguson, *Church History*, 259.
6. Elliott, "Theodoret," 540.

The full and final over-reaction to Constantinople's Christological correction, however, came one generation later. As happens so often in church history, the student went beyond his teacher not in stature but in error. Whereas Theodore of Mopsuestia may have started down the road to theological error with his over-emphasis on the independence of Christ's two natures, his student embraced it fully and headed straight for the ditch. With him, the church was on the road to Ephesus.

THEOLOGICAL DECLENSION AND DISPUTATION

Theodore's student Nestorius (~381–451/52) showed great potential for Kingdom usefulness moving up through the ecclesial ranks to positions of greater importance and influence. Beginning as a presbyter, he served as the head of the monastery in Antioch. From there Eastern Emperor Theodosius II (401–450), in a politically charged move, appointed him to the bishopric in Constantinople, the imperial capital, whereupon Nestorius established a reputation as a defender of orthodoxy. As such his words carried much gravitas and could not escape the attention of friends or foes.

Just as the differences between Word-Flesh Christology and Word-Man Christology divided the Alexandrians from the Antiochenes, so too did the question of Mary as *theotokos*—the God-bearer. While the westerners embraced this title as a means of highlighting the incarnation without undermining Christ's deity, the Antiochenes refused this distinction for Mary out of concern that such a designation made too much of Mary and too little of the Word. Such an emphasis on his human birth, they believed, undermined Christ's divine nature by implying that the unchangeable had changed. Instead, still wishing to honor the fullness of Jesus's humanity, they argued that Mary served as the mother of the man assumed by God.[7] As such, this rejection of the label became the theological starting point for Diodore and Theodore's christological developments as they carefully sought to maintain the distinction between Christ's two natures. In keeping with the teaching of his tradition and his teacher, Nestorius strongly opposed any who would grant Mary the title "mother of God" and defended those who stood with him in his opposition.

Nestorius's insistent rejection of *theotokos* fueled his Christology and the opposition to it in the years immediately preceding the Council of Ephesus. In 428, Nestorius's chaplain publicly denounced what he perceived to

---

7. Ferguson, *Church History*, 260.

be the error of *theotokos*. When public outcry arose from the Alexandrian-leaning people of Constantinople, Nestorius defended his faithful servant. One year later, Proclus, a presbyter in Constantinople, preached in favor of the doctrine. Nestorius, in attendance for this sermon, publicly rebutted Proclus's position. The notion of *theotokos*, he reasoned, dissolved the distinction between Jesus's two natures, ultimately undermining his humanity. So strong was his argument for the full humanity of Christ, some feared that Nestorius actually denied the deity of Christ.

In his "First Sermon Against the Theotokos," Nestorius kept the theological flames burning when he asked, "Does God have a mother?"[8] He answered his own rhetorical question in the negative. To say "yes," he posited, would make Paul, the author of Hebrews according to Nestorius, a liar in that Hebrews 7:3 draws a parallel between Melchizedek and Jesus by stating that Christ was "without father, without mother, without genealogy."[9] Explaining Mary's role in the incarnation, he added, "A creature did not produce the Creator, rather she gave birth to the human being, the instrument of the Godhead."[10] According to Nestorius, God "formed out of the Virgin a temple for God the Logos, a temple in which he dwelt."[11] His insistence on drawing such a firm distinction between Christ's deity and his humanity arose from two concerns. First, Nestorius's affirmation of the impassibility of God required the passibility of the human nature be limited to just that nature. They must remain separate, he contended. Second, the passibility of the human nature was necessary so that Jesus could fulfill the Law as a human in the same way that Adam had transgressed it. As he said,

> Consequently, Christ assumed the person of the debt-ridden nature and by its mediation paid the debt back as a son of Adam, for it was obligatory that the one who dissolved the debt come from the same race as he who had once contracted it. The debt had its start from a woman, and the remission had its start from a woman.[12]

Christ having put on human nature as one does a garment, as no mere human, however. "He is at once God and man."[13] This man Jesus, because

---

8. Nestorius, "First Sermon against the *Theotokos*," 124.
9. Ibid.
10. Ibid., 124–25.
11. Ibid., 125.
12. Ibid., 126–27.
13. Ibid., 129.

Section II—Historical Christological Councils

of the connection between the human and the divine, merits worship as no other human does. As he concluded, "I divide the natures, but I unite the worship."[14]

Not to be left out of a good theological debate, the Alexandrians weighed in early on in the growing controversy over the doctrine they held so dearly. Cyril (~380–444), bishop of Alexandria, wrote Nestorius in 429 to give a defense of *theotokos*. Exegeting John 1:14, Cyril pointed out that the subject of the sentence is "the Word," the second person of the Trinity. The "flesh," he continued, is an attribute—a trait—the Word took on in the incarnation.

> For we do not say that the nature of the Word was changed and became flesh, or that it was converted into a whole man consisting of soul and body; but rather the Word having personally united to himself flesh animated by a rational soul, did in an ineffable and inconceivable manner become man, and was called the Son of Man, not merely as willing or being pleased to be so called, neither on account of taking to himself a person, but because the two natures being brought together in a true union, there is of both one Christ and one Son; for the differences of the natures is not taken away by the union, but rather the divinity and the humanity make perfect for us the one Lord Jesus Christ by their ineffable and inexpressible union.[15]

There was no change in either nature, he reasoned. In the incarnation, Cyril explained, the *logos* united himself to the flesh in what he termed the hypostatic union.[16] The two, without surrendering their own attributes, became one in being and purpose.

Furthermore, Cyril continued, Mary's unique role in this union was indisputable and invaluable. "Since, for us and for our salvation, he personally united himself to an human body, and came forth of a woman, he is in this way said to be born after the flesh; for he was not first born a common man of the holy Virgin, and then the Word came down and entered into him, but the union being made in the womb itself." Cyril also argued that this complete union of the two natures was necessary for Christ's humiliation on the cross as the very real man Jesus suffered and died when the divine Word alone could not. Yet, responding to the Antiochene notion that

---

14. Ibid., 130.
15. Cyril of Alexandria, "The Epistle of Cyril to Nestorious," 197–98.
16. Ferguson, *Church History*, 261.

Christ's two natures existed side-by-side, separate in nature but united in ethical action, Cyril pointed out that the Bible repeatedly speaks of Jesus's life, death, and resurrection just as it did of his birth, as one event that occurred to the Son of God as a whole not an occasion peculiar to his human nature alone. As he wrote, "We worship, confess one Christ and Lord, not as worshiping a man with the Word."[17]

Finally, Cyril closed his letter with a clear summation of the Alexandrian position. In the incarnation Jesus "partook of the flesh and blood like to us; he made our body his own, and came forth from a woman, not casting off his existence as God, or his generation of God the Father, but even in taking to himself flesh remaining what he was." As such Jesus was at once in one person both fully God and fully man and not two persons, the divine and the human, sharing one earthly existence. Therefore, Cyril concluded, with the "holy Fathers" of the church, the church must continue "to call the holy Virgin, the Mother of God, not as if the nature of the Word or his divinity had its beginning from the holy Virgin, but because of her was born that holy body with a rational soul, to which the Word being personally united is said to be born according to the flesh." Thus, he defended the language of *theotokos* until the end, arguing that it adequately expressed both Mary's role in Christ's birth and the reality of the union of his two natures in that event. To reject the one necessarily meant the rejection of the other. That, he believed, would be tantamount to heresy.[18]

Nestorius responded in kind. He wrote a letter. In keeping with his reputation as a defender of orthodoxy, Nestorius appealed to the now-revered Nicene Creed as the definitive explanation of Christ's nature(s). The creed, he pointed out, used language that speaks of Christ's two natures side-by-side, never speaking of them as conjoined or united. The creed, he contended, devoted considerable energy to highlighting the deity of Christ, clearly speaking of the deity alone when it spelled out that he was "one Lord Jesus Christ" and "of one substance with the Father." Only later in the creed does it explain that he "was incarnate and was made man." The two natures, Nestorius argued, were completely separate.

Another letter arrived from Cyril. In his second letter, Cyril still sought correction via conciliation. Acknowledging Nestorius's reference to the Nicene Creed, he believed his opponents' understanding of the creed was flawed. "It is incumbent on us to be true to these statements and

---

17. Cyril, "The Epistle of Cyril to Nestorious," 14:198.
18. Ibid.

Section II—Historical Christological Councils

teaching," he wrote, "and to comprehend what is meant by saying that the Logos from God took flesh and became human."[19] Agreeing that nothing of the divine nature was changed in the incarnation, Cyril thought the creed intended to do more than explain his immutability. "On the contrary," he continued, "we say that in an unspeakable and incomprehensible way, the Logos united to himself, in his hypostasis, flesh enlivened by a rational soul, and in this way became a human being and has been designated 'Son of man.'"[20] Through this union came "one Christ and one Son out of the two."[21] As such, Christians worship not two messiahs but one. Finally, this hypostatic union of the two natures in one being justified the calling of Mary *theotokos*, as it was she who gave fleshly birth to him who was both God and man.[22]

Trying to maintain the filial tone of Cyril's letter, Nestorius responded once more. Having admitted that he was taken aback by the sternness of Cyril's letter, he offered forgiveness and then proceeded to dissect Cyril's "all-wise utterances" that contained such "astonishing teaching."[23] In his rebuttal Nestorius admitted that believed himself to be squarely within the pale of orthodoxy concerning Christ's two natures and the impassibility of the divine. "I do not see how he reintroduced as passible and newly created one who had first been proclaimed as impassible and incapable of a second birth—as if the qualities which attach naturally to God the Logos are corrupted by his conjunction with his temple."[24] Like all Antiochenes, the impassibility of Christ's deity stood as the central issue for Nestorius. As he understood Scripture, the humanity of Jesus and not the deity suffered, for the divine could not suffer as that would represent a change in his nature. Thus, Mary in no way could be construed to be the "Mother of God," *theotokos*. God was pre-existent and immutable, incapable of suffering. Instead, he suggested that Mary's role was that of "Mother of Christ," *christokos*, the one who could and would suffer in his humanity.[25] Accordingly, Nestorius defended to the end, his belief that the two natures of Christ remained two: the one generated by God and the other born of a woman.

---

19. Cyril of Alexandria, "Second Letter to Nestorius," 132.
20. Ibid., 132–33.
21. Ibid., 133.
22. Ibid., 134–35.
23. Nestorius, "Second Letter to Cyril," 135.
24. Ibid., 137.
25. Ibid.

> The body therefore is the temple of the Son's deity, and a temple united to it by a complete and divine conjunction, so that the nature of the deity associates itself with the things belonging to the body, and the body is acknowledged to be noble and worthy of the wonders related in the Gospels.[26]

The humanity served the needs of the deity, sharing only the honor worthy of the greater nature by association rather than the weaknesses of the flesh.

In Nestorius's mind it was Cyril, not himself, who committed theological error. "To attribute also to [Jesus], in the name of this association (the incarnation), the characteristics of the flesh that has been conjoined with him—I mean birth and suffering and death—is, my brother, either the work of a mind which truly errs in the fashion of the Greeks or that of a mind diseased with the insane heresy of Arius and Apollinarius and the others."[27] Finally, having labeled Cyril a heretic and defended himself as being in line with the teachings of the Father, Nestorius closed with wishes for good health and continued prayers—for himself.

The bishop of Rome, Celestine (d. 432), caught wind of the debate raging between Alexandria and Antioch and dispatched John Cassian (360–435) to craft a response to Nestorius. His response, "On the Incarnation," arrived in 430. From the opening pages and their reference to the pestilence of heresies like Arianism and Paganism to his appeal to the theological greats that preceded him—men like Athanasius and Augustine—John's agreement with Cyril's position is clear. Needless to say, his arguments, though quite long and thorough, failed to convince Nestorius. For that reason, Celestine convened a synod in Rome that same year in which Nestorius's views were condemned as heterodox.

---

26. Ibid., 138.

27. Ibid., 139. Ironically, it was Nestorius who shared some similarities with the heretics. Like Arius, Nestorius desired to maintain a strict distinction between the deity of the Word and humanity of the man Jesus to preserve the immutability of God. For Arius this meant denying the absolute deity of Christ, choosing instead to argue that Christ was a created being of the highest order and thus worthy of worship but nonetheless less than God. For Nestorius this meant denying a real union of the two natures. Christ's deity was distinct from his humanity. Like Apollinarius, Nestorius's defense of the reality of the two natures required that he explain the relationship between the two. Apollinarius maintained that the divine in essence conquered or subjected the human, replacing the human spirit with the divine and, as a result, diminishing the human nature. Nestorius, accepting the Council of Constantinople's rejection of the Apollinarianism, argued for the real presence of both natures in their fullness but proposed another solution that placed those two natures at potential odds with one another and diminishing the unity of Christ.

A second synod gathered in Alexandria. To no one's surprise, the Antiochene's position received outright rejection there as well. Once more, Cyril wrote to Nestorius, this time to inform him of their corporate decision to denounce his position. After introductory niceties, the harshness of the Cyril's words set in. "If you injured yourself alone, by teaching and holding such things, perhaps it would be less matter," he remarked. "But you have greatly scandalized the whole Church, and have cast among the people the leaven of a strange and new heresy."[28] Affirming the Nicene Creed once more, Cyril appealed to the theological heritage of the church to support his position concerning the unity of the incarnate Christ.

> Confessing the Word to be made one with the flesh according to substance, we adore one Son and Lord Jesus Christ; we do not divide the God from the man, nor separate him into parts, as though the two natures were mutually united in him only through a sharing of dignity and authority (for that is a novelty and nothing else), neither do we give separately to the Word of God the name Christ and the same name separately to a different one born of a woman; but we know only one Christ, the Word from God the Father with his own flesh.[29]

He further affirmed Mary as *theotokos*. "And since the holy Virgin brought forth corporally God made one with flesh according to nature, for this reason we also call her Mother of God."[30] In their decision, as Cyril reported it, the Alexandrians declared Nestorius's teaching errant and the Antiochenes's presupposition concerning Mary fallacious.

Moreover, to the letter Cyril attached twelve anathemas denouncing Nestorius's position, declaring it heretical, and excommunicating him and any who would share his sentiments. Here too, the *theotokos* lay at the root of the debate. According to the first anathema, "If anyone would not confess that the Emmanuel is very God, and that therefore the Holy Virgin is the Mother of God inasmuch as in the flesh she bore the Word of God made flesh: let him be anathema."[31] The remaining eleven anathemas repeated the various arguments Cyril offered in his earlier letters. In the end, the decision of the Alexandrian synod was clear: either one must accept their conclusions or there would be no theological peace.

28. Cyril of Alexandria, "The Epistle of Cyril to Nestorius," 14:201.
29. Ibid., 202.
30. Ibid., 205.
31. Ibid., 206.

While Cyril's last letter and anathemas nicely summarized his view, they offered little opportunity for reconciliation. The Alexandrians, and the now the Romans also, would accept nothing less than total victory. Nestorius refused to recant his position, and the church universal once more found itself at a crossroad. The church would travel onward with Cyril or Nestorius, the Alexandrians or the Antiochenes, or alone. But she could not remain in the middle of the road and watch the head-on collision between the two camps any longer. Neutrality ceased to be an option. The church had to decide which way she was going to go in regards to the relationship of Christ's unity or risk losing her own.

COUNCIL OF EPHESUS

Recognizing the severity of the situation, Nestorius implored Theodusius II to convene a council to resolve the issue once and for all—assuming that the emperor's support would swing sentiment in his favor. Sensing the need for unity within the fragmented Roman Empire, Theodosius, the emperor of the eastern half of the Roman Empire, along with his cousin, Valentinian III (419–55) the Western Emperor, ordered the bishops to assemble and bring final resolution to the debate that had raged between Cyril and Nestorius, the Alexandrians and the Antiochenes, and the East and the West. Writing to Cyril, the emperor noted, "It is our will that the holy doctrine be discussed and examined in a sacred Synod, and that be ratified which appeareth agreeable to the right faith, whether the wrong party be pardoned by the Fathers or no."[32] So, in June of 431, a large contingent of bishops from across the empire answered the call and began to gather in the Church of Mary to determine the fate of Nestorius and *theotokos*.

As if the location chosen for the council wasn't fortuitous enough, the events themselves foreshadowed the outcome as they unfolded. Many of the invited parties were late in arriving. First, the emperor's emissary, carrying the edict that would define the purpose and authority of the council, was tardy. Second, Nestorius and his contingent failed to appear on time as well. With the arrival of the emperor's orders, however, Cyril and the others moved to begin the council without the accused. Initially some bishops balked but were persuaded to proceed. The determining factor, it would seem, was a strong sentiment among Cyril's party and others of resentment toward the influence of Constantinople and Antioch.

32. Quoted in, "The Third Ecumenical Council," 14: 192–93.

Section II—Historical Christological Councils

When the council opened on June 22, 431, one hundred fifty-three bishops were present, all from the West or ecclesiologically unaligned in this theological fray. The Antiochenes remained unaccounted for. Cyril presided over the proceedings. After the emperor's directions were read, role was called. The secretary called Nestorius's name three times to no avail. He refused to join the assembly seeing that his fate was predetermined. In fact, he posted guards at the doors to his quarters to keep himself from being taken before the council by force.

Without the accused, the council moved forward. The emperor's clear instructions included the admonition that only the bishops were to participate in the discussions and that none of them were to be permitted to leave Ephesus until the matter was settled. After the emperor's directions were read and attendance was taken, the Nicene Creed was read aloud to set the accepted theological parameters for the debate to follow. Once that standard had been set, the bishops first considered Cyril's letter to Nestorius "on account of his aberration from the right faith."[33] Upon finishing the reading, Cyril asked his audience, "Wherefore I desire your holiness to say whether rightly and blamelessly and in accordance with that holy synod (Nicaea) I have written these things or no."[34] Going around the room, the bishops, from the greatest to the least, concurred. Cyril's theological formulations as expressed in his earlier dispatches to Nestorius concerning the incarnation were in keeping with the Nicene Creed.

Next the council heard Nestorius's second letter to Cyril read aloud. Once more, Cyril sought their opinion. Did they think the teachings of Nestorius were in keeping with the earlier council? "All the bishops cried out together: Whoever does not anathematize Nestorius let him be anathema." Together, they cried out, "We all anathematize Nestorius as a heretic."[35] After hearing Cyril's second letter and accompanying anathemas, excommunication followed. "We have come, with many tears, to this sorrowful sentence against him, namely, that our Lord Jesus Christ, whom he has blasphemed, decrees by the holy Synod that Nestorius be excluded from the episcopal dignity, and from all priestly communion."[36]

Four days after the council first convened, John, the bishop of Antioch, arrived with a contingent of forty-three bishops from Syria. Bad weather

---

33. "Extracts from the Acts," 14:197.
34. Ibid., 199.
35. Ibid.
36. "Decree of the Council against Nestorius," 14:218.

delayed their timely arrival. Seeing that Nestorius's fate had already been decided, John's group held their own council. As one might suspect, the outcome was vastly different. They found Cyril at fault and deposed him for wrongly convening the council without everyone in attendance.

Rather than producing unity, thus far the Council of Ephesus created nothing but further dissension as the bishops allied themselves with their respective theological parties. Theodosius, the older and more influential of the two joint emperors, recognized the dangers of further division. He compelled Celestine, whom the council had already deferred to via his earlier letter to Cyril, to intervene.

The bishop of Rome commissioned a small party led by two bishops under his influence to go to Ephesus as his representatives. This group arrived in July. Taking their seats as the second session of the Council of Ephesus began, they read a letter from Celestine appealing for a strong defense of apostolic teaching and that of the Council of Nicaea that all previously concurred was in agreement with the apostles. The council, he urged, must do whatever necessary to protect the purity and unity of the church. Thus, with Theodosius's implied support and Celestine's imprimatur, the council stood by their original decision. Without issuing a new, expanded creed, leaning wholly upon the Nicene Creed as their expression of orthodox faith, the Council of Ephesus declared Nestorius a heretic. His excommunication stood. Convinced that he was wronged, Nestorius accepted their decision and went into exile. He returned once more to the monastery from which he had begun this theological journey.

CONCLUSION

Having soundly rebuked Nestorius at Ephesus, the bishops returned to their posts. Peace, however, did not return as quickly. With Nestorius an entire tradition had been found wanting and marginalized by the church at large. The Antiochenes limped home with bruised egos and diminished respect. Two years later, in 433, the tardy protagonist John of Antioch reached out to the bishops of the West in hopes of breaching the divide created by the Nestorian controversy.

John dispatched another bishop from the East with a letter full of promise and compromise. This letter, now known as the Formula or Formulary of Reunion, sought a via media, a theological explanation concerning the two natures of Christ to which all Christian brothers could subscribe.

Section II—Historical Christological Councils

Hoping for the best but anticipating the worst, John's ambassador of good will was welcomed with open arms as was John's overture of grace.

John's proposal, strongly affirming the Nicene Creed and accepting the decisions of Ephesus, as repeated verbatim in Cyril's response to him, said,

> Therefore we confess that our Lord Jesus Christ, the only-begotten Son of God, is complete God and complete human being with a rational soul and a body. He was born from the Father before the ages, as to his deity, but at the end of the days the same one was born, for our sake and the sake of our salvation, from Mary the Virgin, as to his humanity. This same one is coessential with the Father, as to his deity, and coessential with us, as to his humanity, for a union of two natures has occurred, as a consequence of which we confess one Christ, one Son, one Lord. In accordance with this concept of the unconfused union, we confess that they holy Virgin is Mother of God, because the divine Logos was made flesh and became a human being and from the moment of conception itself united to himself the temple which he took from her.[37]

Jettisoning their brother Nestorius for the sake of peace, John and the other Antiochenes acknowledged that Cyril and the Alexandrians' explanation of the hypostatic union of Christ's two natures was correct and acquiesced concerning Mary's role as *theotokos*. To this, Cyril gladly agreed. As he wrote, "Having read these your holy words, and finding that we ourselves think in the same way . . . we gave glory to God the Savior of all, and we rejoiced with one another that your churches and ours have a faith in agreement with that of the inspired Scriptures and the tradition of the holy fathers."[38]

The peace for which Christ prayed (John 17:20–21) and the church fought at Ephesus would be short-lived. With correction came over-correction once more. Cyril died and was replaced by a man of near equal ability but far less grace, seeking domination rather than reconciliation. When the next theological controversy arose a decade later in the teachings of Eutyches, the church found itself once more on the road to destruction.

---

37. Cyril of Alexandria, "Letter to John of Antioch," 141–42.
38. Ibid., 142.

INTERACTIVE PERSONAL SEMINAR

Chapter Summary

As each of the ecumenical councils addressed the theological questions of its era, it opened up a new line of exploration for the next. The Council of Nicaea defined the deity of Christ while the Council of Constantinople defended his humanity. The Council of Ephesus was left to think through the manner in which Christ's two natures related to each other while remaining faithful to the conclusion of Scripture and the earlier councils.

Key Terms

- Christology
- Word-Flesh Christology
- Word-Man Christology
- Theotokos
- Anthropotokos
- Christokos
- Hypostatic Union
- Anathema

Advanced Questions

1. Is acceptance of the hypostatic union necessary for salvation?
2. In what ways does an affirmation of theotokos support a high view of Christ's humanity?
3. The Council of Ephesus did not provide a new or updated creedal statement. Why not?
4. Could the Council of Ephesus have done more to prevent the rise of new problems like Eutychianism?

Section II—Historical Christological Councils

Theological Questions

1. Explain the theological difference between Cyril's view of Mary as *theotokos* with Nestorius's argument for *christokos*.
2. Was Nestorius's teaching worthy of the harsh rebuke of the Council of Ephesus? Why or why not?
3. Using Scripture, provide support for both Nestorius's and Cyril's positions.
4. In what ways does one's theological presuppositions drive their hermeneutical method?

Issues to Research

- Consider the role of political allegiances in the life of the church during the early days of Christendom.
- Consider the use of *theotokos* by these early councils and its later use by the Roman Catholic Church. Did the councils affirm the Catholic doctrine or does the Catholic doctrine reveal a departure from the theology of the early church?
- The bishop of Rome played a role in the proceedings leading up to and at the Council of Ephesus. Does this role validate the argument that the bishop of Rome was considered the *prima inter pares* (the first among equals) and thus already fulfilling the role of pope as some have argued or just that Celestine was an important ally during these debates.
- What modern Christological debates might be settled by appealing to the Council of Ephesus?
- Compare the use of the term "heresy" in its historical sense with how it is often used by the modern church.

7

Christology and The Chalcedon Council

Marvin Jones & Justin Carter

INTRODUCTION

The Council of Chalcedon is a defining moment in Christianity. The deliberations of the Council produced the theological creedal milestone that both modern Protestants and Catholics adhere. The famous Chalcedonian Creed established christological orthodoxy that has stood the test of time. The significance of the Chalcedonian Creed is that neither one sixteenth-century Protestant Reformer nor one Catholic Theologian has declared the Creed inadequate.

The story of Chalcedon is the product of theological inquiry ever since the Arian Crisis was the focal point of the 325 Nicene Council. Yet in certain ways, Chalcedon is built upon the decisions of Council of Ephesus in 431. Even though the attempt of all the councils was theological unity, the church could not achieve unity as the creeds often led to more questions than answers. The Council of Ephesus was no exception.

The Council of Ephesus ended in 431, but like its predecessors, it did not bring lasting unity to the church. The political changes within the fourth century also precipitated an ecclesiastical change which meant the climate was ripe for controversy. By 451, a mere twenty years had passed since the Ephesus Council dealt with Nestorianism, the church found itself with the christological problem once again at the forefront.

PRELUDE TO CHALCEDON

Between the First Council of Ephesus and the Council of Chalcedon the preaching of Eutyches (c. 378–454 AD) created another theological controversy within the church. The controversy itself appears to be concerned, not so much with Eutyches's teaching *per se,* but with competing views of the authority of the *Formulary of Reunion*[1] agreed upon between Cyril of Alexandria and John of Damascus in 433 AD.[2] In the four years before Chalcedon, two synods were held concerning Eutyches. The first condemned him as a heretic and the second exonerated him. These two synods were the Synod of Constantinople in 448 AD (the Home Synod of Flavian) and the Second Council of Ephesus in 449 AD. Before the events of these councils can be discussed, Eutyches and his own theology[3] must be examined.

Eutyches

Very early in his life, Eutyches became a monk near Constantinople.[4] He was ordained as a priest and eventually was elected as archimandrite of a great monastery. Eutyches was involved in many prestigious relationships, including being godfather to Chrysaphius, the Emperor Theodosius II's grand chamberlain, as well as a friendship with Cyril of Alexandria and other people connected with Cyril. He also served as a member of a monastic delegation that lobbied against Nestorius during the Nestorian controversy. Shenouda Ishak comments:

> For this Eutyches was highly esteemed and influential both in political and ecclesiastical circles. With the intention of combating the Nestorians, he fought against all the upholders of Nestorius's popular slogan 'Christ in two natures.' His keen opposition to

1. See Peter Beck's Chapter, *The Council of Ephesus,* for more explanation.
2. Samuel, *The Council of Chalcedon Re-Examined,* 23 and n. 85.
3. This survey will not consider later developments of Eutychianism or Monophysitism.
4. At the Home Synod, he claimed to have been a monk for seventy years, which would have nearly been his entire life. See Ishak, *Christology and the Council of Chalcedon,* 107.

Nestorianism led him to be accused in 448 A.D. by Eusebius of Dorylaeum of the opposite heresy of denying Christ's real humanity.[5]

The accusation from Eusebius of Dorylaeum led to his deposition at the Home Synod in 448 AD and the crescendo of events leading to Chalcedon. The exact teaching that led to Eusebius's accusation is unclear. Eutyches did not have the precise theological articulations of his good friend Cyril and seemed to shift his views under pressure. During his examination at the Home Synod, he declared that Christ had two natures before the incarnation and one nature after. Eusebius appears to have believed that Eutyches meant that Christ had a heavenly flesh and therefore did not share in full humanity—a point that Eutyches denied.

The appropriate question to ask and examine is what exactly did Eutyches believe? The Home Synod, hoping to find a solution to the problem, probed Eutyches on his christological position. The Synod concluded he denied Christ's real humanity, which was similar to the heresies of Apollinaris and Valentinus. Thus, the council condemned Eutyches for the same previous heresies. However, Eutyches's actual statement at the council does not seem to make this error. The minutes of the Home Synod were read at the Second Council of Ephesus. Paragraph 505 of those minutes reads:

> Eutyches the presbyter said: "This is what I believe: I worship the Father with the Son, the Son with the Father, and the Holy Spirit with the Father and the Son; I acknowledge that his coming in the flesh was from the flesh of the Holy Virgin, and that he became man perfectly for our salvation. This I confess before the Father and the Son and the Holy Spirit and before your holiness.[6]

During the Second Council of Ephesus, Eutyches also clearly anathematized heretics such as Mani, Valentinus, Apollinarius, and Nestorius.[7]

Eutyches obstinately maintained throughout the proceedings that Christ is of two natures before the incarnation and of only one nature afterwards. Leo Davis summarizes Eutyches's concerns with ascribing two natures to Christ after the incarnation: "To affirm two natures was for him to affirm two concrete existences, two *hypostases*, two persons in Christ. The genuine humanity of Christ and the importance of his historical reality were in danger of being swept away by an imprecise terminology and an

5. Ibid.
6. *Acts of the Council of Chalcedon*, 1:220.
7. Ibid., 1:158.

unbalanced emphasis on Christ's divinity."[8] Beyond these theological concerns, Eutyches firmly believed himself to be completely in line with the council of Nicaea and several notable theologians, including Athanasius, in rejecting the phrase "two natures" in regard to the incarnate Christ.[9]

Eutyches clearly stated at the Home Synod that he believed Christ's flesh came from the Holy Virgin and that Christ possessed full humanity. Eutyches thought the accusations against him were unfounded. In Cyrillian fashion though, again, not with Cyril's precision, he maintained that Christ had two natures before the incarnation and one nature after the incarnation.

Reaction to Eutyches

From the extant material alone, it seems that Eutyches's imprecise articulations led others like Eusebius to be suspicious of his theology. Whether Eutyches's opposition was right to be suspicious, however, is unclear. Richard Price argues that Flavian, who at the urging of Eusebius called the Home Synod, misrepresented Eutyches during the synod and to Leo after the Synod. Leo, likewise, misunderstood Eutyches's position when he wrote his *Tome*.[10] In order to better understand the condemnation of Eutyches, attention must now be drawn to the Synod of Constantinople and the Second Council of Ephesus.

THE SYNOD OF CONSTANTINOPLE, 448 AD (THE HOME SYNOD OF FLAVIAN)

Eusebius of Dorylaem brought his case against Eutyches to the patriarch Flavian and the Home Synod—a semi-permanent council of bishops at Constantinople.[11] Flavian eventually ordered Eutyches to appear before the Synod, despite Eutyches's plea that his vow of seclusion and his ill health did not permit his attendance. Eutyches finally joined the Synod to end rumors that he was organizing the monks against the bishop.

---

8. Davis, *The First Seven Ecumenical Councils*, 171.

9. Leo the Great, *The Letters and Sermons of Leo the Great*, Ep. 21.1.6–7. The letter is written from Eutyches to Leo. This letter demonstrates Eutyches belief about the Council. This does not necessarily mean that he understood the Council of Nicaea or Athanasius correctly.

10. Price, *Acts of the Council of Chalcedon*, 1:116.

11. Davis, *First Seven Ecumenical Councils*, 173.

On November 8, 448 AD, during the first session of the Synod of Constantinople, Eusebius of Dorylaeum presented and read the formal indictment, and emissaries were sent to deliver the first summons to Eutyches. Four days later, a second session consisting of thirty bishops discussed Cyril's second letter to Nestorius, the acts of the first session of the Council of Ephesus and the letter of John of Antioch—which contained the *Formulary of Reunion* of 433 AD. These discussions clarified the nature of the Christian faith which then became the basis for deciding the case of Eutyches. At the seventh session on November 22, Eutyches was interrogated and condemned. When he was pushed to affirm that Christ maintained two natures after the incarnation and to anathematize all who hold contrary views, he responded "But I have not found them clearly in the scriptures . . . nor have the fathers said all these things. So if I anathematize, woe unto me that I condemn my fathers."[12] The synod cried out "Let him be anathema."[13] Eutyches responded that in his reading of Cyril and Athanasius he only found them to speak of two natures before the incarnation, never after.

Eutyches's interrogation centered on whether he would confess "two natures after the union" and whether he affirmed that Christ was "consubstantial with us." Eutyches was clear on the first question, as was described above: he confessed that the Lord was of two natures before the union, but one nature after the union. On this point, he quickly declared his agreement with Cyril and Athanasius. Regarding the phrase "consubstantial with us," however, Eutyches was reluctant to use it. V.C. Samuel points out that this was

> not because he denied the reality and perfection of Christ's manhood, nor because he refused to admit his real birth from Mary, but because Christ for him was God incarnate. The manhood which God the Son assumed in the incarnation was not the manhood of a man, but of God the Son who accepted on himself an incarnate state. In other words, Eutyches was trying in his own way to exclude a doctrine of two Sons, which he feared was implicit in the phrase."[14]

Eutyches was not an instructed theologian, so he found it difficult to spell out this idea properly. Regardless, the Synod declared that anyone who denies two natures after the union does not have the orthodox faith, and

---

12. Ishak, *Christology and the Council of Chalcedon*, 137.
13. Ibid.
14. Samuel, *Chalcedon Re-examined*, 21–22.

Flavian gave the verdict that Eutyches was a follower of Valentinus and Apollinarius. This declaration removed Eutyches from headship of his monastery and led to the excommunication of the monks who followed his opinions.

THE SECOND COUNCIL OF EPHESUS, 449 AD

At the heart of the Home Synod's decision was their understanding of the *Formulary of Reunion*. They adopted the Antiochene view of the *Formulary*, which understood the document as authoritative. Eutyches, however, appears to approach the document from the Alexandrian view, which affirmed the *Formulary* to be a statement between John of Antioch and Cyril of Alexandria on the basis of John's acceptance of the Council of Ephesus and not as an authoritative statement of faith to be placed along with the Creeds. The Second Council of Ephesus in 449 AD, under the leadership of the bishop of Alexandria, pushed an agenda following the Alexandrian view of the *Formulary*.

Eutyches, dissatisfied with his deposition by the Home Synod, immediately sent an appeal to the Councils of Rome, Jerusalem, Alexandria, Thessalonica, and Ravenna. His letter to Pope Leo contained his personal confession of faith that he hoped would gain Leo's support for his defense.[15] At the same time, Flavian also sent a letter to Leo, informing him of the Synod's accusation and subsequent sentence upon Eutyches.[16] Leo received Eutyches's letter rather quickly, but for some unknown reason, did not receive Flavian's letter for several more months. By February 18, 449 AD, Leo grew concerned that he had not yet heard from Flavian and wrote to him requesting more information about the Synod. That same day, he wrote Emperor Theodosius II expressing his concerns with Eutyches's letter, believing that an injustice had been done but desired more full information concerning the Synod's findings.[17] Flavian then responded with an extended account of the heresy of Eutyches,[18] prompting Leo to respond

---

15. Leo the Great, *Ep.* 21.1. This letter is written from Eutyches to Leo.
16. Leo the Great, *Ep.* 22.4. This letter is written from Flavian to Leo.
17. Leo the Great, *Ep.* 23–24.
18. Leo the Great, *Ep.* 26. This letter is written from Flavian to Leo.

on May 21[19] acknowledging the receipt of the letter. Approximately three weeks later, Leo sent his (now famous) *Tome* to Flavian on June 13.[20]

The *Tome* reveals that Leo was convinced, by Flavian's letter, that the Home Synod had acted correctly in the matter. However, Theodosius II had already been convinced by Eutyches and Dioscorus of Alexandria that further action was necessary to settle the matter between Eutyches and Flavian. On March 30, an empirical decree was issued ordering a representative council to meet in Ephesus. Leo responded on June 13 and accepted the invitation. However, he could not attend personally and informed Theodosius of the names of those who would represent him.[21] Leo further informed the Emperor that he was sending the *Tome* with Flavian with the hope that the *Tome* would help defend Flavian.

Even though he had accepted the invitation, Leo confided in Flavian that he still did not think a general council was necessary.[22] There was nothing that Leo or Flavian could do to prevent the council from taking place. Adding to Leo's and Flavian's frustration, the *Tome* arrived on time but was deemed to have arrived too late to be read at the council. Thus, Leo's *Tome* did not have any influence in the council's proceedings. Ironically, the Emperor's summons required attendees to arrive on August 1, and the council would begin on August 8. The *Tome* was there a month in advance of the council.

There were also other events taking place that ensured the new council would be problematic at best. Prior to the Council of Ephesus convening in the fall of 449, the Home Synod itself was put on unofficial trial by Eutyches's supporters in April. They charged Flavian's notaries with falsification and corruption. On April 13, the minutes of the Home Synod were scrutinized, and several witnesses recounted how Flavian had pressed Eutyches to accept a stronger dyophysite formula. Eutyches, following Cyril from nearly twenty years earlier, also rejected Flavian's dyophysite position. However, this piece of information was missing from the official minutes, revealing them to be "doctored to protect Flavian" from accusations of Nestorianism.[23]

19. Leo the Great, *Ep.* 27.
20. Leo the Great, *Ep.* 28.
21. Leo the Great, *Ep.* 29.
22. Leo the Great, *Ep.* 36
23. Ishak, *Christology and the Council of Chalcedon*, 152.

Further accusations against Flavian were leveled on April 27. An imperial official noted that Flavian had discouraged some of Eutyches's supporters from attending the trial, which gave no hope for fairness at the proceedings. Their findings damaged Flavian's reputation as an impartial judge during the Synod and almost certainly worked against him at the forthcoming council.

Ephesus 449 Convenes

The Second Council of Ephesus met in two sessions. The first session met on August 8 and the second on August 22. The first session opened with the reading of the imperial letters, which outlined the priorities of the council, particularly the conflict between Eutyches and Flavian and the eradication of Nestorianism. Some argued that Leo's *Tome* should be read at the outset of the council, but Dioscorus believed that the best decision was to move straight to the council's business outlined in the Emperor's instructions. Since Leo's *Tome* was merely a letter to Flavian, it did not hold precedence over the business of the council. Thus, Dioscorus opened discussions about the conflict between Eutyches and Flavian.

After the minutes of the Home Synod were read, Dioscorus, the other leaders of the council, and one hundred twelve bishops[24] agreed to accept Eutyches's profession of faith and reinstatement. Once Eutyches and his monks were exonerated, the council then moved to depose Flavian. The bishops accused Flavian and Eusebius of Nestorianism and of unjustly condemning Eutyches. After the verdict of condemnation, Flavian and Eusebius were treated as prisoners. Unfortunately, Flavian died soon after the council.[25]

The second session of the council concerned itself with the unfinished business of condemning and deposing other "Nestorian" bishops. They followed the order from Theodosius II to eject from the church all who favored the error of Nestorius. Once this work was done, the council adjourned and was praised and supported by Theodosius. Leo, however, was not pleased. He was upset that his *Tome* had not been read and honored at the council, but W.H.C. Frend argues "it was good that Leo's *Tome* was not read, for in

---

24. A total of 130 bishops were in attendance.

25. "It is commonly held that he died four days after being brutally manhandled after his condemnation, but Frend and Chadwick argue that Flavian died in exile, perhaps in February, 450 AD." See Ishak, *Christology and the Council of Chalcedon*, 163–64.

that atmosphere its author and his representatives would have been excommunicated then and there."[26] Nevertheless, Leo rejected the conclusions of the council, writing on July 20, 451 AD to the Empress Pulcheria[27] that the meeting at Ephesus was a "meeting, not of judges but of robbers."[28] For Leo, the controversy had not yet ended. He believed his *Tome* contained the solution to the christological problem facing the church.

LEO'S TOME

The Councils of Ephesus (431) and Chalcedon (451) were forced to deal with Nestorius and Eutyches. Gerald O' Collins states, "the whole controversy with Nestorius, like that with Eutyches twenty years later, continued to shift the theological attention away from Christ's death and resurrection to his incarnation and the relationship between his human and divine natures."[29]

The previous attempts for solutions by Eutyches (that after the incarnation there was only one nature) and Nestorius (the two natures were connected by a neutral entity) were not only held in suspect, but were condemned by ecclesiastical councils and synods. Even though both positions were disregarded ecclesiastically, they still had widespread support throughout the church. It is obvious the church as a whole was struggling to achieve a christological balance that could explain the relationship between the two natures of Jesus Christ. Leo's *Tome* attempts to give an adequate christological explanation that addresses the errors of Nestorius and Eutyches.

Leo's Christology

For over a year Leo had tried to have his letter to Flavian read at the synods. Within his letter are the seeds of the famous Chalcedonian christological definition. The accomplishment of Leo's theology builds upon a strong Western, i.e. Latin, tradition that had not changed. Men such as Tertullian,

---

26. Frend, *The Rise of Christianity*, 767.

27. Emperor Theodosius II died on July 28 after being thrown from his horse while hunting. His sister, Pulcheria, ascended to the throne after her brother's death.

28. Leo the Great, *Ep.* 95.2. This comment has given rise to nicknaming the Second Council of Ephesus 449 as "The Robbers' Synod."

29. O' Collins, *Christology*, 194.

Hilary, Ambrose, and Augustine contributed to the two natures/one person Christology that Leo proposed in his letter. Aloys Grillmeier states "On 16 July 450, Leo sent a Roman delegation to the East to give events a new turn by direct negotiations. To this delegation Leo again gave his *Tomus ad Flavianum*, this time with an anthology of extracts from the Fathers."[30] The Latin christological tradition, as demonstrated by Leo, did not struggle with the christological formula as the Greek Eastern tradition.

The premises that Leo purports in his letter will become part of the theological foundation for the Chalcedonian Creed. Leo writes, "Therefore in the entire and perfect nature of very man was born very God, whole in what was his, whole in what was ours."[31] The theological concept that refers to the Divine Word and the God-Man are the same. The properties of each entity form the identity of the person on earth. Thus, each property (divine and human) was retained during the incarnation.

The second premise refers to both natures existing in Christ without the mixture or mingling of the natures together. "For each of the natures retains its proper character without defect; and as the form of God does not take away the form of a servant, so the form of a servant does not impair the form of God."[32] There is no third entity, or a mixture of properties, to form the identity of Christ. "He who becomes man is the Son of the Father who has already existed from eternity and is thus pre-existent as a person. A new person does not come into being when the human nature is taken, nor does this result in two persons."[33] Each proper nature, both human and divine, retained in Christ's person, does not diminish the property of the other or form a new person.

The third premise refers to the actions of each property. They perform separate functions but work in unison of operation. "For each 'form' does the acts which belong to it, in communion with the other; the Word, that is, performing what belongs to the Word, and the flesh carrying out what belongs to the flesh."[34] Leo has no reservation claiming that the properties of each nature were separate and unaffected by the incarnation. This point

---

30. Grillmeier, *Christ in Christian Tradition*, 529. See above where the letter was not read at the Ephesus Council deemed arriving too late for adequate reading and understanding.

31. Leo the Great, *Ep.*28.3. Letter from Leo to Flavian.

32. Ibid.

33. Grillmeier, *Christ in Christian Tradition*. 532.

34. Leo the Great, *Ep.*28.4 Letter from Leo to Flavian.

will lead to the fourth premise, which is one of the clarifying focal points of Leo's Christology.

The *communication of idioms*[35] is a theological hallmark and the fourth premise of Leo's *Tome*. The communication between the two natures forms one person which in effect denies the Nestorian "two sons" problem. Leo's concept of Christ's person is that there is communication between the two natures. This premise is the foundation upon which Christ is constituted. "Therefore in consequence of this unity of person which is to be understood in both natures."[36] Even though the two natures never mix or comingle, the communication between the two natures form the person of Christ as a single being.

Leo cites the death and resurrection of Christ as proof that the two natures were existent in the Lord after death. The death of Christ demonstrates that the weakness of the flesh or human nature was the means of the Lord's death, yet the divine nature is coeternal and consubstantial with the Father. Leo appeals to the Apostle's Creed for support. "Wherefore we all, in the very Creed, confess that 'the only begotten Son of God was crucified and buried,' according to that saying of the Apostle."[37] The death of Christ reveals the human nature and the property inherent to the nature of death. So the weakness of flesh allows the accomplishment of the atonement of Christ.

The resurrection demonstrates that the human nature was still existent in Christ's person. For example, when Thomas touched the side of the Lord, he was touching the actual, real body of the Lord. "He allowed himself to be handled with careful inquisitive touch by those who were under the influence of doubt . . . he came to his disciples when the doors were shut…that the properties of the Divine and the human nature might be acknowledged to remain in him without causing a division, and that we might in such sort know that the Word is not what the flesh is, as to confess that the one Son of God is both Word and flesh."[38] Leo knew he had the weight of the Latin Western tradition supporting him. This fact gave Leo

---

35. Grillmeier, "Communication of Properties (Communication of Idioms)," 70–72. yields this following definition. The two natures, deity and humanity, "was the dynamically unifying concept of the communion of idioms. The idiomata signify the things which are proper or peculiar to a nature."

36. Leo the Great, *Ep.*28.5 Letter from Leo to Flavian.

37. Ibid.

38. Ibid.

boldness in making his case for Christ's person existing in two natures as foundational for Chalcedon.

THE COUNCIL OF CHALCEDON

The Council of Chalcedon was called into being by the Empress Pulcheria. Leo had persuaded the Empress to convene the council in Italy to avoid the errors of the Ephesus II council. One also wonders if this location would allow him to exercise great control over the proceedings and subsequent findings. Empress Pulcheria and Marcian (her husband) also saw the need for supervision but decided upon a location closer to her capital. "In May of 451, Marcian sent out letters summoning bishops to a council that would meet in September in the city of Nicaea. The choice of venue, of course, was no accident. As Dioscorus had sought to be a second Cyril at Ephesus II, so Marcian and Pulcheria reached back to an earlier conciliar model, wishing to cast themselves as the new Constantine and Helena presiding over the Second Council of Nicaea."[39]

The location was moved to Chalcedon for three specific reasons: 1) the Huns were attacking Illyricum, which meant that Marcian was directing military operations and thus unable to attend Nicaea; 2) the facilities at Nicaea were not adequate to support the 350–500 attendees at the council; and 3) Chalcedon was much closer to Constantinople which meant it would be an easy boat ride from the palace. Thus, the council location moved to Chalcedon and convened on October 8, 451.[40]

The Actions of Chalcedon

The council opened on October 8 with the reading of the Council of Ephesus 449 minutes. The minutes from the Home Synod followed. According to Davis, "When the reader finished the letter of Cyril accepting the Formula of Union of John of Antioch quoted in the acts, the bishops cried out: 'This we believe.' Shouts were heard against Dioscurus, 'murderer of Flavian.'"[41] The results of the ordeal left Dioscurus standing alone at the council. He still insisted the condemnation of Flavian was appropriate

---

39. Price, *Acts of the Council of Chalcedon*, 1:39.
40. Ibid., 39–40.
41. Davis, *First Seven Ecumenical Councils*, 181.

given that he, like Eutyches, believed that Christ had only one nature after the incarnation.

By October 10, the council's imperial commissioner wanted the bishops to write a doctrinal statement. However, the bishops read documents that were declared orthodox. Those letters were Cyril's letters to John of Antioch, his second letter to Nestorius, Leo's *Tome* to Flavian, and the Creeds of Nicaea and Constantinople. The new creed would wait until the closing days of the council.

Regardless of the timing, the imperial commissioners knew that a formal creed must be adopted to ensure the success of the council. The creed must be not only adopted by the council as a whole but also signed by each individual attendee. Their signatures would ensure ecclesiastical peace for the empire. The rationale for the Cyril and Leo letters being read early in the proceedings worked in favor of the imperial commissioners' desire to have a creed drafted. When those letters were read they gave impetus to the council as Cyril's letters condemned Nestorius, whereas, Leo's *Tome* condemned Eutyches. Cyril's letters also provided "a sound interpretation of the creed (Nicaea)."

The bishops delayed formalizing a new creed, but time and opportunity were on the imperial commissioners side. In order to force the bishops to determine the exact meaning of their findings, the imperial commissioners put forward a very blunt question: Are you for Leo or Dioscurus? They answered with affirmation of Leo's Christology, so a commission was formed to draft a formal creed.

THE CHALCEDON DEFINITION OF FAITH

The bishops of Chalcedon upheld the Nicene and Constantinople Creeds as orthodox. They also accepted the proceedings from the Council of Ephesus. This had the effect of acknowledging three previous councils as ecumenical in scope. The new Chalcedon Creed must be in conformity to the previous council creeds if it was going to be imperial and ecclesiastically binding. The goal was to formulate and adopt a creed that stated the unity of the person of Christ while recognizing the distinct natures that formed the person. Such and endeavor had not been attempted before.

Section II—Historical Christological Councils

EXCURSUS

The Chalcedonian Creed

Following therefore the holy fathers, we confess one and the same our Lord Jesus Christ, and we all teach harmoniously [that he is] the same perfect in Godhead, the same perfect in manhood, truly God and truly man, the same of a reasonable soul and body; consubstantial with the Father in Godhead, and the same consubstantial with us in manhood *(homoousion)*, like us in all things except sin; begotten before the ages of the Father in Godhead, the same in the last days for us; and for our salvation [born] of Mary the Virgin *(theotokos)* in manhood, one and the same Christ, Son, Lord, unique; acknowledged in two natures, without confusion, without change, without division, without separation-the difference of the natures being by no means taken away because of the union, but rather the distinctive character of each nature being preserved, and each combined in one Person and *hypostasis*—not divided or separated into two Persons, but one and the same Son and only-begotten God, Word, Lord Jesus Christ; as the prophets of old and the Lord Jesus Christ himself taught us about him, and the symbol of the Fathers has handed down to us.

Since we have determined these things with all possible accuracy and care, the holy and ecumenical Council has decreed that no one shall allowed to bring forward another Creed, nor to compose or produce of think out or teach [such] to others. But those who dare either to compose another Creed, or propound, or teach, or deliver another Symbol to those who wish to turn to the knowledge of the truth from paganism or Judaism, of from any kind of heresy—if they are bishops or clerics, the bishops shall be expelled from the episcopate, the clerics from the clergy; if they are monks or laymen, they shall be anathematized.[42]

The Theology of the Creed

The theology of the Chalcedon Creed was designed to present a fresh solution to the person of Christ while acknowledging the earlier Creeds as viable. The language of the Creed addressed not only the contemporary problems with the last twenty years but upheld the ecclesiastical stance

---

42. *The Chalcedon Creed*, 373–74. Scholars are divided on the name of the Creed. Most call it a "Definition of the Faith," while other call it "The Chalcedon Creed."

against Arianism at Nicaea. The Chalcedon Creed is a remarkable work that still sets the standard for christological studies for both Protestants and Catholics.

Arianism

Chalcedon held the stance against Arianism by supporting the Nicene Creed. The phrase *"consubstantial with the Father"* continued to deny the Arian premise that the Son was the created firstborn. The Son is presented, in the Chalcedon Creed, as co-eternal and of the same substance as the Father. The fact that Chalcedon attached the Nicene Creed before the Chalcedon Creed signified the approval of the Nicene Council. Chalcedon was not trying to replace the earlier creeds but strongly desired to recognize the validity of earlier creeds.

Apollinarianism[43]

The council affirmed that Christ had a sound, reasonable mind. Apollinarius diminished Christ by having an inferior humanity juxtaposed to the Lord's deity. The result is that Christ had a divine mind and a divine spirit but a human body. The implication is that Christ was not completely human.

The council's definition stated the direct opposite of Apollinarius. The phrase *"the same perfect in manhood, truly God and truly man, the same of a reasonable soul and body; consubstantial with the Father in Godhead, and the same consubstantial with us in manhood (homoousion)"* depicts the real humanity of Christ. Davis accurately states, "The bishops thus renounced any notion of the hypostatic union which would jeopardize the differences of the natures or deny that their union was accomplished without confusion." Basically, the council affirmed the reality of Christ's human nature.

Nestorianism

Nestorianism was addressed in the phrase *"acknowledged in two natures, without confusion, without change, without division, without separation- the difference of the natures being by no means taken away because of the*

[43]. For a lengthy discussion see Peter Beck's chapter on *The Council of Ephesus*.

union, but rather the distinctive character of each nature being preserved, and each combined in one Person." Chalcedon "broke new ground"[44] by giving the definition that Christ is two natures in one person. No earlier creed addressed the issue in such declarative fashion. For that matter, no other creed had the opportunity to do so, as the focus was more trinitarian than christological.

Chalcedon's theological focus was a strong affirmation that Christ was one person in his essence. In other words, there was not a third entity that each nature had access to in the Lord's mind. This seemed to be a safeguard against the Nestorian position, which allowed for that possibility.

The bishops also used the term *theotokos* in referring to the incarnation. The theological effect the Chalcedon stated was that a real union occurred at the Lord's birth. The council viewed the incarnation of the coming of God into human flesh. This allowed the council to state that both natures are preserved in the one person. The bishops took the position that Christ is a unified person that does not vacillate between two natures but possesses both in his personhood.

Eutychianism

The Eutychian problem and the ensuing political fiasco was the reason the council was called into being. The council utilized the phrase, *"but rather the distinctive character of each nature being preserved, and each combined in one Person and hypostasis – not divided or separated into two Persons, but one and the same Son and only-begotten God, Word, Lord Jesus Christ;"* to strongly address Eutyches.

Eutyches and his followers proposed the errant theological concept that Christ had two natures prior to the incarnation but not after the event. The issue that the council addressed was the negative implication that Eutychianism presented. If the Lord assumed a body while possessing only one nature, then logically humanity had to be absorbed by the divine. The council acted strongly against this by stating that each nature was preserved in one person. The two natures are "not divided" but are "preserved" into one person. The language is strongly representative of Leo's *Tome*.

---

44. O'Collins, *Christology*, 196.

CONCLUSION

The significance of Chalcedon is profound. The Chalcedon Creed has established the boundaries of orthodoxy concerning the person of Jesus Christ. In the immediate context, the Chalcedon Creed settled the long dispute between the Alexandrian and Antiochene schools of hermeneutics. The council decided in favor of the Antioch method of interpretation. Their focus upon duality of natures that was so prevalent in the Antiochene School was maintained. Yet, the council did not dismiss the Alexandrian School altogether. They also affirmed Christ's unity, which is the focal point of the Alexandrian hermeneutic.

The Negative Impact of Chalcedon

Even though a settlement was reached, the creed still had problems. For one, the creed did solve a theological issue but did not heal the rift in the church on a practical level. The Egyptian churches never adopted the Chalcedon Creed. Harold O.J. Brown observes:

> The goal of the council was to reestablish harmony between the quarreling Eastern patriarchates and bring Alexandria and Antioch into harmony with Rome . . . Chalcedon's condemnation of what it considered the Christological extremes of Nestorianism and monophysitism suppressed views only within the empire. Nestorianism would enjoy a great expansion into Asia, while the continuing hostility of the Monophysites would facilitate the loss of Egypt to the Moslems.[45]

Brown maintains Chalcedon did not have a safeguard within the creed to ward off heresy. For that matter "Chalcedon narrowed the definition of orthodoxy so much that it excluded many who really belong in it."[46] The Egyptian churches drifted away from the orthodox position over time and eventually embraced the error of monophysitism.[47]

The second issue that was neglected was the hypostatic union. The manner in which the natures communicated was not clearly delineated. For example, even though Christ has two natures in one person, does orthodoxy allow for the Logos to die and resurrect or is that strictly relegated to

---

45. Brown, *Heresies*, 181.
46. Ibid.
47. This is the position that had one nature that was both divine and human.

Christ's human nature? If the suffering occurs only per the human nature, then what happened to the Logos during the process? Did the divine nature become passive or withdraw altogether?[48] These questions and any attempt to answer them was not forthcoming from the council. The idea of christological speculation was still left open.

The third problem with the creed is that it set the boundaries in negative terms. The four infamous negatives, *"without confusion, without change, without division, without separation"* depict Christology in those boundaries but did not give a concrete positive definition of the person of Christ. In other words, Christianity knows what or who Christ is not, but no positive definition describes what or who Christ is in his personhood. This area of Christology is still a theological concern nearly sixteen hundred years later.

The Positive Impact of Chalcedon

The Chalcedon Creed set the standard for christological orthodoxy from 451 to the present. "The Creed of Chalcedon became the standard for measuring orthodoxy; where either its affirmation of Christ's deity or this humanity is rejected, it means that historic orthodoxy has been abandoned."[49] Chalcedon has never been set aside or condemned by succeeding councils or creeds. The christological definition is still the hallmark for theological orthodoxy: Christ has two natures in his personhood.

---

48. In the 19th century the Kenosis theory developed concerning from these issues. See my chapter on Philippians as the Kenosis theory is addressed there.

49. Brown, *Heresies*, 183.

INTERACTIVE PERSONAL SEMINAR

Chapter Summary

Chalcedon addressed the issue of the dual natures of Jesus Christ. Yet the council did not meet or operate within a vacuum. They inherited the previous Councils' conclusions (Nicaea, Constantinople, and Ephesus). By adopting the now famous Chalcedon Creed they paid homage to the previous Councils. Their Creed was destined to be the hallmark of christological orthodoxy that has permeated the church to this very day.

Key Terms

- Christology
- Human Nature of the Lord
- Divine Nature of the Lord
- Communication of Idioms
- Hypostatic Union
- Monophysitism

Key People

- Leo The Great
- Cyril
- Flavian
- Dioscurus
- Eutyches

Advanced Questions

1. How is hypostatic union portrayed in the Scriptures through the Lord's life?
2. In what way did Chalcedon support the incarnation?

Section II—Historical Christological Councils

3. The Council of Chalcedon provided the famous Chalcedon Creed. Why was this necessary?
4. Did politics have too much influence in the theology of the church?
5. Did Chalcedon intentionally try to set the standard for Christianity or was it a by – product of the Council? Depending on your answer, is the Chalcedon Creed still valid for contemporary Christianity?

Theological Questions

1. Explain the theological difference between Euthyches's view of two natures before the incarnation and one after with Leo's view that both natures are present after the incarnation.
2. Was Nestorius, who was condemned at Ephesus, vindicated by Chalcedon? Why or why not?
3. In what way[s] does one's theological presuppositions drive this/her hermeneutical method?

Issues to Research

- Consider the role of political allegiances in the life of the church during the early days of Christendom.
- Did Leo, who first used the term "Pope," take advantage of the political situation to secure the prominence of Rome?
- Review the 27 Canons adopted by Chalcedon? Why did they reject the 28th Canon? (hint: This question will take in-depth research).
- Should contemporary Christians refer to Chalcedon to settle modern christological issues?

Section III

Contemporary Christological Applications

8

The Person and Work of Jesus
From New Testament Portraits to Theological Statements

Adam Harwood

A TEXT IS BETTER understood when its author clarifies his assumptions. For that reason, I will begin this chapter by disclosing a few theological-hermeneutical assumptions. My first assumption is that Jesus was and is God. The early church worshiped Jesus and considered him to be divine *not* because particular creeds claimed he was divine; rather, the early church justified in its creeds its prior and current actions of worshipping Jesus and belief that Jesus was and is divine. Such a view of Jesus can be seen in the Gospels and continuing throughout the New Testament in Jesus's references to the Father, the divine titles Jesus used to refer to himself, and Jesus's actions which can be attributed only to God. Some religious scholars claim that Jesus was only a man who was wrongly believed to be divine.[1] I affirm, along with the broad Christian tradition, that Jesus was and is the Word who became flesh, the eternal Son of God, and truly God and truly man.

---

1. Bart Ehrman, for example, claims that Jesus never claimed to be God and that Jesus's followers mistakenly thought he had been raised from the dead, which led them to ascribe to him a divine status wrongly. For his argument, see Ehrman, *How Jesus Became God*. For a reply to Ehrman's thesis, see *How God Became Jesus*.

Section III—Contemporary Christological Applications

My second assumption is that the Bible is a reliable record of the life and ministry of Jesus. Certain questions concerning textual variants in the manuscript tradition are difficult to answer, and the historical-religious context of the first century might never be known fully. Even so, those difficulties do not preclude one from affirming that the Bible was inspired by God and is a trustworthy account of Yahweh, his relationship with Israel, and Israel's Messiah Jesus. The biblical portraits of Jesus in this chapter have been gleaned from the New Testament. Although much insight can be gained from sorting through the Old Testament to search for implicit and explicit references to the coming Messiah, this study will proceed by focusing only on the New Testament texts. And even though it would be illuminating to reconstruct a chronological account of the life and ministry of Jesus from the New Testament, I have chosen to trace his life through following a fixed-canon approach primarily.[2]

My third assumption is that the New Testament provides all the necessary and reliable data for understanding the person and work of Jesus. This data does not distinguish between the person of Christ and the work of Christ. The New Testament simply testifies of Jesus. Also, the data extracted from Scripture is imperfectly and continually formulated by the church. Further, although God inspired the New Testament, the creeds enjoy no such status. The creeds have emerged as the church has attempted to clarify its beliefs when confronted in particular contexts which specific questions. The wider Christian community accepts only four of those creeds. Many more creeds were written which do not enjoy such widespread acceptance, and dozens of confessions have been written which express the views of denominations and movements, rather than the wider Christian consensus.[3] The result is a priority in theological authority in which Scripture is primary, followed by a sensitivity to the interpretation of Scripture throughout the history of the church.

---

2. Surveying the New Testament books in their canonical order rather than according to the order in which the texts were written frees me from making judgments about the order in which the books were written.

3. For a basic explanation of the differences between creeds and confessions, see Holcomb, *Know the Creeds and Councils*, 9–24.

NEW TESTAMENT PORTRAITS OF JESUS

Matthew

Four hundred years following the prophetic ministry of Malachi, the New Testament breaks the silence with these words: "The historical record of Jesus Christ, the Son of David, the Son of Abraham" (Matt 1:1).[4] In Matthew's Gospel, Jesus is Israel's long-awaited Messiah, who inaugurates and teaches about the kingdom of heaven as well as fulfills Old Testament promises by his birth, life, death, and resurrection for sins. Matthew's demonstration that Jesus is the promised Messiah begins in the first chapter with the genealogy, which is presented in three sections of fourteen generations each.[5] The three sections mark the times of Abraham (1:2–6a), David (vv. 6b–11), and the exile (vv. 12–16). As a descendant of David and Abraham, Jesus fulfills the promises to the great king as well as the father of the nation ("the Son of David, the Son of Abraham," v. 1). Also, Jesus fulfills the promise of the restoration of the nation from exile. Additionally, Matthew emphasizes the fulfillment of Old Testament prophecies in the life of Jesus. Some version of the fulfillment formula, "This was to fulfill what was spoken by the prophet," is used ten times in this Gospel. As examples: In Matt 1:22–23, the virgin birth of Jesus fulfills Isa 7:14; in Matt 2:15, the escape to and return from Egypt fulfills Hos 11:1; and in Matt 27:9–10, Judas's betrayal of Jesus for thirty pieces of silver fulfills Zech 11:12–13.

The "kingdom of heaven" is mentioned 50 times in this Gospel, and Jesus speaks 44 of those occurrences.[6] At his birth, the wise men look for the king of the Jews (Matt 2:2); at his trial, the governor asks Jesus if he is the king of the Jews (27:11). Frank Matera summarizes the plot of Matthew with the kingdom motif as follows:

---

4. Unless otherwise stated, Bible quotations in this essay are from the Holman Christian Standard Bible. In canonical order, the silence was broken by Matthew. In time, however, several other NT authors probably penned their works before Matthew composed the Gospel that bears his name. Thanks to Dr. Charles Ray Jr. for bringing this distinction to my attention.

5. The actual numbers of generations are 13, 14, and 13. However, "ancient counting often alternated between inclusive and exclusive reckoning." A comparison of the genealogies in Matthew and Luke reveals that some of the generations were omitted to make the numbers work in the presentation. That should not violate any sensibilities because the word which is rendered "the father of" or "begat" can simply mean "was the ancestor of." Blomberg, *Matthew*, 53.

6. These numbers include the phrases "kingdom of God" and "Father's kingdom," as well as occurrences of the word "kingdom" which refer to God's kingdom.

> God sends Jesus to save his people from their sins by inaugurating the kingdom of heaven. Jesus will accomplish this through his ministry of teaching, preaching, and healing, and by shedding his blood for the forgiveness of sins. Aware that the kingdom of heaven will destroy his rule, Satan tries to prevent Jesus from accomplishing this mission.[7]

Matthew twice describes the ministry of Jesus as "teaching in their synagogues, preaching the good news of the kingdom, and healing every disease" (4:23; 9:35; cf. 11:1–5). Chapter 13 contains parables of the kingdom, two of which Jesus explains. According to Darrell Bock, the parable of the sower (vv. 1–9, 18–23) teaches: "Many will be exposed to the kingdom and hear about it, but only some will internalize what they have heard and bear fruit for it."[8] The other parable in the chapter which Jesus explains is the wheat and the weeds (vv. 24–30, 36–43), in which the Son of Man at the end of the age will separate the sons of the evil one from the sons of the kingdom.

After Peter's confession that Jesus is the Messiah and Son of God (16:16), Jesus began his journey to Jerusalem where he would suffer, be killed, and then raised on the third day (16:21). Matthew records the rejection and vindication of Jesus as Israel's Messiah (21:1–28:20).

Mark

In Mark's Gospel, Jesus is the Son of Man who has all power and authority, yet gave his life as a ransom for many (10:45).[9] The Old Testament backdrop is that the Son of Man was given authority by God to judge the nations (Dan 7:13–14). Jesus identifies with this figure of divine authority by declaring the forgiveness of sin (Mark 2:10), lordship over the Sabbath (Mark 2:28), and his cosmic and future return (Mark 13:26). Even so, Jesus adds to the concept of Son of Man the element of *suffering* for the people.[10]

---

7. Matera, *New Testament Christology*, 27.

8. Bock, *Jesus According to the Scripture*, 200.

9. Although this section focuses on the title Son of Man, other titles are mentioned such as the Christ and Son of God.

10. The idea that one man would die on behalf of many people was not a new idea. Isaiah 52:13—53:12 refers to the Suffering Servant, whose death provides atonement for the sins of the nation.

In this first half of the Gospel, Jesus is a figure of power and authority. John the Baptist announces Jesus's ministry as the coming of God's kingdom (1:15). Men literally drop their nets to follow him (vv. 16–20), and he taught with authority (v. 22). A demonized man screams out the identity of Jesus, "the Holy One of God" (v. 24). Jesus gives commands to evil spirits and they obey (vv. 25–26). Jesus demonstrates his authority by working miracles. He calms the seas (4:35–41), casts out evil spirits (5:1–20), heals the sick, and raises the dead (5:21–43). His power to deliver people and his authority over creation is comprehensive.[11] Jesus has all power and authority.

The hinge on which this Gospel turns is Peter's confession of Jesus as the Christ. In the background of the first half of the Gospel echoes this unanswered question: "Who is Jesus?" Until chapter 8 no one answers it. The narrator reveals the answer in 1:1 ("Christ, the Son of God"). God the Father announces the answer in 1:11 ("You are my Son, whom I love."). Satan and the demons know the answer in 1:24, 34. But the people do not answer correctly. The question is raised again in 4:41 when Jesus calms the seas, "Who is this?" The turning point comes at 8:29 when Peter is the first person in the Gospel to answer correctly, "You're the Christ."

After Peter's confession Jesus again tells them to keep their answer to themselves, perhaps because Jesus had a timeline in mind for his journey to the cross or because they did not understand his mission. Whatever the reason for this messianic secret, Jesus resists their efforts to promote his cause because they want to gather support for a conquering Christ rather than a suffering Christ. Jesus explains that he—the Son of Man—would suffer, be rejected by the religious crowd, and finally killed. Then he will be raised on the third day. Jesus predicts his suffering and death three times (8:31–32; 9:31–32; 10:32–34). Each time, the disciples give a poor response (Peter rebukes Jesus, 8:32; they debate who is the greatest, 9:33–34; and they desire chief seats in the kingdom, 10:35–41). In each case, Jesus clarifies for his disciples what it means to follow him. They are to take up their crosses (8:34–38), prefer the last seat (9:35–37), and serve others (10:42–45). Following the Son of Man involves suffering and serving.

In chapter 13, Jesus predicts the coming of the Son of Man. In chapter 14, he is anointed for burial, serves the last supper, and is arrested and tried. In chapter 15, the Son of Man suffers and dies on the cross. The identity of Jesus has been stated by the narrator (1:1), the Father (v. 11), and demons

---

11. Bock, *Jesus According to Scripture*, 167.

(chs. 1, 3, and 5). Although Peter confesses him as the Christ, Peter still fails to understand that Jesus would be a *suffering* Christ. In 15:39, a Roman soldier at the foot of the cross is the first person in the Gospel to correctly understand the identity of Jesus, declaring, "This man really was God's Son!"[12] Jesus was buried in a borrowed tomb. On the third day, the women find the burial stone has been rolled away, his body is gone, and an angel tells them, "You are looking for Jesus the Nazarene, who was crucified. He has been resurrected! He is not here! See the place where they put Him" (16:6b).

Luke (Gospel & Acts)

In this two-volume Gospel and book of Acts, Luke produces historiography (historical writing) about the birth and ministry of Jesus as well as the birth and growth of the church. Luke claims to draw from eyewitness accounts to reconstruct these events (1:1–4). The coming of John the Baptist and Jesus is announced by the angel Gabriel (1:5–33), and the Messiah is conceived when the Holy Spirit overshadows Mary (vv. 34–38). The child's arrival was announced by angels (2:8–20), and as a baby, he was recognized as the promised redeemer of Jerusalem (v. 38).

Luke 9:51—19:27 has come to be known as the travel narrative, so named because 9:51 states Jesus "determined to journey to Jerusalem." These ten chapters document Jesus's resolve to go to Jerusalem to die. Jerusalem killed its prophets, and Jesus would be its most notable murder. The travel narrative reveals a theme of reversal and surprise in the stories and parables of Jesus. Consider these examples:

- A victim's true neighbor is a despised Samaritan, not his fellow Jew (10:29–37).
- The moment the rich fool reaches his goal in life, he loses his life (12:13–21).
- The invited guests will not come to the great banquet but the losers of society will come; thus the insiders are left *out*, but the outsiders are brought *in* (14:16–24).
- In all three stories of the lost sheep, coin, and son (ch. 15), something lost is found, and there is a celebration. The set of stories culminates

---

12. Strauss, *Four Portraits, One Jesus*, 192, 195.

in a party for the returning prodigal son in which the "sinful" son is honored with a feast! The older brother, who is obedient but self-righteous, will not participate.

- A poor widow receives justice from an evil judge because of her nagging. If that is the response of an evil judge to persistence, then imagine the response of a loving heavenly Father (18:1–8).
- Two men pray at the temple. The religious leader goes away *without* God's forgiveness, but the tax collector leaves *with* God's forgiveness (18:9–14).
- The episode with Zacchaeus is the pinnacle of the travel narrative (19:1–10). As a chief tax collector, he was a traitor to his people and the ultimate outcast. Jesus reaches out to the lowly—even in a tree—to offer salvation. If Zacchaeus can be saved, then *anyone* can be saved.[13]

The greatest reversal and surprise of Luke's Gospel is found in the crucifixion. Jesus, the Son of God, is killed. Then Jesus kills death through his resurrection, which is both a surprise and a reversal.

The Christology of the book of Acts can be found in the promise of Acts 1:8 and the speeches of Peter, Stephen, and Paul. Acts 1:8 serves as a statement around which Luke organized the narrative of the ethno-geographic expansion of the gospel. Jesus promised his disciples, "But you will receive power when the Holy Spirit has come on you, and you will be My witnesses in Jerusalem, in all Judea and Samaria, and to the ends of the earth" (1:8). The book of Acts is primarily the story of the Holy Spirit empowering believers in their witness of Jesus from the Word of God to all people. The witness of the earliest group of Spirit-filled Jews (ch. 2) breaks through the ethno-geographic boundaries to reach Samaritans (ch. 8) as well as God-fearing Gentiles in Caesarea (ch. 10) and full Gentiles in Ephesus (ch. 19).

The speeches of Peter identify Jesus as Israel's Messiah who suffered and was killed in Jerusalem, but whom God raised, and who will return as judge and king. In light of these truths, all people must repent of their sin and believe in Jesus (2:14–36; 3:11–26; 10:34–43). Stephen retold the story of Israel rejecting its prophets. Jesus was greater than Joseph and Moses, who were designated by God (7:9—10, 20), rejected by God's people (vv. 9, 27), and who delivered God's people (vv. 12–15, 36).[14] In addition to

13. Strauss, *Four Portraits*, 274–75.
14. Hamilton, *God's Glory in Salvation Through Judgment*, 428–29.

the improper focus on Jerusalem and the temple, Stephen declared to the Sanhedrin that their rejection of the Law and prophets comprised their rejection of God (vv. 51–53). Jesus welcomed the martyred Stephen.

Paul delivered six speeches in the book of Acts. Paul's first speech—addressed to the Jews of Pisidian Antioch—is especially relevant when considering the person and work of Christ. Jesus is King David's descendant and Israel's Savior (13:23). The rulers and residents of Jerusalem, failing to recognize God's Word, succeeded in persuading the Romans to put him to death; but God raised Jesus from the dead (vv. 27–30).[15] In fulfillment of OT promises, Jesus is the Son of God and holy one who would not see decay (vv. 33–37). Forgiveness of sin and justification which was not available through the Law is now available through Jesus (vv. 38–39).

In the Gospel of Luke, Jesus tells of reversal and surprises. In the book of Acts, believers are empowered by the Spirit in their witness of Jesus to all people, as seen in the ethno-geographic expansion of the gospel as well as the speeches of Peter, Stephen, and Paul.

John's Gospel & Letters

This section will explore the Christology of John's Gospel and his letters.[16] Near the end of John's Gospel, he explains why he wrote of these signs of Jesus: "so that you may believe Jesus is the Messiah, the Son of God, and by believing you may have life in His name" (John 20:31b). John testifies about Jesus with a goal in mind that people might believe in Jesus, which would result in those believers having life in his name. Similarly, near the end of 1 John, the apostle wants those who believe in him to *know* they have eternal life (1 John 5:13). John Stott makes an important distinction between the stated purposes of the books: "For it is one thing to receive life; it is another to know that we have received it."[17]

The person and work of Christ can be seen in a variety of ways in John's Gospel. Jesus is the pre-existent and divine Word that became flesh, was rejected by his creation, in whom is life, and who reveals the Father

---

15. Matera, *New Testament Christology*, 78, writes: "Prior to Jesus' resurrection, the general resurrection of the dead was merely a hope. By raising Jesus from the dead, however, God has begun to fulfill the promise made to Israel."

16. Because of its unique message as well as its place at the end of the canon, the book of Revelation will be the final biblical portrait considered.

17. Stott, *The Incomparable Christ*, 41.

(1:1–18). The Gospel presents eight witnesses to the divinity of Christ: John the Baptist (1:34), the works of Christ (5:36), the Father (v. 37), the Scriptures (v. 39), Christ himself (8:14), the Holy Spirit (15:26), believers (v. 27), and the author of the Gospel (19:35).[18] The seven miracles, also called signs, reveal God's glory in Jesus and result in the disciples trusting him (2:11). The seven signs were: changing water into wine (2:1–11), healing the official's son (4:43–54), healing the man at Bethesda (5:1–15), feeding the five thousand (6:1–14), walking on water (vv. 16–21), healing the man born blind (9:1–12), and raising Lazarus (11:1–44). Jesus identifies himself in seven "I am" statements with Yahweh, the covenant name of God: the bread of life (6:35); the light of the world (8:12); the door (10:7); the good shepherd (vv. 11–14); the resurrection and the life (11:25); the way, the truth, and the life (14:6); and the true vine (15:1).

The theology of John's Gospel can be outlined according to 14:6, in which Jesus declares himself to be the life, the truth, and the way to God. Those who believe in Jesus, the Messiah, Son of God, and Son of Man are promised eternal life. Jesus is the truth in that he is the Word of God and he fulfilled OT promises, as seen in his "I am" statements as well as the replacement motif concerning the Jewish festivals of Passover (ch. 6), Tabernacles (chs. 7–8), and Dedication (ch. 10). Jesus is the way to God for those who believe and obey, by God's grace, through faith and the working of his Spirit.[19] The uniqueness and divinity of the person of Christ made possible the work of Christ. And the "crowning achievement" of his work was his sacrificial death as the Lamb of God for the sins of the world (1:29, 35; 19:34b–35).[20]

John provides in his letters doctrinal, moral, and social tests to undermine false confessions of faith in Christ and to confirm genuine confessions. Liars are those who deny Jesus has come in the flesh (doctrinal test, 1 John 2:2), claim to walk with God but walk in darkness (moral test, 1:6), and claim to love God but hate certain people (social test, 4:20). Stott writes, "Conversely, (1) we know the Spirit of God because he acknowledges Christ (1 Jn 4:20; cf. 2 Jn 9); (2) we know that we know him because we obey his commandments (1 Jn 2:3); and (3) we know that we have passed

---

18. Stevens, *Doctrines of the Christian Religion*, 82.
19. Schreiner, *The King in His Beauty*, 503–36.
20. Pate, *The Writings of John*, 40.

out of death into life because we love our Christian brothers and sisters (1 Jn 3:14)."[21]

Paul (Romans–Philemon)

If one were to read only Paul's letters, very little would be known about the life of Christ. Jesus was born of a woman and under the Law (Gal 4:4), was a descendant of David (Rom 1:3), came "in flesh like ours under sin's domain" (Rom 8:3b), and had brothers (1 Cor 9:5; Gal 1:19). James Dunn observes that "the life of Jesus seems to be of little more than an assumed and hidden antecedent to the all-important record of his death." Rather than thinking Paul did not care about the life of Jesus, it is more likely that Paul took for granted that his audience was aware of Jesus's life and teachings. Paul will focus on Jesus as the Messiah of Israel (1 Cor 1:23; Rom 9:3) as well as the "eschatological counterpart" of the first Adam (Rom 5:12–21; 1 Cor 15:21–22).[22]

Paul's letters were occasional. They were not drafted according to later categories of systematic theology to present organized statements about the person and work of Christ. Nor were they written as works of biblical theology, providing precise definitions and explanations of the Old Testament titles, allusions, and imagery applied to Jesus. Rather, Paul's understanding of the identity and mission of Jesus emerged as he addressed the concerns and questions particular to each letter's recipient. Paul understood Christ as the fulfillment of God's mission to and with Israel to reconcile the world to God.

Paul referred to his life before encountering Christ as one who was zealous for the Law (Gal 1:14; Phil 3:4–6). Early in his life, Paul opposed followers of Christ because of his devotion to Yahweh. When God revealed to Paul that Jesus was his Son and Israel's Messiah (Gal 1:16), Paul reinterpreted the story of Israel in light of the person and mission of Jesus. As examples of this integration of Jesus into the story of Israel: God answers the judgment, condemnation, and death resulting from Adam's transgression with God's grace resulting in the justification of those who receive the gift (Rom 5:15–17; 1 Cor 15:21–22). Jesus is the fulfillment of the promise to Abraham (see Gal 3 [esp. vv. 8, 29] and Rom 4). Jesus is the promised descendant of David (Rom 1:2–3). Jesus, already in nature God, took the

---

21. Stott, *Incomparable Christ*, 41.
22. Dunn, *The Theology of Paul the Apostle*, 184, 202.

form of a servant and was obedient in his life and death then exalted by the Father and worshiped as Lord (Phil 2:6–11; cf. Isa 45:22–23).[23] The term Lord is a "key Christological title, used about 180 times in the undisputed Pauline letters."[24]

Also, the activity of Jesus is described by Paul in the way the functions of Yahweh are described in the Old Testament. Like Yahweh, Jesus is Creator, Ruler, Judge, and Savior. In 1 Cor 8:6, Paul connects Jesus with the *Shema* as well as the creative work of God the Father. Similarly, all things were made by and for Christ (Col 1:15–17). Repeating the concepts in Ps 110:1 of the right hand of God and enemies under his feet, Paul declares the rule of Jesus by proclaiming all things under the feet of Christ (1 Co 15:24–28) and urges Christians to understand Christ's position at the right hand of God (Col 3:1). Just as Yahweh is the Judge of all nations (Ps 96:13), Jesus will judge humanity (Phil 2:16; Rom 2:16; 2 Cor 5:10). Just as Yahweh is recognized as the Savior (Exod 15:2; Deut 32:15; Isa 43:3; Ps 68:20), Paul identifies Jesus as the one to call on to be saved (Rom 10:9, 12–13) and as the one who saves (Titus 2:13).[25]

Jesus is the Christ, who died for sinners (1 Cor 15:3), which is the good news that Paul identifies as the center of his ministry.[26] God is reconciling the world in Christ. The true people of God are those who receive his Messiah, Jesus. The mystery now revealed is that Gentiles are now included among the people of God (Eph 3:3–6). Yahweh has been faithful in his promises to Israel, even when he included the Gentiles (Rom 9–11). This gospel is for all people, first to the Jews then for the Gentiles (Rom 1:16). The message is that Christ died for sinners. He redeemed us from the curse by becoming cursed for us (Gal 3:13). We have redemption through his blood (Eph 1:7) and have been declared righteous by his blood (Rom 5:9).

Hebrews

In the book of Hebrews, the new covenant with God through Jesus is in every way better than the old covenant. Jesus is compared with and found better than major elements and figures in Judaism. In the first three verses,

---

23. For more on Phil 2:6–11 as an early Christian confession, see Longenecker, *Studies in Hermeneutics*, 127–29.
24. Hurtado, *Lord Jesus Christ*, 108.
25. Wright, *The Mission of God*, 109–121.
26. In 1 Cor 2:2, Paul vows to know nothing except Christ crucified.

Section III—Contemporary Christological Applications

Jesus is compared to and regarded as superior to the prophets. God has spoken through his Son, who is the heir of all things, the agent of creation (Heb 1:2), and the exact representation of God. Jesus sustains all things, provided purification for sins, and sat down at the right hand of God (v. 3). In Heb 1:4–14, Jesus is superior to angels. Jesus has a better name (vv. 4–5). Angels worship and serve Jesus (vv. 6–7). Jesus has an eternal throne (vv. 8–9), was involved in creation (vv. 10–12), and God promises that he will conquer his enemies (v. 13).

Hebrews 2:1–4 introduces the first of five warning passages in the book.[27] These passages concern salvation provided by the Son. In Hebrews 2, for example, the audience is warned: "How will we escape if we ignore such a great salvation?"

The main idea in Heb 2:5–18 is that Jesus is superior to angels despite and because of his humanity. Humans are lower than angels in God's created order (Heb 2:7; Ps 8:5). Accordingly, when Jesus became flesh, he was made lower than the angels (Heb 2:9). The purposes and results of the incarnation include:

- to taste death for everyone (v. 9)
- to be perfected through suffering (v. 10)
- to be our brother and of the same family (vv. 11–13)
- to destroy the devil, who holds the power of death (v. 14)
- to free us from the fear of death (v. 15)
- to help Abraham's children (v. 16)
- to be a faithful and merciful high priest (v. 17)
- to atone for our sins (v. 17)
- to help those who are being tempted[28] (v. 18)

Although Jesus was made lower than the angels, he was greater than angels and accomplished the salvation of humans.

---

27. The other warning passages are: 3:7–19; 6:4–6; 10:26–31; and 12:15–17.

28. The HCSB translates *peirastheis* as "tested." This is a legitimate grammatical option, which is also preferred by other major English translations such as the NRSV and NLT. The context of the verse does not provide a clear indication which meaning might have been intended by the original author. Either "tested" or "tempted" are reasonable translation choices. I prefer "tempted," which is used in translations such as the ESV, NIV, and NASB.

The book of Hebrews weaves together the theme of the superiority of the new covenant in Jesus with the warnings concerning salvation. Jesus is better than Moses, who led rebellious people in the desert (Heb 3). Those who believe God's good news rather than harden their hearts enter God's Sabbath (4:1–13). Jesus is the high priest for those who obey God (4:14—5:10, esp. 5:9). Spiritually mature people believe and teach the fundamentals of faith in and obedience to Christ (5:11—6:12). Like Abraham, those who hope in Christ will receive God's promise because Jesus is a greater high priest than Melchizedek (6:13—7:20). Christ is the priest of a better covenant (ch. 8), a better tabernacle (ch. 9), and a better sacrifice (ch. 10). Rather than being written in stone, the new covenant will be written on hearts and minds (8:10). Rather than offering sacrifices in an earthly tabernacle, Jesus offers new covenant sacrifices to God himself (9:24). Rather than the blood of bulls and goats, which never takes away sin, Jesus in the new covenant offers his body in accordance with God's will and which cleanses from sin (10:4, 10–12). The author encourages his audience to believe God, like the Old Testament witnesses (11:1—12:1a); to focus on Jesus, "the source and perfecter of our faith," who endured suffering on the cross at the hands of sinners (12:1b-4); and to endure suffering as discipline from a loving father (12:5–12).

James, Peter, and Jude

James

James mentions the name of Jesus only twice (1:1; 2:1). However, when those references are combined with the other uses of "Lord," which seem to refer to Jesus, James presents Jesus as Lord and Christ (1:1; 2:1), glorious (2:1), the object of our faith (2:1), and coming (5:7–8). Despite the scarcity of explicit references to Jesus in the book, it is permeated with his teaching. Thematic parallels between the book of James and the teachings of Jesus are illustrated in the following table:

Section III—Contemporary Christological Applications

The Use of the Jesus Tradition in James[29]

Theme	James	The Synoptic Tradition
Blessing on the "poor"	1:9; 2:5	Matt 5:3; Luke 6:20
Mercy	2:13	Matt 5:7
The tongue	3:2, 5–6, 8	Matt 12:34–37
Gehenna	3:6	Matt 5:22, 29–30; 10:28; 18:9; 23:15, 33; Mark 9:43, 45, 47; Luke 12:5
A tree and its fruit	3:10–12	Matt 7:15–20
Peacemakers	3:18	Matt 5:9
Admonition against the "rich"	1:10–11; 5:1	Luke 6:24; 12:13–21
The fleeting value of temporal riches	5:2–3	Matt 6:19–21; Luke 12:33–34
Letting one's "yes" be yes, and one's "no," no	5:12	Matt 5:34–37

This emphasis on reproducing the teachings of Jesus rather than providing explicit statements about Jesus led one New Testament scholar to remark that the book of James has "an implied Christology."[30]

1 Peter

The book of 1 Peter was written to encourage those who were suffering because of their devotion to Christ by pointing them to him. Suffering strengthens and purifies one's faith, which will be revealed when Christ returns (1:6–7). Like some of Peter's audience, Jesus also experienced unjust suffering, without protest or retaliation (2:18–25). Suffering can yield opportunities to be a faithful witness for Christ (3:8–18). Jesus suffered in his body; his followers might suffer as well, which will result in their sanctification (4:1–6). Suffering *for* Christ allows believers to participate in the sufferings *of* Christ and the revelation of his glory (4:12–19). God who called saints to glory in Christ will restore and strengthen those who have suffered (5:1).[31] Frank Matera correctly states, "The contribution of 1 Peter to Christology is more practical than speculative." He explains that "by fo-

---

29. Sweeney, "James, Letter of."
30. Witherington III, *The Many Faces of the Christ*, 202.
31. Stott, *Incomparable Christ*, 77–78.

cusing on the sufferings of Christ, 1 Peter shows the intimate relationship between Christology and the Christian life: the *past* suffering of Christ is the *present* condition of believers, while the *present* glory of Christ is the *future* glory of those who follow the steps of the suffering Christ."[32]

2 Peter & Jude

Because of their textual and thematic similarities, 2 Peter and Jude will be considered together. One New Testament scholar has written about 2 Peter: "The Christology of the letter is superficial, fixed only on Christ's return but lacking any full-orbed view of Christ."[33] Although not fully developed, the view of Jesus in the letter is robust. In the first two verses, Jesus is called God, Savior, Christ, and our Lord. Jesus is also identified with one or more of those titles in 1:8, 11, 14, 16; 2:1, 20; 3:2, 18. The most significant christological nugget from the book other than the titles is that false teachers denied the truth of Jesus's return (3:3–7). Jude 1 states that believers are kept by Jesus Christ, and verse 4 refers to ungodly men who deny Jesus Christ.[34] Richard Bauckham summarizes the Christology of Jude as follows: "Jesus is the eschatological agent of God's salvation and judgment" and the Christ.[35]

Revelation

The book of Revelation provides a graphic depiction of the victory of God in Jesus Christ. Because multiple christological titles and themes have been discerned in this book, only the most prominent will be addressed in this section.[36] In Rev 1:5, Jesus is called the faithful witness, the firstborn from the dead, and the ruler of the kings of the earth.[37] These three concepts ap-

---

32. Matera, *New Testament Christology*, 184. Emphasis his.

33. Schreiner, *1, 2 Peter, Jude*, 253.

34. Schreiner, *1, 2 Peter, Jude*, 440, argues that the men denied the lordship of Christ by their sinful behavior.

35. Bauckham, *Jude and the Relatives of Jesus*, 312–13.

36. This section draws heavily from the outline and insights of Osborne, *Revelation*, 34–36.

37. Patterson, *Revelation*, 60–61, writes: "There is a sense in which Jesus may be observed here in his three ministries as prophet (faithful witness), priest (conquering for man the wage of sin exacted against man through his victory over death), and king (ruling all other kings)."

Section III—Contemporary Christological Applications

pear throughout the book. As the faithful witness (also in 3:14 and 19:11), Jesus is the model for his followers who are called to persevere in their witness of him (6:9; 11:7; 12:11). As the firstborn from the dead, Jesus was the first of many who will be raised to resurrection life (2:7, 11; 20:6; 22:2–3, 14, 17), and he will judge humanity when all people are raised (20:14; 21:4). As the ruler of the kings of the earth, Jesus defeats the enemies of God. Jesus, identified with God, is the slain and conquering Lamb of God. This identification of Jesus with God and as the Lamb of God will be explored below.

In the book of Revelation, Jesus is identified with God in various ways. For example, the same titles applied to God are applied to Jesus. Also, the same actions executed by God are executed by Jesus. This identification of Jesus with God can be seen in this brief list of parallels:

Themes or Actions in the Book of Revelation which refer to both God and Jesus

Title or Action	God	Jesus
Alpha and Omega	1:8; 21:6	1:17; 22:13
sits on the throne	1:4; 3:21b; 5:13	3:21a; 5:6; 22:1
exerts wrath	14:10, 19; 15:1	6:16
is worshipped	4:9–11; 5:13	5:9–13

In short, Jesus is God.

Perhaps the most important theme in the book is that Jesus is the Lamb. The word lamb (*arnion*) is used 28 times in Revelation to refer to Christ. No other New Testament author uses that word in reference to Christ.[38] The slain Lamb conquers. The blood of Jesus sets people free (Rev 1:5), and he is the slaughtered Lamb who is the only one in heaven worthy of worship and to open the scroll (5:6–14). His blood brought redemption (5:9; 7:14) as well as the defeat of Satan (12:11). The "wrath of the Lamb" causes fear (6:16), for he is on the throne (5:6; 7:17), he judges from the Lamb's book of life (13:8; 21:27), and he welcomes his people into God's presence (7:9–10; 14:1; 21:22–23; 22:1–3). Nijay K. Gupta concludes:

> Revelation relishes in the marvelous irony that the glorious, holy, and benevolent character of God could be unveiled in the actions of such a seemingly innocuous figure (Jesus) who appears to the

---

38. Only twice in the New Testament is Jesus called the "Lamb of God" (*ho amnos tou theou*, John 1:29, 36). Paul refers to Christ as the Passover Lamb (*pascha*, 1 Cor 5:7), Philip identifies Jesus with the lamb of Isa 53:7 (*amnos*, Acts 8:32), and Peter refers to Jesus as a lamb (*amnos*) without defect or blemish (1 Pet 1:19).

world as little more than a discarded animal. However, triumphing over death and evil, this lamb is slain, not as the sign of human and cosmic power against what is weak, but as the climax of the plan of God to redeem his world through a purifying, self-giving sacrifice.[39]

Although some readers of the book of Revelation speculate on obscure interpretations and possible connections to historical events, a stronger case can be made that the message of Revelation concerns the victory of God through Jesus the Lamb, who is the slain conqueror.

The last chapter of the Bible's last book ends with repeated promises from Jesus to return soon (Rev 22:7, 12, 20). Recalling that promise is a fitting way to end a survey of New Testament Christology. Everything the biblical authors declared about the identity and work of Jesus in history culminates in his future return, which will transition the present age to a new heaven and earth. Because of the person and work of Christ, his people will dwell eternally in the presence of the triune, thrice-holy, loving, creator and redeemer, God.

THEOLOGICAL STATEMENTS ABOUT JESUS

Stanley Hauerwas once quipped, "The Church seldom knows what it believes until someone gets it wrong."[40] Responding to theological errors has prompted the church to reflect on doctrinal questions and develop theological statements to clarify its views. The first four ecumenical councils focused primarily on the identity of Christ. Conflict over Arianism resulted in the affirmation at Nicaea in 325 that Jesus is truly God. Next, Apollinarianism prompted a clarification at Constantinople in 381 that Jesus is truly human. Then, Nestorianism was rejected at Ephesus in 431 for the view that Jesus is one person. Finally, all of those views, as well as Eutychianism, were addressed at Chalcedon in 451 to clarify that Jesus had two natures. A summary of those debates will be provided below with an attempt to ground the ecumenical views in the biblical text.

Arius (270–336), a church leader from Alexandria, denied that Christ was truly divine. In his attempt to be faithful to the Scriptures, he and his followers taught only God the Father was Creator and wrongly inferred that the Son was a created being. They justified this view by citing Jesus's

---

39. Gupta, "Christology."
40. Hauerwas, "Foreword," in *Heresies and How to Avoid Them*, x.

Section III—Contemporary Christological Applications

claim that "the Father is greater than I" (John 14:28b) as well as the New Testament references to Jesus as God's Son, claiming that at some point in eternity past, the Father existed prior to the Son. As a result, this heretical saying about Jesus became popular during the debate: "There was a time when he was not." Borrowing from Greek philosophy, the Arians likened Jesus to a demiurge which had emanated from the One. The Arians believed Jesus was truly man and semi-divine (existing prior to creation), but they did not believe he was *truly* divine.

Alexander, the bishop of Alexandria, excommunicated Arius and condemned Arianism. Emperor Constantine summoned a council at Nicaea in 325. The resulting creed, which reflects a rejection of Arianism, describes Jesus as "Lord Jesus Christ, the Son of God, the only-begotten of his Father, of the substance of the Father, God of God, Light of Light, very God of very God, begotten, not made, being of one substance with the Father."[41] The biblical connection with many of the statements in the creed is obvious. For example, in the Gospels Jesus is affirmed as Lord and Christ (both terms are ascribed to Jesus in Luke 2:11) as well as Son of God (Matt 14:33; Mark 1:1; Luke 1:35; John 20:31). The phrase "only-begotten of the Father" reflects the New Testament texts which refer to Jesus as the only-begotten from the Father, or one and only Son, such as John 1:14, 18; 3:16, 18; and 1 John 4:9.[42] The remaining phrases in the creed reflect post-canonical doctrinal development rather than the restatement of biblical titles or terms.[43] The subsequent phrases were included to communicate the view that Jesus is truly divine, a concept which is found throughout the New Testament.

Although condemned by the creed in 325, Arian views continued. Semi-Arians taught that Jesus was *homoiousios* (of a "similar being") with the Father, but the creed had declared Jesus was *homoousios* (of the "same being") with the Father. This theological difference boiled down to a single iota. Athanasius (ca. 296–373) emerged as a defender of the full divinity of Christ. In *On the Incarnation*, Athanasius argued against the view that Christ was created by God as follows: Only the Creator can create

---

41. "The Nicene Creed," NPNF2, 14:3.

42. The proper translation of *monogenēs* has been debated in recent years. However, both translations ("only-begotten" and "one and only") result in an affirmation of the full deity of the Son. For more information on this debate, see Pendrick, "Monogenēs," 587–601, and Skarsaune, "A Neglected Detail in the Creed of Nicaea (325)," 34–54.

43. See Holmes, *The Quest for the Trinity*, 43–44, for a brief account of how a phrase in Ps 36:9 ("in your light we see light") made its way into the creed ("God of God, Light of Light") via patristic hermeneutics.

and redeem creation, and God created and redeemed creation in Christ; also, only God should be worshiped, and the Bible portrays Jesus receiving worship. Also, if Christ had not been truly divine, then there would have been no atonement because there would have been no perfect and divine sacrifice for sin.[44] The debate over the identity of Christ continued until the language of the Nicene Creed was more widely accepted at the second council, which was held at Constantinople in 381.

Apollinarius of Laodicea (ca. 310–390) was both a friend of Athanasius and a defender of the full divinity of Christ. However, he fell short of affirming the full humanity of Christ. Instead, Apollinarius taught that the Logos was the life-animating principle of Christ, rather than affirming that Jesus had a truly-human *psuchē* (soul) and *nous* (mind). This view of Christ is problematic for two important reasons. First, the view approaches Docetism, a wrong teaching that Jesus only seemed to be human. If Jesus lacked a human mind and will, then he was not truly human. Scripture affirms, however, that he was "born of a woman" (Gal 4:4) and that he was tempted in every way and so is able to help humans who are sometimes tempted (Heb 2:18). Second, denying the full humanity of Jesus creates a difficulty for the doctrine of the atonement because, as Gregory of Nazianzus famously declared, the unassumed is unredeemed (*Ep.* 101).[45] Jesus became human to save humans.[46] The writer of Hebrews explains that Jesus became flesh to be our brother and of the same family (Heb 2:11–13) and to destroy the devil (v. 14). These and other achievements would not be possible if Jesus were not truly human. The Council of Constantinople (381) declared Apollinarian teachings to be unorthodox. Also, the council reaffirmed the language of 325 that Jesus was *homoousios* (of the "same being") with the Father and affirmed the full divinity of the Spirit.

After the questions concerning the full humanity and full divinity of Christ were clarified by the church at the end of the fourth century, another problem arose, which was how to describe the unity of humanity and divinity in one person.

---

44. For Athanasius's arguments, see his *On the Incarnation*. Although this work provides a contemporary defense of the orthodox position, Lewis Ayres does not provide an extended treatment of *On the Incarnation*, explaining there is no evidence it had any significant impact on fourth-century readers. Ayres, *Nicaea and its Legacy*, 5.

45. See Nazianzus, *To Cledonius the Priest Against Apollinarius*, NPNF2 7:439–42.

46. For an explanation and critique of Apollinarianism, see Kelly, *Early Christian Doctrines*, 289–301, and Grillmeier, *Christ in Christian Tradition*, 329–40.

Section III—Contemporary Christological Applications

Nestorius (386–451) was accused of dividing the one person of Christ into two persons. Nestorius was the patriarch of Constantinople. In 428, his first year in office, one of his bishops preached a message in which he spoke against applying the term *Theotokos* (God-bearer) to Mary. The next month, Nestorius preached a Christmas message in which he argued against using the term. Nestorius thus inserted himself into a heated debate between groups that argued whether Mary should be called *Theotokos* or *anthropotokos*. The term *Theotokos* was regarded inappropriate by some because "the incarnate God did not die." The term *anthropotokos* was considered inappropriate by others because the preexistent Christ had no mother. Instead, Nestorius suggested the term *Christotokos*. Cyril of Alexandria, however, was not impressed with Nestorius's new term. In his *Letter to the Monks of Egypt*, Cyril wrote that Nestorius was "vomiting out a pile of stupid little words" by questioning his use of the term *Theotokos*.[47] Nestorius asked rhetorically when Mary would have given birth to God. Cyril thought Nestorius was trying to revive Arianism and answered that the *Logos* was preexistent and became flesh in Mary and possessed a human soul. In this way, Mary was the mother of God.

Nestorius instigated political trouble for himself when he removed a robe from the church which Pulcheria (the emperor's powerful sister) had dedicated under the auspices of her consecrated and perpetual virginity. Nestorius might have removed the robe only because he thought that the symbol was unnecessary, but the implication was that she was no virgin. Nestorius entangled himself in a theological argument with powerful people and he lost. By 430, less than two years after his infamous Christmas message, Nestorius had been condemned. The next year, another council met to depose and excommunicate him as well as to affirm the use of the term *Theotokos*. He was banished, and his writings were burned. Later Nestorians clearly regarded the union of humanity and divinity in Christ as the union of two persons, but it is not clear that the originator of the movement held that view. In other words, Nestorius may not have been a Nestorian. Rather, Nestorius might have been a victim of both political forces and an imprecise theological vocabulary.[48]

---

47. Cyril of Alexandria, *Epistle* 1, 246.

48. After his condemnation at Ephesus in 431, Nestorius wrote *The Bazaar of Heracleides*. For a primary source account of his view, see this work which was unavailable to most readers until a sixteenth-century Syriac edition of the work was discovered in Turkey in 1895.

Because no Bible verse declares Jesus to be one person in two natures, one is left to draw inferences from Scripture. Although complexity can be discerned within the Godhead, such as God referring to himself in both singular and plural forms (Gen 1:26–27), "Jesus always spoke of himself in the singular."[49] Also, even Scriptures which refer to both human and divine traits refer to Jesus as a single subject (Gal 4:4; 1 Tim 3:16).

Shortly after this controversy was settled, the Formulary of Reunion (433) stated that Christ was "consubstantial (*homoousios*) with the Father in Godhead and consubstantial with us in manhood."[50]

Eutyches (375–454), a monk in Constantinople, was accused of wrongly teaching that these two natures of Christ united into one nature at the incarnation. Before the incarnation Christ had two natures, Eutyches taught, but after the union of divinity and humanity Christ had only one nature.[51] The problem with his view is that such a hybrid nature would be a *tertium quid* that is neither divine nor human. The Eutychian view has been compared to combining the colors blue and yellow, which would result in green, a third color which is neither blue nor yellow.[52] The theological implications of this view would be devastating, for if Christ must be truly divine and truly human to redeem humanity, then the single-natured Christ of the Eutychian view was neither of those natures thus humanity would not have been redeemed. Eutychianism and other problematic views were condemned at Chalcedon in 451, and it was asserted that there is one Christ "in two natures, without confusion, without change, without division, without separation." This statement drew boundaries around an understanding of Christ which would yield centuries of presenting in fresh terms and models the union of humanity and divinity in Christ while also clarifying what sort of moves would be outside the boundaries of an orthodox interpretation of Scripture.

CONTEMPORARY SIGNIFICANCE

It would be tragic if the theological and historical claims in this chapter remained only in the reader's files (or bookshelf) only to pull out when contemplating christological arguments. Rather, the truths considered in this

---

49. Erickson, *Christian Theology*, 661.
50. *The Oxford Dictionary of the Christian Church*, 3rd rev. ed., s.v. "Christology."
51. Kelly, *Early Christian Doctrines*, 330–34.
52. See Williams, "Nestorianism," 34–35, and Holcomb, *Know the Heretics*, 123–24.

Section III—Contemporary Christological Applications

chapter are relevant for today. Consider four statements of the doctrine's contemporary significance. First, because of the incarnation of the eternal Son, God the Father can be known. As the Apostle John writes, "No one has ever seen God. The One and Only Son—the One who is at the Father's side—He has revealed Him" (John 1:18). Likewise, Paul declared Jesus to be "the image of the invisible God" (Col 1:15a). Although contemplation of God, who is spirit (John 4:24), can be difficult to ground in understandable terms, it is a truism that if you want to know about God, then learn about Jesus.

Second, Jesus is the prototype for humanity. Christians sometimes wrongly think of themselves as the model for humanity and wonder if Jesus can truly relate to the human condition. That is exactly backward. Instead, Jesus is the model human being and everyone else is the model for humanity which has been stained and scarred by sin. If we want to know what it means to be truly human, then we should look to Jesus. He was without sin (2 Cor 5:21) and he committed no sin (1 Pet 2:22). Jesus did not give in to temptation but submitted himself to the Father and withstood temptation's full weight. Because the eternal Son became truly human and he was truly tempted, he can genuinely sympathize with the human condition and intercede for us with the Father (Heb 4:14–16).

Third, the incarnation of the eternal Son reveals God's free and loving desire to know and be known by his creatures. The decision for God the Son to become flesh, like God's trinitarian act of creating all things, was a free act which God knew would result in a fallen humanity and would require redemption if a relationship were to be reestablished. These stages of creation, fall, and redemption should be understood in light of God's love for his creation, including all people, as well as God's desire for all people to turn from their sinful condition and be restored to their Creator (see 2 Pet 3:9 and 1 Tim 2:3–4). Jesus said he came "to seek and to save the lost" (Luke 19:10). Rather than remain in the comfort and glory of heaven, God the Son became flesh to reveal the Father then suffer rejection by those he created (John 1:10–11) to take away the sin of the world (John 1:29).

Fourth, the incarnation demonstrates the holiness and justice of God. Rather than pass over the sins of humanity, God the Father judged his Son, who took on himself the sin of the world so that all who believe/trust in him are righteous (Rom 3–4). Similar to the conditions under the old covenant, when the holy God required blood sacrifices to atone for sin, Jesus under the new covenant was the once-for-all sacrifice and atonement for the sin of the world (Heb 9). The incarnation of the Son provided the only perfect sacrifice of atonement for a holy and just God. Jesus was truly human because only a human sacrifice could atone for human sin, and Jesus was truly God because only God himself could satisfy the requirements of a holy God.

Section III—Contemporary Christological Applications

INTERACTIVE PERSONAL SEMINAR

Chapter Summary

The New Testament provides a variety of complementary portraits of Jesus and later theological statements summarized orthodox affirmations of the full divinity and humanity of Christ as well as the view that those two natures exist in one person.

Key Terms

- Messiah/Christ
- Son of God
- Son of Man
- Lord
- Arianism
- *homoiousios*
- *homoousios*
- Apollinarianism
- Nestorianism
- *Theotokos*
- *anthropotokos*
- Eutychianism

Questions

1. Select one Gospel and compare it with Paul's presentation of Jesus. Should the differences be considered contradictory or complimentary views? Please provide examples to support your answer.

2. In what ways does one's view of the person/identity of Christ inform one's view of his work accomplished by his life, death, and resurrection? Support your answer by citing several New Testament texts.

Issues to Research

1. Discuss the relationship among the doctrines of the incarnation, atonement, and the Trinity.
2. Explore the historical views of the atonement.
3. Evaluate contemporary theological views of Jesus, such as those offered by liberation theologians, feminist theologians, or contemporary Roman Catholic and Eastern Orthodox theologians.

9

Christological Preaching in the Contemporary Church

Philip Caples

INTRODUCTION

THE DAY HAS ENDED, and the excitement has begun to subside. The public announcement of the call to the ministry is complete. The pastor has announced that I will be preaching my first sermon in two weeks; but wait that means I must prepare a sermon and deliver it to the church. Where do I start other than in the Bible? What will I say that the people have not heard in another sermon? How will the church respond to my sermon? These questions have raced through the minds of countless young preachers right after arriving home from announcing that God has called them into the Gospel Ministry. As the young minister seeks to answer these questions a sense of inadequacy and anxiety began to build. Therefore, what is the best approach for preaching Christ through the Old (OT) or New Testaments (NT)?

Serious expositors of Scripture agree that Christ should be the central focus of the sermon. However, maybe a more basic approach offers insights for young pastors seeking to develop their own understanding of this important task. Therefore, to preach Christ-centered messages in a contemporary world will involve examining the importance of the preacher's personal preparation for the preaching event and the importance of sermon development for drawing attention to preaching Christ in a consistent manner.

THE PERSONAL WALK OF THE PREACHER

In the early years of a preacher's pulpit ministry, he needs to decide who or what will give direction in his life. The best practice for any minister is to allow Scripture to be the mandate for life and ministry. In other words, a Christ-centered sermon cannot emerge from an individual who is not Christ-centered in his personal life. To protect the personal walk of a minister, a pastor should evaluate both his life and ministry. To accomplish this task, a preacher should examine his personal life, his family life, his church life, and his life within his church and community.

Understanding the personal life of a minister revolves around three important facts: a true salvation experience, a genuine call to ministry, and a high view of Scripture. An effective preaching ministry begins with a true conversion or regeneration experience. The importance of a believer sharing the gospel cannot be overlooked because the preacher is called to proclaim the good news. As Paul wrote, "How then shall they call on Him in whom they have not believed? And how shall they believe in Him of whom they have not heard? And how shall they hear without a preacher? And how shall they preach unless they are sent? As it is written: *"How beautiful are the feet of those who preach the gospel of peace, who bring glad tidings of good things!"*[1] As this writer has communicated for over twenty-five years, one cannot give away what one does not possess.

Equally important to salvation for the effective minister is a genuine call from God to prepare and preach the gospel. Stephen F. Olford argues that preachers must be faithful and fearless in their preaching.[2] The Bible has recorded numerous faithful and fearless proclaimers of truth. In Exodus 3, God called Moses through a burning bush to deliver God's people from Egypt back to the Promised Land. The Bible records in Acts 9 that

---

1. *The New King James Version*, Ro 10:14–15. With the remaining Scripture referenced in this chapter being from the New King James Version, the writer will abbreviate this translation by using NKJV.

2. Olford, *Anointed Expository Preaching*, 14–15.

Section III—Contemporary Christological Applications

Saul of Tarsus had been breathing threats and killing the disciples of the Lord.[3] The call from God for any minister will be unique. However, the call from the Lord is imperative because his call on a minister's life will prove to be helpful throughout the life of a faithful preacher.

Preparing to preach the word also demands a high view of the Holy Scriptures. The biblical basis for this statement is found in 2 Timothy 3:16–17 which states, "All Scripture *is* given by inspiration of God, and *is* profitable for doctrine, for reproof, for correction, for instruction in righteousness, that the man of God may be complete, thoroughly equipped for every good work."[4] The words "inspiration of God" literally means "God-breathed." To preach the inspired Scripture allows a minister to share with a congregation absolute truth on a subject matter without feeling pressured about addressing a particular topic. The preacher is only the messenger of the Lord. Tony Merida in his book *Faithful Preaching* rightly wrote, "A high view of Scripture should lead to a high view of biblical preaching."[5]

With these biblical mandates in place, a minister can embrace his task of preaching the word knowing how God made him. As the Psalmist wrote, "For You formed my inward parts; You covered me in my mother's womb. I will praise You, for I am fearfully *and* wonderfully made."[6] Further an individual can accept how the Lord has wired him and seek to love who God has made him to be. Acceptance of one's self as an individual will help a person to embrace the place of service as an assignment from the Lord, which will empower an individual to prosper in an effective preaching ministry. However, a minister must constantly evaluate his spiritual life seeking to combat pride, arrogance, and selfishness.[7]

Evaluating one's spiritual life needs to include looking at his relationship with his family. Too many horror stories exist of pastors who have come home from the office to hear a spouse say, "I cannot live with a pastor any longer. I have filed for divorce." These statements obviously are filled with a lot of pain both from the perspective of the wife and the husband. However,

---

3. *The NKJV*, Ac 9:1.
4. *The NKJV*, 2 Tim. 3:16–17.
5. Merida, *Faithful Preaching*, 31.
6. *The NKJV*, Ps 139:13–14b.

7. For Scripture verses that warn against pride, arrogance, and selfishness, see Prov. 16:18–19; 8:12–13; 16:5; 21:3–4, 24; 29:23 for just a few verses to consider. The point of this material is to show the reader that sin has no place in the life of an effective preacher. While one will sin daily, one must be quick to confess known sin to maintain a life of holiness and purity as a faithful man of God.

ministry demands extensive time from a pastor and too many times family members begin to feel that they are being given leftover time or no time at all. Therefore, how can this type of pain and problem be avoided?

While one cannot give an exact formula for ensuring that this never happens, maybe a couple of suggestions might be offered. First, a pastor needs to make time for his wife. The Apostle Paul encouraged both the wife and the husband to walk with great wisdom and mutual respect for each other. For the wife, wisdom and respect revolve around her willingness to "submit to your own husbands, as to the Lord."[8] On the other hand, Paul urged the husband to "love your wives, just as Christ also loved the church and gave Himself for her."[9] This mutual love and respect is solidified by both wife and husband setting aside time for each other. This principle can be incorporated by having a date night where both parties reserve or block out time in their schedule to enjoy each other's company.

Secondly, the wife and husband need to make time for the family. While a Christian family should enjoy worshipping and attending church together, a pastor and his family must spend quality time making memories with their family outside of church as well. A pastor who does not make time for his wife and children will not be effective in the larger context of the church because growing Christians will see that he is not living a balanced life. The lack of a balanced life will show in his preaching.

Evaluating a minister should involve examining his relationship with his church family. Knowing the church family is vitally important for developing an effective Christ-centered sermon. Congregations are filled with people who have different backgrounds, needs, and ways of viewing church work, culture, and the minister's place and role within each. The minister must develop his message with this knowledge in mind in order to connect the Word of God with the congregation. However, he must also communicate his message, knowing his audience as well. Congregations go through various seasons of life where they face hurt, loss of important and influential people, or other extreme challenges.[10] Christ-centered sermons along with a loving pastoral spirit in a minister will enhance the power of the gospel in a church family.

Similarly, a minister needs a good relationship with his community when seeking to make a difference with his preaching. The ultimate goal

---

8. *The NKJV*, Eph. 5:22.
9. Ibid., Eph 5:25.
10. Duduit, *Preaching with Power*.

Section III—Contemporary Christological Applications

of every church is to reach their community for Christ. Research demonstrates that many churches are disconnected from their community.[11] The disconnection is related to the leadership style of the pastor and either his inability or unwillingness to engage the community as the local minister. The positive aspect of this problem is that it can be resolved.

However, a greater concern exists. How will the pastor relate to the community outside of the pulpit ministry? Social media is an inexpensive way to reach the community. However, a minister needs to watch his social life. His theological training will not be helpful if he disqualifies himself with the very people that he is trying to reach. Preparing the preacher is very important to preaching a Christ-centered sermon. However, a more academic approach to preaching a Christ-centered sermon needs to be explored as well.

THE PREACHER'S SERMON DEVELOPMENT

To start developing a true expository message on a christological passage, one needs to start with the Bible. However, more specific than just starting with the Bible, a minister needs to study the importance of the different genres within Scripture. In other words, an expositor will develop an expository sermon using different techniques depending on the particular biblical genre of narrative, law, poetry, prophecy, or wisdom literature in the Old Testament (OT). Equally, biblical students will use different means to develop a sermon from the narrative, an epistle, or apocalyptic literature in the New Testament (NT).[12] Furthermore, sermon development will need to give attention to embedded genres in Scripture such as miracles, pronouncement stories, parables, along with major themes like the Kingdom of God and Christian ethics.

As a student moves beyond the hermeneutical concerns, one must determine an approach for developing a homiletical outline. The minister has several options for consideration. They include: the rhetorical exposition

---

11. Caples, "Community Identity and Pastoral Leadership: A Small Church Paradox." This paper was part of a research doctoral seminar that was submitted to Dr. Reggie Ogea and Dr. Steven Echols as part of the requirements for the course PREA9413: Pastoral Leadership on April 9, 2009.

12. For further discussion on genre studies, see Klein, Bloomberg, and Hubbard, *Introduction to Biblical Interpretation*, ix-xii; Corley, Lemke, and Lovejoy, eds., *Biblical Hermeneutics*; Fee and Stuart, *How to Read the Bible*; Fee, *New Testament Exegesis*; Stuart, *Old Testament Exegesis*.

approach, the key word approach, the exegetical approach, the pure exposition approach, the hybrid homily approach, the Puritan approach, the question and answer approach, the problem-solving approach, the inductive approach, and finally the sermonic plot approach.[13]

Once the approach is identified, students need to work with the biblical text using the homiletical features associated with the chosen type of sermonic approach. For a deductive or inductive sermon, a student would begin to develop the formal elements of the sermons. John A. Broadus may have been the first preacher and scholar to use the term formal elements. For Broadus, the formal elements included the basic arrangement of the homiletical outline based on the proposition of the biblical text under examination. Additionally, the introduction and conclusion were part of the formal elements as well.[14] However, scholars like Harold Bryson, James C. Taylor, Haddon Robinson, Jerry Vines and Jim Shaddix, and others provided a more formal approach to the development of the *formal elements*. Depending on the author that one is reading, abbreviations vary, but they represent the same basic part of the formal elements.[15]

Once the formal elements are developed and the outline is completed, the student should begin to work on the functional elements of the sermon: explanation, application, and illustration. The basic task of the explanation section is to explain the biblical text based on a prepositional outline of the text. Students can use a host of materials to help develop this section. One can use computer-based programs like Accordance Bible Software, Logos Bible Software, or a number of other technological based programs.[16]

---

13. For more discussion on each approach for developing an expository sermon, see Merida, *Faithful Preaching*, 92–95.

14. Broadus, *On the Preparation and Delivery of Sermons*, 77–126.

15. Bryson and Taylor in their book *Building Sermons to Meet People's Needs* provide the abbreviations E.T.S., Essence of the Text in a Sentence, E.S.S., Essence of the Sermon in a Sentence, Objective of the Sermon, Probing Question, and Unifying Word as their Formal Elements. Merida, *Faithful Preaching* uses M.P.T.—Main Point of the Text, M.P.S.—Main Point of the Sermon, Objective, Question, and Key Word; Vines and Shaddix, *Power in the Pulpit*—C.I.T.—The Central Idea of the Text, Proposition of the Text, The purpose of the Text, Objective of the Text, and the Unifying Word. These basic parts are used with inductive and deductive sermons approaches using the key word method. If one does not use the key word method, then the student would only use the textual statement, the applicational statement of the sermon, the objective of the sermon, and possibly a transitional statement.

16. See Addendum 2.

Section III—Contemporary Christological Applications

Equally, students can use commentaries both on computer-based software or hard-copy to help learn about the meaning of the text.

The application section is developed using biblical truth to find relevance with its audience. Shaddix writes, "We think of application as linking the importance of the truth of a text with the hearer's situation and need by not only leading them to accept what has been stated but to act upon its counsel."[17] Shaddix continues that a minister who desires to make an accurate application of a biblical text should seek to find relevance of a text in the following areas and in the following sequence: theological, universal, generational, cultural, communal, and individual.[18]

The final functional element of a sermon is the illustration. The purpose of an illustration is to illumine the eternal truth of the biblical text. Merida argues that an illustration should both help a person understand the biblical text and the application of the text better. Also, he states that an illustration should intensify the meaning of a particular text, argue for a particular issue, and inspire or motivate hearers to action.[19]

While this chapter has not provided all the material that a student needs to develop and to preach a doctrinal, Christ-centered sermon, it has provided the basic steps along with several helpful suggestions for resources for further study. Perhaps the next section will prove the most helpful as the student engages an actual Bible passage that has been previously discussed in the book. The goal of the next section is to develop expositional outlines that can be used to preach the biblical text.

CONTEMPORARY SIGNIFICANCE

As you read through this book, you have been introduced to the following biblical passages: Phil. 2:5–11, John 1:1–4, Col. 1:15–20, and Heb. 1:1–4. To help students further understand the art of developing a Christ-centered sermon from these christological passages, the writer would like to present the formal elements of a deductive key word method approach to developing an expository sermon. This writer will use an adaptive approach for the formal elements combining the works of Bryson and Taylor, Vines and Shaddix, Merida, and John R. W. Stott's book *Between Two Worlds: The*

---

17. Shaddix, *The Passion Driven Sermon*, 109.

18. For further discussion on how to develop an accurate application of a particular Bible passage, See Shaddix, *The Passion Driven Sermon*, 109–21.

19. Merida, 107–08.

Challenge of Preaching Today.[20] These outlines will include the following terms: *Then Statement, Now Statement, Objective, Question,* and the *Unifying Word.*[21]

The formal elements of a sermon based on Phil. 2:5–11 would be:

Then Statement: Paul urged the Philippian believers to live a humble life.[22]

Now Statement: Christians need to live a humble life.

Objective: I want my people to live a humble life.

Question: How can Christians live a humble life?

Unifying Word: Steps

The basic outline for this biblical passage would be:

The first step involves possessing the mind of Christ. Phil. 2:5

    Explanation

    Application

    Illustration

The second step involves learning from the example of Christ. Phil. 2:6–9

    Explanation

    Application

    Illustration

---

20. Stott, *Between Two Worlds.*

21. For further understanding, the *Then Statement* is a sentence of 16 words or less that states what the biblical text meant at the time of its writing by the original author. The *Now Statement* is a sentence of 16 words or less that helps the preacher communicate what the meaning of the sermon for a contemporary audience. The *Objective* helps identify the purpose of the sermon and it follows the basic pattern of *I want my people to . . .* The *Question* probes the *Now Statement* to help develop the outline of the sermon, which will be used to communicate the message of the biblical text. The *Unifying Word* is a word that unifies the major division of the sermon to help provide simplicity, clarity, and unity for the sermon so that the preacher is only communicating the truth of the text rather than multiple truths from the text.

22. Anders, *The Holman New Testament Commentary. All* Then Statements are adapted from the information in this commentary series and this commentary series is an excellent help for students learning to develop a Then Statement.

Section III—Contemporary Christological Applications

The third step involves embracing the humility of Christ. Phil. 2:10–11

Explanation

Application

Illustration

The formal elements of a sermon based on John 1:1–4 would be:

Then Statement: John urged his audience to embrace the attributes of Jesus as God's only begotten Son.[23]

Now Statement: People need to embrace the attributes of Jesus as God's only begotten Son.

Objective: I want my people to embrace the attributes of Jesus as God's only begotten Son.

Question: What are the attributes of Jesus that people should embrace?

Unifying Word: Attributes

The basic outline for this biblical passage would be:

The first attribute of Jesus for an individual to embrace is His eternal nature John 1:1–2.

Explanation

Application

Illustration

The second attribute of Jesus for an individual to embrace is His creative nature John 1:3.

Explanation

Application

Illustration

The third attribute of Jesus for an individual to embrace is His redemptive nature John 1:4

Explanation

---

23. Gangel, *The Holman New Testament Commentary*.

Application

Illustration

The formal elements of a sermon based on Col. 1:15–20 would be:

Then Statement: Paul urged the Colossian believers to submit to the supremacy of Christ.[24]

Now Statement: Christians need to submit to the supremacy of Christ.

Objective: I want my people to submit to the supremacy of Christ.

Question: Why should Christians submit to the supremacy of Christ?

Unifying Word: Reasons

The basic outline for this biblical passage would be:

The first reason relates to Him being God Col. 1:15.

    Explanation

    Application

    Illustration

The second reason relates to Him being the Creator of the Universe Col. 1:16–17.

    Explanation

    Application

    Illustration

The third reason relates to Him being the Head of the Church Col. 1:18–20.

    Explanation

    Application

    Illustration

The formal elements of a sermon based on Heb. 1:1–4 would be:

---

24. Anders, *The Holman New Testament Commentary.*

Section III—Contemporary Christological Applications

Then Statement: The writer of Hebrews urged his audience to embrace the superiority of Jesus.[25]

Now Statement: Christians need to embrace the superiority of Jesus.

Objective: I want my people to embrace the superiority of Jesus.

Question: Why should people embrace the superiority of Jesus?

Unifying Word: Reasons

The basic outline for this biblical passage would be:

The first reason to embrace the superiority of Christ relates to His position with the Father Heb. 1:1–2.

>Explanation
>
>Application
>
>Illustration

The second reason to embrace the superiority of Christ relates to His power from the Father Heb. 1:3.

>Explanation
>
>Application
>
>Illustration

The third reason to embrace the superiority of Christ relates to His performance for the Father Heb. 1:4.

>Explanation
>
>Application
>
>Illustration

As you work through the biblical text and examine these formal elements and outlines, you may have some ideas that differ. The main point to remember is that the individual who is exegeting a Bible passage does not want to bring a bias or a presupposition to the text because it may cause the interpreter to take the biblical material out of context. However, every interpreter will choose different words to emphasize the meaning of a biblical passage under examination. The only caution is to allow the text to drive

---

25. Lea, *The Holman New Testament Commentary.*

the movement of the Bible passage rather than allowing a commentary or the mind of the interpreter to go beyond the original context of the biblical material. To help you see what the writer is seeking to share, please reference numerous commentaries and other works for assistance.[26]

This chapter has not answered all of the questions concerning the preaching of a christological sermon. Rather, this chapter has sought to offer a general overview of how to work with a christological Bible passage based on prior knowledge of a foundational course in sermon preparation and delivery.[27] Yet, the reader has been given a few valuable insights on preparing the preacher and preaching Bible passages that will connect with a contemporary audience and make the truth of Scripture come alive for the audience.

This professor/pastor prays that this chapter has led you to delve deeper into the subject of studying the biblical text and preaching for the purpose of seeing transformation take place in the life of an individual for the glory of Christ. As Paul wrote to young Timothy, "I charge *you* therefore before God and the Lord Jesus Christ, who will judge the living and the dead at His appearing and His kingdom: Preach the word! Be ready in season *and* out of season. Convince, rebuke, exhort, with all longsuffering and teaching."[28] The preacher will never know on this side of eternity the true impact of every sermon that he preaches. However, he does know this according to Isaiah 55:11, "So shall my word be that goes forth from my mouth; It shall not return to me void, but it shall accomplish what I please, and it shall prosper in the thing for which I sent it."[29]

So, until we either meet at a preaching conference, a classroom, or another event on earth or until we meet in our eternal home of heaven, stay true to the Lord Jesus Christ and his wonderful Word.

---

26. See Addendum 1 for an example of how to work through an expository outline seeking to preach a christological message.

27. The introductory preaching class at Louisiana College is RL442: Introduction to Sermon Preparation and Delivery. For this class, the professor uses *Faithful Preaching* written by Tony Merida, which provides a deeper understanding on how to develop the Formal and functional elements of a sermon.

28. *The New King James Version*, 2 Tim. 4:1–2.

29. Ibid., Isa. 55:11.

Section III—Contemporary Christological Applications

INTERACTIVE PERSONAL SEMINAR

Chapter Summary

Preaching through a christological passage follows the same steps as preaching basically any expository sermon. Assuming the student has had a basic preaching course on sermon preparation and delivery, this chapter has discussed the importance of a preacher preparing himself physically, spiritually, and emotionally for the preaching assignment. In this preparation, the preacher should evaluate various relationships to ensure effective delivery of the sermon. Also, the preacher should follow the basic principles of preparing an expository sermon developing both the foundational and functional elements of the sermon. Lastly, the homiletical principles were practiced using the four Christological passages that were discussed earlier in the book.

Key Terms

- Preparation of the Preacher
- Foundational Elements of the Sermon
- Functional Elements of the Sermon
- Propositional Outline for Sermon Development

Advanced Questions

1. What steps do you take to prepare your heart before working with a Bible passage?
2. How would you explain the biblical terms in the explanation section of the sermon to a group of children in the 5th and 6th grades?
3. What steps will you take to help your Sunday School/Discipleship teachers become better prepared to teach their biblical material to their perspective classes each week?
4. What steps will you take to help your Sunday School/Discipleship teachers become better prepare to apply the biblical material to their perspective classes each week?

Theological Questions

1. Explain the term "Image of the Invisible God" taking into account the background of Colossians and Genesis 1.
2. Explain the term "firstborn of all creation" and then compare it to the term "firstborn from the dead."
3. Explain the phrase "reconcile everything to himself" in Col. 1:20 in light of God's redemptive-plan of salvation for all of humanity.

Issues to Research

- Consider the historical, political, and social background for the book of Colossians.
- Consider how preaching through the book of Colossians prepares a pastor to preach on contemporary cultural issues. Pay close attention to the Colossian Heresy, and then note key challenges within contemporary cultural that challenge Christian orthodoxy.
- What role does the biblical genre of a Bible passage have to do with preparing and preaching through a book of the Bible?
- How does direct application differ from indirect application? Note material from the Church Fathers when seeking to research this question.
- How does ancient rhetoric help us understand the writings of Paul?

10

Christology for the Twenty-First Century

Marvin Jones

THE EARLY CHURCH LEFT modern Christians with a rich christological heritage that demonstrates they were trying to pass on the pure tenets of the faith to succeeding generations. The insight of the early church was twofold: 1) they addressed their own cultural need for clarity as to the identity of Jesus Christ, 2) they wanted to make certain the Christians following them understood their identification of Jesus Christ.

The contemporary church must now review early christological definitions for various purposes. The first rationale, for christological review, is so that the contemporary church maintains a commitment to proclaim the ancient faith in its own cultural expressions. The person of Jesus Christ is still relevant to culture. The challenge that modern Christianity must accept is to present Christ to increasingly pluralistic Western societies. In order to reclaim the Christian mandate to spread the gospel to every generation, contemporary Christians must have a fundamental understanding of the person of Christ that is relevant to its own culture.

To present historical Christology is to have a viable alternative to competing voices. Sectarianism, via American pluralism, allows religious groups to proclaim a Christ that does not resemble the biblical presentation of the Son of God. Certainly within the context of religious freedom, it is imperative for the contemporary church to examine these truth claims, to evaluate them for content, and either accept or reject them based upon the adherence to the Scriptures and historical definitions. Alternative christological theories dot the landscape of the American cultural terrain. The solution for the contemporary church is to lay a biblical, historical, and christological foundation that undergirds the ministry of the ecclesia.

In Western Europe and the Muslim world, the process of christological verification must be a priority. The task of exalting Jesus in a culture that has relegated him to a myth is a challenge to embrace. Jesus Christ as savior can be presented in his humanity, who identifies with doubting people; yet, as God, he offers redemption to those from their doubts.

The second rationale for understanding historical Christology is to hear the proclamation of Jesus Christ resound with authority in contemporary pulpits. The pastor, elder, or preacher must arm himself with the biblical understanding of the text supported by the historical, ecclesiastical, and christological definitions. The contemporary church must preach Christ—dead, risen, alive, and savior of humanity—to a contemporary world. The preaching of Christ will distinguish between a cold orthodoxy of the past and transform the contemporary church into a living and viable orthopraxy. The contemporary church must re-learn that worship, ministry, education, and proclamation propel the body into the triune presence of the living God. When this lesson is re-learned, then and only then, will the world see Christ revealed in his purpose i.e. the redemption of humanity.

The third and final rationale for understanding historical Christology is for the contemporary church to establish theological parameters for contemporary discussions on gender, sexuality, and race. Whatever one says about Jesus Christ, the constrictions of his humanity were not fluid. His anatomy depicted a specific human gender that was not changeable. His death was accomplished in his gender. For that matter, his gender was lived in the *imago dei* as all humanity. The accomplishment of the cross was not confined to gender issues but was a calling to redeem both genders. The contemporary world is confused by gender roles and the contemporary church has not addressed the issue with a biblical resolution.

Redefining sexuality is at the forefront of contemporary culture. The question the contemporary church must answer is how does Christ, in his incarnation, relate to sexual beings? Various answers have been given that range from celibacy, marriage approval, to the contemporary expression of homosexual approval, and even promiscuity. The contemporary church must reclaim a biblical definition of sexuality for humanity. The modern

Section III—Contemporary Christological Applications

response to contemporary culture's sexual dilemma must flow from the Scriptures. Yet the response presented to culture must be in terms of sanctity without perversity. Jesus Christ does sanctify human sexuality in its proper role within the physical body just as his redeeming and sanctifying ministry was presented in the proper role within his physical body.

Racial acceptance is a challenge for the contemporary church. The church's history has a murky record when attempting to resolve racial injustices. The contemporary church's knowledge of the person of Jesus Christ in his Jewish humanity is hardly considered as constructive to the racial dilemma. In all likelihood, if Jesus were alive today as a Jewish man, he would identify by experience with those who were racially separated from societal mainstream. The separation of people based upon skin color is a denunciation of God's creation of humanity. One cannot deny the creation of different races with different skin color. The problem that contemporary culture faces is that there is no biblical solution advanced by the contemporary church. Creation, as God's image, means that all humans have been and will be created in the *imago dei*.

Unfortunately, racial separation has become systemic in Western culture. One of the failures of the contemporary church is the abandonment of creation's biblical mandate (humanity's *imago dei*), the denial of creedal confessions, and loving the world with racial limitations. This approach hinders the gospel. The call for racial reconciliation must start with the biblical mandate, recognizing creation's existence as *imago dei*, stemming from the person of Jesus Christ. The thrust of this argument reflects back to the early church's ecclesiastical definition. Christ, a man whose race was despised, entered the world to love all races.

The agenda for christological studies is challenging but worthy of the church's time to think through and adopt theological solutions to engage a culture that wants answers to valid questions. The presence of the triune God in the contemporary church is a compelling reason to proclaim Jesus Christ to a hurting world with those answers. This gospel proclamation, with a proper biblical Christology, will evangelistically transform culture as it is designed to do. This book has been a small attempt to introduce historic Christology so that the contemporary church will have a biblical foundation for its ministry.

Addendum 1
Sermon Brief: Col. 1:15–20

SUBMITTING TO THE SUPREMACY OF CHRIST

Tommy got off the school bus one afternoon and wanted to go fishing. His father had taken him fishing numerous times at the lake behind their house, and they usually caught fish. What would it hurt if he walked to the lake and fished from the bank? It would not hurt anything. Besides the fact, if he threw all the fish back into the lake, his father and mother would not know that he even went fishing. However, one problem emerged that Tommy had not considered. Tommy caught a large bass and when he went to land the fish, he fell into the lake.

He had been wet before, so it should not pose a problem. However, Tommy had forgotten one small issue. His father and mother had told him to not ever go fishing until they got home from work. The supreme command of his parents had been forgotten and now Tommy faced a dilemma.

According to Norman Geisler, "Three purposes seem to have been in Paul's mind as he wrote Colossians. First, he sought to show the deity and supremacy of Christ in the face of the Colossian heresy (1:18; 2:9). Second, he wanted to lead believers into spiritual maturity (1:28; 2:6–7). Third, he wanted to inform them about his state of affairs and elicited their prayers on his behalf (4:2–8).[1] Therefore, in these verses, *Paul urged the Colossian believers to submit to the supremacy of Christ.*[2]

---

1. Geisler, "Colossians," 668.
2. Ibid.

Addendum 1

Christians face many situations daily that create a battlefield in their minds. Some situations revolve around their faithfulness or unfaithfulness to Christ while living in a pluralistic world. Other situations may challenge their doctrinal view on the persons of God, Christ, and the Holy Spirit. However, *Christians need to submit to the supremacy of Christ*. With Christians needing to submit to the supremacy of Christ, a question emerges for us to consider. *Why should Christians submit to the supremacy of Christ?*

The first reason relates to Him being God Col. 1:15. In verse 15, two phrases need more explanation: the image of the invisible God.[3] and the Firstborn over all Creation.[4] Also, one would look at any social, political, or otherwise background issues associated with these phrases or words within this particular verse.

As one sought to apply this major division, the preacher would look at the theological significance of these phrases and words for a twenty-first-century audience. On these phrases, attention would be given to the person of Jesus being God, the firstborn of creation, and the need for believers to submit to the Lordship of Jesus both for salvation and living out one's salvation within the community of faith, the larger context of the community, and within the world.

Tommy needed to remember that as a Christian he was responsible to submit to the leadership of his parents. To submit to his parents helped him to align with his commitment to Christ as Lord. To practice disobedience revealed the lack of supreme allegiance that Tommy was willing to embrace in his relationship with Christ.

The second reason relates to him being the creator of the universe Col. 1:16–17. In these verses, one would want to study the phrases,

all things were created by him,[5] through him and for him, things in heaven and on earth, visible and invisible,[6] and the hierarchy of angelic beings—thrones or powers or rulers or authorities.[7]

Naturally, one would follow the same principles for the application section and then provide another illustration that would illumine the importance of Jesus as the Creator of the Universe.

---

3. Ibid., Geisler, 672.
4. Ibid.
5. Ibid., Geisler, 673.
6. Ibid.
7. Ibid.

If this writer were preaching this sermon, he would take another look at little Tommy's life seeking to continue the same story.

The third reason relates to him being the head of the church Col. 1:18-20. In these verses, one would look at the following words or phrases: The Head of the body, the church, the Beginning and the Firstborn from among the dead, note the purpose clause that starts with the words "so that" in everything he might have the supremacy. At this point in the explanation, the question should be asked why because the text is about to state a reason for him having supremacy: all God's fullness dwell[s] in him[8] to reconcile to himself all things.[9]

With these words drawn to the attention of the audience and explained in light of their context, the preacher would make another theological point of application and move toward a practical application, sharing how the church should submit to the authority of Christ as the head of the church because of his position, deity, and purpose, which was to reconcile and redeem sinful humanity back unto God.

Tommy should have listened to his parents.

The preacher would transition at this point and merely restate the reasons for a believer or non-believer to submit unto Christ, and then he would simply state the objective of the sermon: *I want my people to submit to the supremacy of Christ*, which would be followed with the invitation and call for response.[10]

---

8. Ibid.

9. Ibid., Geisler, 674.

10. As a reminder, the preacher needs to work with the explanation section of the text based on an outline of the biblical text. The words or phrases that I chose will emerge from an outline, which can be seen in Addendum 2.

Addendum 2
Propositional Outline of Col. 1:15-20

15   He is the image of the invisible God,
            the firstborn of all creation.
16   For
       by him all things were created,
            in heaven and on earth,
            visible and invisible,
            whether thrones or dominions or rulers or authorities

       all things were created through him and for him.
17   And he is before all things,
            and in him all things hold together.

18   And he is the head of the body, the church.

       He is the beginning, the firstborn from the dead,
            that in everything he might be preeminent.
19   For
            in him all the fullness of God was pleased to dwell,
20   and through him to reconcile to himself all things,
            whether on earth or in heaven, making peace by the blood
                of his cross.

Bibliography

Akin, Danny. "The Person of Christ." In *A Theology of the Church*. Nashville, TN: B&H, 2014.
Allen, David. *Hebrews*. The New American Commentary. Nashville, TN: B&H, 2010.
Anatolios, Khaled. *Retrieving Nicaea*. Grand Rapids, MI: Baker Academic, 2011.
Anders, Max. *The Holman New Testament Commentary: Galatians, Ephesians, Philippians, and Colossians*. Nashville, TN: B&H, 1999.
Apollinarius of Laodicea. *On the Union in Christ of the Body with the Godhead. The Christological Controversy*, edited and translated by Richard A. Norris. Philadelphia, PA: Fortress, 1980.
Arius. *Arius Letter to Alexandria*. In *The Trinitarian Controversy*. Philadelphia, PA: Fortress, 1980.
Athanasius. *Contra Arianos*. In *Select Writings and Letters of Athanasius, Bishop of Alexandria*, Nicene and Post Nicene Fathers, second series, vol. 4, edited by Philip Schaff and Henry Wace, 1:16. Peabody, MA: Hendrickson, 1994.
———. *On The Incarnation of The Word*. In *Select Writings and Letters of Athanasius, Bishop of Alexandria*. Nicene and Post Nicene Fathers, second series, vol. 4, edited by Philip Schaff and Henry Wace, Peabody, MA: Hendrickson, 1994.
Ayres, Lewis. Nicaea and its Legacy: *An Approach to Fourth-Century Trinitarian Theology*. Oxford, EN, Oxford University Press, 2004.
Barnard, L. W. "The Enigma of the Epistle to Diognetus." In *Studies in the Apostolic Fathers and Their Background*, 172. New York: Shocken, 1966.
Barrett, C.K. *The Gospel According to St. John*. Philadelphia, PA: Westminster, 1978.
Barth, Markus. *Colossians*. New York, NY: Doubleday, 1994.
Bartholomew, Craig. *Introducing Biblical Hermeneutics: A Comprehensive Framework of Hearing God in Scripture*. Grand Rapids, MI: Baker, 2015.
Basil. *Letter 236*. In *Basil: Select Letters and Works*. Nicene and Post-Nicene Fathers, second series, vol. 8, Translated by Blomfield Jackson and edited by Philip Schaff and Henry Wace, Peabody, MA: Hendrickson, 2012.
———. *On The Holy Spirit*. In Basil: Select Letters and Works. Nicene and Post-Nicene Fathers, second series vol. 8, Translated by Blomfield Jackson and edited by Philip Schaff and Henry Wace, Peabody, MA: Hendrickson, 2012.
Bauckham, Richard. *Jesus and the God of Israel*. Grand Rapids, MI: Eerdmans, 2008.
———. *Jude and the Relatives of Jesus in the Early Church*. London, EN: Bloomsbury, 1990.

Bibliography

Behm, Johannes. "Μορφῄ" In *Theological Dictionary of the New Testament* 4:750–51. Grand Rapids, MI: Eerdmans, 1999.

Behr, John. *The Nicene Faith*. Vol. 2. Crestwood, NY: St Vladimir's Seminary Press, 2004.

Berkhof, Louis. *The History of Christian Doctrines*. Grand Rapids, MI: Baker, 1996.

Bird, Michael F., ed. *How God Became Jesus: The Real Origins of Belief in Jesus' Divine Nature*. Grand Rapids: Zondervan, 2014.

Blomberg, Craig L. *Matthew*. New American Commentary 22. Nashville, TN: Broadman & Holman, 1992.

Bock, Darrell L. *Jesus According to the Scripture: Restoring the Portrait from the Gospels*. Grand Rapids, MI: Baker Academic, 2002.

Borchert, Gerald. *John 1–11*. The New American Commentary, 30. Nashville, TN: B&H, 1996.

Broadus, John A. *On the Preparation and Delivery of Sermons*, edited by Vernon L. Stanfield. San Francisco, CA: Harper One, 1979.

Brown, Colin. "Ernst Lohmeyer's Kyrios Jesus." In *Where Christology Began: Essays on Philippians 2*, edited by Ralph P. Martin and Brian J. Dodd, 12. Louisville, KY: Westminster/John Knox, 1998.

Brown, Dan. *The Da Vinci Code*. New York: Anchor, 2006.

Brown, Harold O. J. *Heresies*. Garden City, NY: Doubleday & Co., 1984.

Bruce, F.F. *The Epistle of Paul to the Philippians and Philemon*. New International Commentary, 82. Grand Rapids, MI: Eerdmans, 1984.

———. *The Epistles to the Colossians, to Philemon, and to the Ephesians*. Grand Rapids, MI: Eerdmans, 1984.

Caples, Philip R. "Community Identity and Pastoral Leadership: A Small Church Paradox." Paper presented for doctoral seminar in PREA 9413: Pastoral Leadership at New Orleans Baptist Theological Seminary, LA., 9 April 2009.

Carson, D. A. *The Gagging of God*. Grand Rapids, MI: Zondervan, 1996.

———. *The Gospel According to John*. Grand Rapids, MI: Eerdmans, 1991.

Clarke, Greg. *Is it Worth Believing? The Spiritual Challenge of The Da Vinci Code*. Kingsford, New South Wales: Matthias Media, 2005.

Cyril of Alexandria. *Epistle 1*. Translated by John McGuckin, Saint Cyril of Alexandria and the Christological Controversy, Crestwood, NY: St. Vladimir's Seminary Press, 2004.

———. *The Epistle of Cyril to Nestorius with the XII Anathemas*. In Nicene and Post-Nicene Fathers, edited by Philip Schaff and Henry Wace, Peabody, MA: Hendrickson, 2012.

———. *Letter to John of Antioch*. In *The Christological Controversy*, 141–42, edited and translated by Richard A. Norris, 103. Philadelphia, PA: Fortress, 1980.

———. *Second Letter to Nestorius*. In *The Christological Controversy*, 132, edited and translated by Richard A. Norris, 103. Philadelphia, PA: Fortress, 1980.

Davis, Leo Donald. *The First Seven Ecumenical Councils (325–787): Their Meaning and Theology*. Collegeville, MN: Liturgical, 1983; Reprint 1990.

Dods, Marcus. Hebrews. *The Expositors' Greek New Testament*, 5 Vol. 4:249. Grand Rapids, MI: Eerdmans, 1988.

Drobner, Hubertus R. *The Fathers of the Church: A Comprehensive Introduction*. Peabody, MA: Hendrickson, 2007.

Duduit, Michael. ed. *Preaching with Power: Dynamic Insights from Twenty Top Pastors*. Grand Rapids, MI: Baker, 2006.

Dunn, James D. G. *The Epistles to the Colossians and to Philemon. The New International Greek Testament Commentary*. Grand Rapids, MI: Eerdmans, 1996.

Bibliography

———. *The Theology of Paul the Apostle*. Grand Rapids, MI: Eerdmans, 1998.

Ehrman, Bart D. *How Jesus Became God: The Exaltation of a Jewish Preacher from Galilee*. New York: Harper One, 2014.

Elliott, Mark W. "Theodoret." In *The Dictionary of Historical Theology*, 540. Edited by Trevor A. Hart. Grand Rapids, MI: Eerdmans, 2000.

Erickson, Millard J. *Christian Theology*, 3rd ed. Grand Rapids, MI: Baker, 2013.

———. ed. *Concise Dictionary of Christian Theology*. Grand Rapids, MI: Baker, 1986.

———. *The Word Became Flesh*. Grand Rapids, MI: Baker, 1991.

Eusebius of Nicomedia. *The Letter of Arius to Eusebius, Bishop of Nicomedia*, In *The Ecclesiastical History of Theodoret*. Nicene and Post-Nicene Fathers second series, vol. 3, translated by Charles Gordon Browne and James Edward Swallow. Edited by Philip Schaff and Henry Wace, Peabody, MA: Hendrickson, 2012.

Fee, Gordon D. Pauline *Christology: An Exegetical–Theological Study*. Peabody, MA: Hendrickson, 2007.

Ferguson, Everett. *Church History*. Vol. 1. Grand Rapids, MI: Zondervan, 2005.

Frend, W. H. C. *The Rise of Christianity*. Philadelphia, PA: Fortress, 1984.

Gangel, Kenneth O. *The Holman New Testament Commentary: John*. Edited by Max Anders. Nashville, TN: B&H, 2000.

Geisler, Norman L. "Colossians." In *The Bible Knowledge Commentary: An Exposition of the Scriptures*, edited by J. F. Walvoord and R. B. Zuck, 668. Vol. 2. Wheaton, IL: Victor, 1985.

Gonzalez, Justo L. *The Story of Christianity*. Vol. 1. San Francisco, CA: Harper and Row, 1984.

Gregg, Robert C., and Dennis E. Groh. *Early Arianism: A View of Salvation*. Philadelphia, PA: Fortress, 1981.

Gregory of Nazianzus. *Oration 31*. In *Cyril of Jerusalem,* In *Gregory Nazianzen*. Nicene and Post-Nicene Fathers second series, vol. 7, translated by Charles Gordon Browne and James Edward Swallow. Edited by Philip Schaff and Henry Wace, Peabody, MA: Hendrickson, 2012.

———. *Oration 42*. In *Cyril of Jerusalem,* In *Gregory Nazianzen*. Nicene and Post-Nicene Fathers second series, vol. 7, translated by Charles Gordon Browne and James Edward Swallow. Edited by Philip Schaff and Henry Wace, Peabody, MA: Hendrickson, 2012.

———. *To Cledonius the Priest Against Apollinarius*. In *Cyril of Jerusalem,* In *Gregory Nazianzen*. Nicene and Post-Nicene Fathers second series, vol. 7, translated by Charles Gordon Browne and James Edward Swallow. Edited by Philip Schaff and Henry Wace, Peabody, MA: Hendrickson, 2012.

Grillmeier, Aloys SJ. *Christ in Christian Tradition*: From the Apostolic Age to Chalcedon. Vol. 1. Atlanta, GA: John Knox, 1975.

———. "Communication of Properties (Communication of Idioms)." In *The Westminster Handbook of Patristic Theology*, 70–72. Edited by John Anthony McGuckin. Louisville, KY; Westminster, 2004.

Gupta, Nijay K. "Christology." In *The Lexham Bible Dictionary*, edited by John D. Barry et al. Bellingham, WA: Lexham, 2015.

Guthrie, Donald. *"Hebrew,"* Tyndale New Testament Commentary Series. Grand Rapids, MI: Eerdmans, 1983.

———. *New Testament Introduction*. Downers Grove, IL: Intervarsity, 1990.

Hamilton, James M. Jr. *God's Glory in Salvation Through Judgment: A Biblical Theology*. Wheaton, IL: Crossway, 2010.

Bibliography

Hanson, R. P. C. *The Search for the Christian Doctrine of God: The Arian Controversy.* Edinburgh, Scotland: T&T Clark, 1988.

Harris, Murray J. *Prepositions and Theology in the Greek New Testament.* Grand Rapids, MI: Zondervan, 2012.

Hauerwas, Stanley. "Foreword." In *Heresies and How to Avoid Them: Why it Matters what Christians Believe,* edited by Ben Quash and Michael Ward. Peabody, MA: Hendrickson, 2007.

Hawthorne, Gerald. *Philippians,* The Word Biblical Commentary, 43. Waco, TX: Word, 1983.

Holcomb, Justin S. *Know the Creeds and Councils.* Grand Rapids, MI: Zondervan, 2014.

Holmes, Stephen R. *The Quest for the Trinity: The Doctrine of God in Scripture, History, and Modernity.* Downers Grove, IL: IVP Academic, 2012.

Hurtado, Larry W. *Lord Jesus Christ.* Grand Rapids, MI: Eerdmans, 2003.

Johnson, Luke T. *Hebrews: A Commentary.* The New Testament Library. Ed. C.C. Black and J.T. Carroll Louisville, KY: Westminster/John Knox, 2006.

Kannengiesser, Charles. *Holy Scripture and Hellenistic Hermeneutics.* Berkley, CA: Center for Hermeneutic Studies, 1982.

———. "St Athanasius of Alexandria Rediscovered: His Political and Pastoral Achievement." In *Coptic Church Review* Vol. 9 (1988) 72.

Kelly, John N. D. *Early Christian Doctrine.* San Francisco, CA: Harper Collins, 1978.

Kent, Homer Jr. *The Epistles of the Hebrews.* Grand Rapids, MI: Baker, 1986.

Kleinknecht, Hermann. "The Greek Use of εἰκών." In *Theological Dictionary of the New Testament* 2:388–89. Grand Rapids, MI: Eerdmans, 1999.

———. "The Logos in the Greek and Hellenistic World." In *Theological Dictionary of the New Testament* 4:76. Grand Rapids, MI: Eerdmans, 1999.

Koester, Craig R. *Hebrews,* Anchor Bible, 185. New York, NY: Doubleday, 2001.

Kostenberger, Andreas J. *John.* Baker Exegetical Commentary on the New Testament, 28. Grand Rapids, MI: Baker, 2004.

Lampe, G. W. H. "Homoousios." In *A Patristic Greek Lexicon,* 959. Oxford, England: Clarendon, 1961.

Lawyer, John E. Jr. "Eucharist and Martyrdom in the Letters of Ignatius of Antioch." In *Anglican Theological Review* 281 (1991).

Lea, Thomas. *The Holman New Testament Commentary: Hebrew and James.* Edited by Max Anders. Nashville, TN: Broadman, 1999.

Leo the Great. *The Letters and Sermons of Leo the Great.* Translated by Charles Lett Feltoe, in *Leo the Great, Gregory the Great,* edited by Phillip Schaff and Henry Wace. Nicene and Post-Nicene Fathers, second series, Vol. 12, Peabody, MA: Hendrickson, 2004.

Letham, Robert. *The Holy Trinity: In Scripture, History, Theology, and Worship.* Phillipsburg, NJ: P&R, 2004.

Lightfoot, J. B. *Epistle to the Philippians.* Grand Rapids, MI: Zondervan, 1953.

———. *St. Paul's Epistles to the Colossians and Philemon.* Grand Rapids, MI: Zondervan, 1973.

Longenecker, Richard N. *Studies in Hermeneutics, Christology, and Discipleship.* New Testament Monographs 3. Edited by Stanley E. Porter. Sheffield, England: Sheffield Phoenix, 2004.

Loofs, F. "Athanasius." In *The New Schaff-Herzog Encyclopedia of Religious Knowledge,* Vol. 1, Grand Rapids, MI: Baker, 1977.

Bibliography

Matera, Frank J. *New Testament Christology*. Louisville, KY: Westminster/John Knox, 1999.

McCready, Douglas. *He Came Down From Heaven: The Preexistence of Christ and the Christian Faith*. Downers Grove, IL: InterVarsity/Leicester, England: Apollos, 2005.

McKim, Donald K. *Theological Turning Points-Major Issues in Christian Thought*. Atlanta, GA: John Knox, 1988.

Melick, Richard. *Philippians, Colossians, Philemon*. The New American Commentary, 32. Nashville, TN: Broadman, 1991.

Merida, Tony. *Faithful Preaching: Declaring Scripture with Responsibility, Passion, and Authenticity*. Nashville, TN: B&H, 2009.

Michaelis, Wilhelm. "πρωτότοκος" In *Theological Dictionary of the New Testament* 6:878. Grand Rapids, MI: Eerdmans, 1999.

Morris, Leon. *The Gospel According to John*. New International Commentary on the New Testament, 4. Grand Rapids, MI: Eerdmans. 1992.

Moule, C.F.D. "The Manhood of Jesus in the New Testament." In *Crisis in Christology: Essays in Quest of Resolution*, edited by William R. Farmer, 53. Livonia, MI: Dove, 1995.

Nestorius. *Second Letter to Cyril*. In *The Christological Controversy*, 135. edited and translated by Richard A. Norris, 103. Philadelphia, PA: Fortress, 1980.

O'Brian, Peter T. *Colossians, Philemon*. Word Biblical Commentary. Waco, TX: Word, 1982.

O'Collins, Gerald. *Christology: A Biblical, Historical, and Systematic Study of Jesus*. Oxford, EN: Oxford University Press, 2009.

Olford, Stephen F. *Anointed Expository Preaching*. Nashville, TN: B&H, 1998.

Olsen, Roger. E. *The Story of Christian Theology-Twenty Centuries of Tradition & Reform*. Downers Grove, IL: InterVarsity Press, 1999.

Osborne, Grant R. *Revelation*. Baker Exegetical Commentary on the New Testament. Grand Rapids, MI: Baker Academic, 2002.

Pannenberg, Wolfhart. *Systematic Theology*. Vol. 2. Grand Rapids, MI: Eerdmans, 1994.

Pate, C. Marvin. *The Writings of John: A Survey of the Gospel, Epistles, and Apocalypse*. Grand Rapids, MI: Zondervan, 2011.

Patterson, Paige. *Revelation*. New American Commentary 39. Nashville, TN: B&H, 2012.

Pendrick, Gerard. "Monogenēs." *New Testament Studies* 41.4 (October 1995) 587–601.

Renwick, A. M. *Story of the Church*. Grand Rapids, MI: Eerdmans, 1958.

Robertson, A.T. "Colossians." *Word Pictures in the New Testament*, 6. Nashville, TN: Broadman, 1930.

———. *A Grammar of the Greek New Testament*. Nashville, TN: Broadman, 1934.

Rusch, William G. *The Trinitarian Controversy*. Philadelphia, PA: Fortress, 1980.

Samuel, V. C. *The Council of Chalcedon Re-Examined: A Historical and Theological Survey*. Madras, India: Christian Literature Society for the Senate of Serampore College, 1977. 23 and n. 85.

Schaff, Phillip. *History of the Christian Church*. Vol. II. New York, NY: Scribner's, 1930.

———. *Nicene and Post-Nicean Christianity: History of the Christian Church*. Vol. II. Grand Rapids, MI: Eerdmans, 1971.

Schreiner, Thomas R. *The King in His Beauty: A Biblical Theology of the Old and New Testaments*. Grand Rapids, MI: Baker Academic, 2013.

———. *1, 2 Peter, Jude*. New American Commentary, 37. Nashville, TN: B&H, 2003.

Bibliography

Shaddix, Jim. *The Passion Driven Sermon: Changing the Way Pastors Preach and Congregations Listen*. Nashville, TN: B&H, 2003.

Shelly, Bruce. *Church History in Plain Language*. Dallas, TX: Word, 1982.

Skarsaune, Oskar. "A Neglected Detail in the Creed of Nicaea (325)." *Vigiliae Christianae* 41.1 (March 1987) 34–54.

Slick, Matt. "*Adoptionism.*" https://carm.org/adoptionism.

Socrates. *Ecclesiastical History* In Nicene and Post-Nicene Fathers, second series, vol. 2, edited by Philip Schaff and Henry Wace, Peabody, MA: Hendrickson, 2012.

Stevens, William Wilson. *Doctrines of the Christian Religion*. Grand Rapids, MI: Eerdmans, 1967.

Stott, John R. W. *Between Two Worlds: The Challenge of Preaching Today*. Grand Rapids, MI: Eerdmans, 1982.

———. *The Incomparable Christ*. Downers Grove, IL: IVP, 2001.

Strauss, Mark L. *Four Portraits, One Jesus: An Introduction to Jesus and the Gospels*. Grand Rapids, MI: Zondervan, 2007.

Studer, Basil. *Trinity and the Incarnation: The Faith of the Early Church*. Collegeville, MN: The Liturgical, 1993.

Sweeney, James P. "James, Letter of." In *The Lexham Bible Dictionary*, edited by John D. Barry et al. Bellingham, WA: Lexham, 2015.

Theodoret. *The Ecclesiastical History of Theodoret*. Edited by Phillip Schaff and Henry Wace, Nicene and Post-Nicene Fathers, 3. Buffalo, NY: Christian Literature, Peabody, MA: Hendrickson, 2004.

Thiselton, Anthony C. *The Hermeneutics of Doctrine*. Grand Rapids, MI: Eerdmans, 2007.

Veith, Gene Edward. "*The Da Vinci Phenomenon.*" World 21 no.20 (2006) 20–21.

Vincent, Marvin. *Philippians and Philemon*. The International Critical Commentary, 57–58. Edinburgh, Scotland: T&T Clark, 1897.

Walker, Williston. *A History of the Christian Church*. New York, NY: Charles Scribner's Sons, 1985.

Wallace, Daniel. "The Gospel of John: Introduction, Argument, Outline," https://bible.org/seriespage/4-gospel-john-introduction-argument-outline.

———. *Greek Grammar Beyond the Basics*. Grand Rapids, MI: Zondervan, 1996.

Wilckens, Ulrich. "χαρακτὴρ" In TDNT 9:421. Grand Rapids, MI: Eerdmans, 1999.

Williams, A. N. "Nestorianism: Is Jesus Christ One Person or Does He Have a Split Identity, With His Divine Nature Separate and Divided from His Human Nature?" In *Heresies and How to Avoid Them: Why it Matters what Christians Believe*. Edited by Ben Quash and Michael Ward. Peabody, MA: Hendricksen, 2007.

Williams, Rowan. *Arius: Heresy and Tradition*. Grand Rapids, MI: Eerdmans, 2001.

———. *Christian Spirituality*. Atlanta, GA: John Knox, 1980.

Witherington, Ben III. *John's Wisdom*. Louisville, KY: Westminster, 1995.

———. *The Many Faces of the Christ: The Christologies of the New Testament and Beyond*. New York: Crossroad, 1998.

Wright, Christopher J. H. *The Mission of God: Unlocking the Bible's Grand Narrative*. Downers Grove, IL: IVP Academic, 2006.

www.ingramcontent.com/pod-product-compliance
Lightning Source LLC
Chambersburg PA
CBHW060609230426
43670CB00011B/2036